THE GREATEST WESTERNS

EVER MADE AND THE PEOPLE WHO MADE THEM

HENRY C. PARKE AND *TRUE WEST* MAGAZINE

INTRODUCTION BY BRUCE BOXLEITNER

TWODOT®

ESSEX, CONNECTICUT
HELENA, MONTANA

A · TWODOT® · BOOK

An imprint of Globe Pequot, the trade division of
The Rowman & Littlefield Publishing Group, Inc.
4501 Forbes Blvd., Ste. 200
Lanham, MD 20706
www.rowman.com

Distributed by NATIONAL BOOK NETWORK

British Library Cataloguing in Publication Information available

Library of Congress Cataloging-in-Publication Data Available

ISBN 978-1-4930-7439-6 (paperback)
ISBN 978-1-4930-7744-1 (ebook)

CONTENTS

ACKNOWLEDGMENTS

WITH GRATITUDE

THIS BOOK WOULD NOT BE POSSIBLE, IN FACT THE NEARLY EIGHTY *TRUE West* articles that have gone into it, would not have been possible, without the extraordinary help of an extraordinary number of extraordinary people. I would like to thank my wife, Stephanie Parke, who edited all of the articles and helped me keep within my allotted word count. My friend and collaborator in audio commentaries and all manner of hijinks, C. Courtney Joyner, who recommended me for the job of film editor for *True West*. Then *True West* editor Meghan Saar, who hired me, and now *True West* editor Stuart Rosebrook, both of whom I've thoroughly enjoyed working with and from whom I've learned so much. *True West* publishers Bob Boze Bell and Ken Amorosano; Ken was instrumental in putting this deal together. I'm grateful for the unflagging support and encouragement of my family in my writing career, from my late parents, Harry Parke and Ursula Parke, my sister Deirdre Holleman, and my daughter Sabrina Parke. I must also thank former Two Dot acquisitions editors Sarah Parke (no relation), who found me, and Lauren Younker, who patiently guided me through this process.

And I must thank the Western actors, writers, directors, producers, art directors, stunt-people, historians, descendants, and all of the other kind people whose interviews give these articles life.

Here they are, roughly in the order of their contributions in the book. Dan Ford (John Ford's grandson), Dennis Devine (Andy Devine's son), Scott Eyeman, Michael B. Druxman, Tommy Kirk, Beverly Washburn, Constance Towers, stuntman Gary Combs, Katharine Ross, Luster Bayless, Robert Duvall, Anita La Cava Swift (John Wayne's granddaughter), Katy Haber, Robert Crawford Jr., Paul Seydor, Bo Hopkins, L. Q. Jones, W. K. Stratton, Mitch Ryan, Matt Clark, Bruce Dern, Stephen Hudis, stuntman Walter Scott, Nicolas Beauvy, Sondra Locke, James Keach, Stacy Keach, Walter Hill, Robert Carradine, Pamela Reed, Ricky Schroder, Kevin Costner, Bill Markley, Daniel Ostroff, Wes Studi, John Fusco, Franco Nero, Tom Selleck, Laura San Giacomo, Simon Wincer, Michael Biehn, Peter Sherayko, Leon Rippy, Tanner Beard, Morgan Woodward, Earl Holliman, Kate Edelman Johnson, Rob

Word, Bruce Boxleitner, Hugh O'Brian, Tim Matheson, Trace Adkins, Patrick Wayne, Christopher Mitchum, Daryle Ann Giardino (Slim Pickens' daughter), Andrew Prine, Barry Corbin, Norman Lear, Mariette Hartley, James Drury, Max Evans, John Wilder, Jesse Vint, Taylor Sheridan, Jim Byrnes, Jeb Rosebrook, Dusty Richards, Lee Martin, Michael Feifer, Paulette Jiles, Eileen Pollack, Robert Utley, Robert Woods, Kelly Reichardt, Dawn Moore (Clayton Moore's daughter), Johnny Crawford, Charlotte Samco (Johnny Crawford's widow), Henry Darrow, Don Collier, Kent McCray, Susan McCray, Chip and Camille Mitchell (Cameron Mitchell's son and daughter), stuntman Steve DeFrance, stuntwoman Jackie Fuller, Robin Weigert, Maria Caso, Brad Dourif, William Sanderson, Anson Mount, Zahn McClarnon, Craig Johnson, Philipp Meyer, Jacob Lofland, Carlos Bardem, Henry Bronchtein, Kevin Murphy, Graham Greene, Michael Horse, Michael Dante, Cody Jones, Andrew Erish, Jon Cassar, Richard Wenk, Walter Mirisch, Royston Innes, Ric Maddox, Craig Hensley, Scott Martin, Lou Diamond Phillips, Gil Birmingham, David Mackenzie, Matthew Holmes, Rafer Johnson, L. P. Leung, Fraser Heston (Charlton Heston's son), Dan Haggerty, Jonathan Nolan, Lisa Joy, Tansy Smith, Petrine Day Mitchum (Robert Mitchum's daughter), Mamie Van Doren, Ernest Borgnine, John Carroll Lynch, Lance Henriksen, Cheryl Rogers Barnett (Roy Rogers' daughter), and Steve Latshaw.

INTRODUCTION BY BRUCE BOXLEITNER

WHEN HENRY PARKE ASKED ME TO WRITE THE INTRODUCTION TO HIS BOOK, he flummoxed me. I really respect Henry, and I would never call myself a writer. What we have very much in common would be our love of Western films and television series, old and current. Another connection is me having been a lifelong fan of *True West* Magazine, which he writes for, and where the articles in this book were first published. They have the best writers, great historians. And Henry is a historian of the Western film and television and has an experience and a knowledge that I don't think they had prior to him. They found the right guy for that spot.

We needed to talk about what he expected of me. I suggested lunch, and when I said I was paying, he agreed. I chose the Sagebrush Cantina, in Calabasas, in the west end of the San Fernando Valley.

I told Henry that I'd moved there in 1978, the second to last year of *How the West Was Won*, with my first wife, Kathryn Holcomb, who played my sister. And we're still very good friends, and we have two wonderful sons together. We had some wonderful years there when Calabasas wasn't all Kardashians. I don't mean to put anybody down, but it changed the face of the place. Now it's all McMansions.

It was a sort of hidden horse community, with bridle trails. I used to ride there with Robert Blake before the crazy times. I had a big black horse that I bought off the show. Calabasas was not anything like the city it's turned into. Back in the seventies, it was a wild west town. None of these four lanes of traffic; it was just one road. The spin-class place across the street was a biker bar; it literally had swinging doors. There was a little antiques shop down the other way, and that was all. And I know this because I had more than a few drinks here many nights. We used to ride our horses over Parkway, Calabasas. They had a hitching rail. We would come down to the cantina on a Saturday night and hitch up, and the horses knew how to get us home.

All this side of the road was just the cantina, the Leonis Adobe, and the gas stations up at the freeway entrance. But this was a legendary area. That freeway, the 101, follows the road they named after the Spanish king, El Camino Real, The Royal Way.

They used to have a well that was known to have had a couple of rustlers dumped down it. And they had a hanging tree that was here for many years, right off to the side of the road. The Leonis Adobe is one of the oldest buildings in Southern California, built in 1844. Miguel Leonis, a cattle rancher, was Basque; his wife, Espiritu, was Chumash and Tongva. And to show how the real West and the movie West can come together, the last people to live in the Leonis Adobe before it became a museum were John Carradine, star of *Stagecoach*, and his family. David and Keith and Bobby grew up there.

There are Facebook pages where people find these old pictures of where Westerns were filmed, and show how they look today. They show Matt Dillon riding down the street, and it's got the Agoura Hills right in the background. *Gunsmoke*, *Wagon Train*, all those shows were shot in Thousand Oaks. I saw *Rawhide* the other day. I can look out from my town house and see the same hills, where they built it all up into suburbia. Real history and movie history can disappear so quickly if someone doesn't write it down. Henry has.

CHAPTER 1
THE CLASSICS

STAGECOACH—1939

More than eighty years ago, director John Ford and screenwriter Dudley Nichols combined their talents, and those of star character-actors Claire Trevor, Thomas Mitchell, John Carradine, and newcomer John Wayne, and made *Stagecoach*, a movie that would forever alter Western film history. It's been called the *Citizen Kane* of Westerns—ironic not only because S*tagecoach* preceded *Kane* by two years, but also because Orson Welles called *Stagecoach* "perfect" and watched it forty times while preparing to direct *Kane*.

Yet it's an apt comparison, because those films changed the future of movies, not by an innovation easy to point out, like Technicolor or 3D, but by utilizing all of the aspects of the filmmakers' arts to tell stories perfectly.

John Ford had been directing films since 1917, beginning with the silent Western three-reeler *The Tornado*, and had made nearly sixty Westerns since then. In 1939, with his first of four Oscars under his belt for 1936's *The Informer*, he could work anywhere he wanted, with studio bosses like Daryl Zanuck and David O. Selznick happy to bankroll any project he'd like. Only now he wanted to make a Western, a genre he hadn't touched in thirteen years, since his silent hit *3 Bad Men*, which he would remake in 1948 as *3 Godfathers*.

Dan Ford, John Ford's grandson, says, "He always preferred to work from shorter projects and expand them, rather than work from novels and cut them down. A lot of his movies came from *The Saturday Evening Post* or *Collier's* magazines." Ford's son Patrick had read the Ernest Haycox story *Stage to Lordsburg* in *Collier's*, and he told his father it might make a good movie.

Rarely read today, Haycox was a very popular, very driven Western author in his day, who started in the pulps but, as Haycox biographer Richard Etulain puts it, "took the Western out of the 'pulps' and took it into the 'slicks,'" that is, higher-quality magazines printed on smoother paper. Growing up poor in

Stagecoach, the *Citizen Kane* of Westerns. George Bancroft as the marshal, John Wayne as the Ringo Kid, and Louise Platt as Mrs. Lucy Mallory are just three of the seven intriguing characters riding a stage through Apache territory in the film that revolutionized Western storytelling. *Courtesy United Artists*

Oregon, Haycox, like so many of his characters, "had hardscrabble origins. He's virtually an orphan by the time he's ten, out on the street, selling newspapers." In his mid-teens he lied about his age to join the Army and fought under Pershing against Pancho Villa on the Mexican border. He fought in World War I, then graduated from the University of Oregon in 1923 with a bachelor's degree in journalism. Ernest Hemingway once noted, "I read *The Saturday Evening Post* whenever it has a serial by Ernest Haycox."

The premise of Haycox's story is simple: a group of strangers boards a stagecoach to Lordsburg, and a series of unexpected challenges, including an attack by Apaches, reveals who rises to the occasion, and who does not.

The usual price for film rights to a *Collier's* story was $1,100, but Ford paid $2,500 for *Stage to Lordsburg*. When he tried to set it up at a studio, Ford came up against two powerful objections: it was a Western, and he insisted on casting an unknown in a pivotal role. The once-popular Western genre had fallen out of favor, except with rural and juvenile audiences. In 1930, Fox had spent $2 million making a Western epic, *The Big Trail*, shot in a new process called Grandeur. Unfortunately, during the Great Depression, exhibitors who had just spent a fortune converting their theaters to play "talkies" had no interest in spending another fortune to convert to wide-screen. Except for in a handful of theaters, the movie played in standard, square 35mm, and it bombed.

The virtually unknown actor Ford wanted to feature was a former college athlete and propman who had accidently wandered into a scene Ford was directing, startling Ford with how photogenic he was. He was groomed by Ford, given small bits in films until he suddenly got a big break and was cast as the lead in *The Big Trail*. His name had been Marion Morrison, but they'd changed it to John Wayne. And now Ford wanted Wayne to star in *Stagecoach*.

"I don't think anybody blames a $75-a-week actor when a $2 million picture goes down in flames," Ford and Wayne biographer Scott Eyman points out. But Wayne had begun starring in B-Westerns and he was "damaged goods as far as they were concerned. After you failed at Fox, you were exiled to Monogram and Republic, and you never got back. It was like Devil's Island." Wayne would star in thirty-three B-Westerns in nine years, until John Ford called. He never did a B-picture again.

Selznick was willing to produce the film, but he wanted stars with big enough names to ensure a profit. Why not Gary Cooper and Marlene Dietrich, instead of Wayne and Trevor? Even though Claire Trevor had been Oscar-nominated in 1937 for *Dead End* (she'd win in 1948 for *Key Largo*), she was seen as a B-movie star. But Ford held firm, and the film was eventually put together, Ford's way, with independent producer Walter Wanger at United Artists.

Dudley Nichols had won an Oscar for *The Informer* and would collaborate with Ford on sixteen movies. What he did so masterfully in adapting *Stage to Lordsburg* was to add urgency, to up the ante for the characters, making them individuals instead of types. No longer just a gambler, John Carradine's character is a ruined Southern gentleman hiding his shame and eager for a chance to regain his dignity. The Army Girl (Louise Platt) is no longer going to meet her fiancé; she is now Mrs. Lucy Mallory, married to an officer and about to give birth. Thomas Mitchell's character is no longer just a drunk; he's a drunk *doctor* who will have to deliver Mrs. Mallory's baby. Malpais Bill, now the Ringo Kid, is still on his way to Lordsburg for revenge on Luke Plummer, played by Tom Tyler, but now Ringo is an escaped convict, and the sheriff (George Bancroft) is along for the ride. Henriette, now Dallas, would never tell Ringo, as in the short story, "I run a house in Lordsburg." Her greatest fear is that he will learn this about her. Now the whiskey drummer (Donald Meek) survives, the Englishman is dropped, and the cattleman is turned into the embezzling banker (Berton Churchill).

About the only character that hardly changes is the driver, originally Happy, now Buck. Rotund, screechy-voiced Andy Devine was ideal for the part, bringing welcome comedy relief. But he knew the other reason he'd been cast. When Ford got impatient and said, "You big tub of lard. I don't know why the hell I'm using you in this picture," Andy replied, "Because Ward Bond can't drive six horses." Andy's son Dennis explains, "He grew up on his father's ranch outside of Kingman [Arizona], so Dad knew how to drive wagons and horses. Dad did all of it [in the film], the driving in and out of towns and stations. But that wasn't Dad on the dry lake, the big chase. Not that he couldn't do it, but because [the studio] was afraid he'd get hurt."

When John Wayne came over from Republic, he brought with him Yakima Canutt, arguably the greatest stuntman who ever lived. Most of the convincing fight scenes performed in films since the mid-1930s are based on techniques Canutt and Wayne developed while working together at "poverty row" studios like Mascot, Republic, and Monogram.

The exterior stagecoach shots were filmed first, in what would become John Ford's personal trademark, Monument Valley. The exteriors for the opening town of Tonto and closing town of Lordsburg were both shot at Republic Studios. The end was originally planned for daylight but was changed to night to hide the fact that it was the same town, and the night-for-night photography is wonderfully pre-*noir noir*.

Andy Devine had seen a rough cut of the film and loved it. But he faced one more scene. Perhaps not so coincidentally, Andy was asked to do a risky stunt on the last day of shooting, so the film could be completed even if something went wrong. Dennis says, "John Ford wasn't stupid, and frankly, my dad was scared of doing that thing."

The scene would come before the big Indian chase. When the stagecoach reaches the hoped-for safety of the river, Buck discovers Geronimo's Apaches (played by Navajos) have burned the ferry. The script called for two trees to be cut down, lashed to either side of the stage, to float the stage across the river. Ford had already discarded the sequence: "The wranglers tell me it can't be done."

"It can be done," Yakima Canutt told Ford, "and I think it will look terrific."

During three days of preparation, Canutt had a Paramount special effects expert build four hollow logs for flotation. Setting up on the Kern River, Canutt rigged an underwater cable to the bottom of the wagon—the cable ran through a pulley to an off-camera truck, which would pull the stagecoach into the river and across to the far side.

Andy faced that last day of shooting with trepidation. "He didn't know what was going to happen—the stagecoach could sink or the horses could drown," his son Dennis says.

Canutt took the reins for the first take, a long shot, and everything went smoothly. The second shot was set up with the camera mounted to the stagecoach roof, looking over the shoulders of George Bancroft, as the marshal, and Andy. Happily, the river crossing went off without a hitch: no retakes needed.

Andy was so relieved, he called up friends to go out and celebrate—Clark Gable and Carole Lombard. They had just sat down with him and his wife, Dorothy, at the Brown Derby and ordered their meals when Dorothy went into labor. Dennis was born January 24, 1939, the day *Stagecoach* wrapped.

The climactic chase, with Apaches tearing after the coach, was shot over three days at Mojave Desert's Lucerne Dry Lake Bed, where Ford had previously filmed the land rush sequence for *3 Bad Men*. The chase is an astonishing collaboration of the skills of Ford and Canutt.

The film was completed for just under $550,000, four days over the forty-three-day shooting schedule. Ford was paid $50,000, less than his then-current rate. Trevor, at $15,000, was the highest-paid cast member, with Wayne, at $3,700, the second lowest, making $34 more than Carradine.

The aftermath of *Stagecoach* is well known. It made John Wayne a star. Wayne and Ford would have a legendary collaboration on a dozen more films, some of the most highly regarded movies in film history. Grandson Dan Ford reveals another outcome of the success. "It was important to [Ford] because he had a big piece of *Stagecoach*, a big money-maker, and it sustained his family for the war years, so he could go off in the Navy." Ford, who saw trouble coming earlier than most Americans, enlisted before the Pearl Harbor attack and went overseas, often handling cameras on the front lines. He achieved the rank of rear admiral and made about a dozen military films, covering subjects as varied as the battle of Midway and sex hygiene.

Claire Trevor had a splendid career as a leading lady in A-movies and a long and happy marriage. Thomas Mitchell had an unbelievable 1939, starring in not only *Stagecoach* but in *Mr. Smith Goes to Washington* and *Gone With the Wind*. He won the Best Supporting Actor Oscar for *Stagecoach*, and receiving the award, commented, "I didn't think . . . I didn't *know* I was quite that good."

It was also a wonderful year for Ernest Haycox. In addition to *Stagecoach*, his novel *Trouble Shooters* became *Union Pacific*, directed by Cecil B. DeMille and starring Joel McCrea and Barbara Stanwyck. He was brought out to Hollywood to be a screenwriter, but didn't care for it and soon returned to Oregon, where he wrote successful novels and more than three hundred short stories. Seven movies were made from his stories in his lifetime. He died at the age of fifty-one in 1950, and his widow lived a comfortable life licensing his stories to films and television, and reportedly watched endless hours of Western TV to make sure his stories *weren't* being used for free.

Considering how successful *Stagecoach* was, and how inexpensive shooting endless stagecoach interiors is, it's surprising it hasn't been more frequently imitated. But what it requires is great writing and great acting, and that's rarely cheap. In 1951's *Rawhide*, Tyrone Power and Susan Hayward are menaced at a stagecoach stop, which certainly has similarities to *Stagecoach*, as do virtually all of the Randolph Scott/Budd Boetticher films of the 1960s.

Other influences are not so obvious. Eyman asks, "Would Alfred Hitchcock's *Lifeboat* exist without *Stagecoach*? [It's] *Stagecoach* on the water, basically." To be fair, others have claimed that *Stagecoach* is just *Grand Hotel* on wheels, but of course, without Apaches.

On television, the economy of the setup inspired episodes of many series, including *The Rebel*, *Cheyenne*, and *The Rifleman*. In fact, Quentin Tarantino explained to *Deadline Hollywood* that these cut-rate *Stagecoaches*, particularly *The Virginian*, *Bonanza*, and *The High Chaparral*, were his inspiration for *The Hateful Eight*. "Twice per season, those shows would have an episode where a bunch of outlaws would . . . come to the Ponderosa, or go to Judge Garth's place . . . and take hostages. There would be a guest star like David Carradine, Darren McGavin, Claude Akins, Robert Culp, Charles Bronson, or James Coburn. I thought, 'What if I did a movie starring nothing but those characters? No heroes, no Michael Landons. Just a bunch of nefarious guys in a room, all telling backstories that may or may not be true. Trap those guys together in a room with a blizzard outside, give them guns and see what happens.'" In 2018, the final segment of the Coen Brothers' *The Ballad of Buster Scruggs*, "The Mortal Remains," is an even more direct descendent of *Stagecoach*.

Then there were the remakes. In 1966, 20th Century Fox released its new take on *Stagecoach*, directed by Gordon Douglas, who'd started directing *Our Gang* comedies and helmed highly regarded Westerns like *Rio Conchos* (1964). Ann-Margaret is Dallas, Alex Cord is Ringo, with Oscar-winner Red Buttons filling in for Donald Meek, Mike Connors for Carradine, Bing Crosby for Mitchell, and Slim Pickens for Andy Devine. Fox's executives spent money on this one: the action is longer and bloodier, the locations are beautiful, and they even commissioned Norman Rockwell to paint one of the handsomest movie posters ever made. They made a film that's adequate if you haven't seen the original but tedious if you have.

And perhaps the studio bosses knew it. As Pauline Kael noted, "Probably in no other art except movies can new practitioners legally eliminate competition from the past. A full-page notice in *Variety* gave warning that 20th Century Fox . . . "would 'vigorously' prosecute the exhibition of the 1939 original . . . one of the most highly regarded and influential movies ever made." Or as John Carradine told *Hollywood Snapshots* author Michael B. Druxman, "They deserved to lose their shirts on the remake. Nobody could have been better than John Wayne, Berton Churchill, Thomas Mitchell, or me. Great classics should never be remade."

The 1986 version of *Stagecoach* is far worse, sadly, as it might have been wonderful. Starring Willie Nelson, Kris Kristofferson, Johnny Cash, and Waylon Jennings, it was planned as a musical, with songs by Willie Nelson. Then half the budget disappeared, and except for the theme by Nelson, the music was never recorded. Kristofferson remembers, "It had a lot of trouble getting started, and we ended up in the stagecoach for most of it." A brief appearance by Lash LaRue toward the end was the only link to a real Western.

Claire Trevor told Druxman, "*Stagecoach* was the only thing I've ever done that couldn't have been done in another medium. It used the motion picture camera and music, folk songs with symphonic arrangements, that, up to that time, had never been done before." She said it best.

OLD YELLER—1957

In 1956, Fred Gipson stunned readers when his new novel began, "He made me so mad at first that I wanted to kill him. Then later, when I had to kill him, it was like having to shoot some of my own folks. That's how much I'd come to think of the big yeller dog." Still read in schools across the country, frequently in conjunction with watching the film, it's often cited as the book that first revealed to readers that the written word could make them cry.

Inspired by the tales Gipson's Texas pioneer grandparents told him, *Old Yeller* is about an adolescent boy, Travis; his kid brother, Arliss; and their mother who, with father away on a cattle drive, are helped by a huge, lop-eared yellow dog who wanders onto their homestead to steal food, and becomes their protector. Walt Disney bought the book and rejected all entreaties to soften its ending: this was the story readers had made a bestseller, and this was the story he would tell.

With only seven characters, the cast had to be strong: Father was Fess Parker, an international sensation as Davy Crockett; lovely Dorothy Maguire, Oscar-nominated for 1947's *Gentlemen's Agreement*, was Mother. And in a memorable appearance, soon-to-be *Rifleman* star Chuck Connors was the neighbor who owns Yeller but kindly trades him for a horny-toad.

But the movie truly belongs to the children and the dog. Tommy Kirk had already starred in *The Hardy Boys* serials on *The Mickey Mouse Club*. He didn't have to audition, "because I was under contract already. The script arrived and they said, you have your wardrobe fittings next Wednesday." Kevin Corcoran, who'd play Arliss, was also a *Mickey Mouse Club* alumnus. "We were about five years apart," Kirk recalls. They would co-star in six Disney movies, including *Swiss Family Robinson* and *The Shaggy Dog*, usually playing brothers. "Kevin was the person I was most close to at Disney. We became very good friends and remained so until he recently passed away."

Beverly Washburn played Lisbeth, diligent daughter of the hilariously shiftless Bud Searcy (Jeff York), the only man left home to look after "the women-folk" during the cattle drive. He'd previously played Mike Fink opposite Fess Parker in the *Davy Crockett* TV series. Washburn, a well-respected child actress, had starred in the pilots of both *Superman* and *Wagon Train*, but unlike the boys, Washburn was not signed to Disney, "And I really didn't think I had a chance (to get the part); they were doing the *Mickey Mouse Club* and there were so many that could have been wonderful. But I went in and read, I met Walt Disney, and when I got the phone call that I had gotten the role, I was just thrilled!" Robert Stevenson, the only Walt Disney director ever to receive an Oscar nomination, for *Mary Poppins*, had directed Washburn twice before and had gone to bat for her.

The big, beautiful mongrel who played Yeller was Spike; he'd been rescued from a shelter by the legendary Weatherwax brothers, who'd trained Lassie. Spike was treated well, Washburn remembers with a laugh. "His dressing room was bigger than mine!" Spike didn't have a stand-in: they couldn't find another dog who looked like him. "Yakima Canutt was in charge of all the animal fights," Kirk explains. "The encounter between the dog and the bear, and the dog and the wolf." Most of what looked like fighting was play, and Canutt, cinema's finest stuntman, made sure that none were hurt.

It was a happy set, in large part due to Stevenson. "He was so gentle and patient and kind," Kirk says. "He's the kind of guy you'd kill yourself to please him." *Old Yeller* was a perfect mix of joy and sadness and hope. Kirk says, "Universal themes, like love and loss, are the stuff of great art, and great artists can tap that vein successfully, even if it's only for a moment." With a screenplay by Gipson and William Tunberg, *Yeller* was a hit, earning a then-remarkable $13.6 million in its initial release, and winning the Motion Picture Exhibitor's 1958 Golden Laurel for Top General Entertainment.

Six years later, Disney released a sequel, *Savage Sam*, from another Gipson novel. They brought back Kirk and Corcoran but not Washburn. "I had a commitment to do another film," she recalls ruefully, "and I wasn't a big enough name that they would wait for me." They should have waited, and done a rewrite. Despite the original screenwriters and a strong cast—Brian Keith, Slim Pickens—*Savage Sam* couldn't decide whether it was a sequel to *Old Yeller* or a remake of *The Searchers*. "I hated the script," Kirk admits. "I hated [director] Norman Tokar." Still, Kirk gave such a powerful performance that he was cast as the youngest offspring in *The Sons of Katie Elder*. Then a party he was attending got raided, and marijuana was found. "And I ended up in a jail cell. And I was immediately replaced on *Katie Elder*." Tommy Kirk and Beverly Washburn remained not only close friends but were neighbors, until his passing in 2021.

Spike would go on to star in two highly regarded Western TV series, with Brian Keith in Sam Peckinpah's *The Westerner* (1960) and as sidekick to Ralph Taeger in 1967's *Hondo*. He also guested ten times, always as a different character, on *Lassie*.

THE HORSE SOLDIERS—1959

Lovely Constance Towers became a star when she played the female lead in two John Ford Westerns back-to-back: 1959's *The Horse Soldiers* and 1960's *Sergeant Rutledge*.

What was Ford looking for in an actress? Towers recalls: "Pappy had a way of looking at women: she was to be respected, kind of on a pedestal. But she had to have a lot of spunk and fire. She was feminine, but had a backbone and was always a lady."

The courtly Ford insisted that Towers be treated that way while filming. "No one ever used bad language around any women on any Pappy Ford set. We had tea in the afternoon, and it was all very gentlemanly. He treated you like a lady wants to be treated; but you had to have a sense of humor, because if you didn't catch the subliminal things that went by you, it was a big disappointment to him."

In *The Horse Soldiers*, Towers played Southern belle Miss Hannah Hunter, whose home is occupied by Union troops under Col. John Marlowe (played by John "Duke" Wayne). Hunter does her best to sabotage the colonel's plans, though she gradually becomes romantically drawn to him, and to his medical officer and nemesis, Maj. Henry Kendall (William Holden).

"I was singing in the Persian Room of the Plaza Hotel [New York City] and [producer] Martin Rackin saw me and invited me to Hollywood to meet Ford. The fact that I was Irish probably didn't hurt. He screen-tested five of us; Gena Rowlands was one, and Joanna Moore. I had a call from an assistant to be at the Blessed Sacrament's church Monday afternoon. I was to sit midway in a pew and wait. I sat, and someone behind me whispered in my ear, 'You got the part.' It was Ford, and he insisted on leaving and not talking to me, which was typical of him. It was always intrigue."

For three months, Ford filmed exterior scenes in Mississippi and Louisiana, with Towers starring opposite two of Hollywood's most dynamic leading men, Wayne and Holden. "They were delightful to work with," she says. "They took care of me."

She refutes claims that the two didn't get along. "They even took an evening off. They cooked up a scheme [claiming that] in the dailies, Duke's teeth looked discolored. He went into Shreveport with Bill, supposedly to have his teeth cleaned, and, of course, they had a night on the town. The next morning, we're all waiting for them on location. Off in the distance, you saw this car driving in fast. They stopped, and John and Bill got out, looking like they hadn't been to bed at all, and Pappy Ford had all the stuntmen lined up to smell their breath.

"But they were very different personalities. John Wayne was as big, friendly, as open as he was on the screen; terrific with fans. He'd be riding all day and acting, come back mud-caked, and he'd stand and talk to young people.

"I heard one young man saying, 'My dad won't let me have the car on Saturday night.' And Duke asked, 'Well, when was the last time you offered to wash that car?' The boy said, 'I haven't.' Duke said, 'Why don't you? Maybe your dad will give it to you. Now I have another piece of advice. When is the last time you told your dad you loved him?' The boy kind of put his head down. 'Go home and try that. That'll work, too.'

"Bill Holden was the opposite. He was very shy, and he believed strongly that the performance he was paid to put on the screen was all he owed the public. People would ask him for his autograph, and he'd refuse. He was the nicest, most polite gentleman, but he was just the opposite of Duke."

The shoot was enjoyable, but it was not easy. "Louisiana has swamps, and anything that happened on my horse, I had to do, except for one horse fall into the water. They had a stuntman do that," she says.

Ford appointed two men to look after her whenever she was on horseback. "Freddie Kennedy and Slim Hightower were wonderful old stuntmen. In the film, one's ahead of me and one's behind me, but we rode through a forest going what felt like a hundred miles an hour through these trees. It was a tough location, but wonderful."

On the very last day on location, during the very last shot, an unexpected tragedy occurred.

"Freddie was doing his last fall," Towers says. "It was a simple shoulder fall, and Duke had told me to stand behind the camera and to run in. And they wouldn't call 'Cut' until I had given Freddie a kiss on the cheek. I ran in, and when I picked up his head, I realized that he was mortally hurt. He'd fallen and broken his neck, so I really was the last person to hold him. He died on the way to the hospital, which certainly cast a pall on the closing shot of the location."

She loved the stuntmen and remembered especially how Ford looked after them: "Pappy didn't pay them until their last weekend, so they would take money home. He gave them enough per diem to survive, but on location, there wasn't much you could do with it, but gamble."

After nearly fifty years, Towers takes great pleasure in her memories: "You take it in stride, then later look back, and it's just amazing. To be in my first big, big film, with those actors, and have it be just joyous all the time, and John Ford guiding everybody. It was a rare and wonderful experience."

TRUE GRIT—1969

"Who is the best marshal they have?"

"The meanest one is Rooster Cogburn. He is a pitiless man, double-tough, and fear don't enter into his thinking."

"Where can I find this Rooster?"

Half a century ago, audiences awaited the premiere of *True Grit* with some trepidation. After all, its star, John Wayne, had lost a lung to cancer. He'd done movies since, but none as vigorous as this, and his recent film, *The Green Berets*, had received a tepid-to-terrible reception due to its gung-ho support of the nation-polarizing Vietnam War. Joyously, his fans' doubts were misplaced. It was a wonderful story, a wonderful film, and Wayne's performance would earn an Oscar.

True Grit is the story of fourteen-year-old Mattie Ross's battle for justice after her father's murderer escapes into Indian Territory. Mattie hires notoriously tough and disreputable Rooster Cogburn and, joined by Texas Ranger Le Boeuf, they try to bring the killer back to Judge Parker's court for trial.

When Wayne read Charles Portis's novel, his Batjac Productions immediately bid for the film rights, only to be outbid by legendary producer Hal Wallis, who four years earlier had produced *The Sons of Katie Elder* with Wayne! Duke confronted Wallis and learned to his surprise that Wallis had bought it intending for Wayne to star.

To write and direct, Wallis brought in the pair he'd teamed for *5 Card Stud*, Marguerite Roberts and Henry Hathaway. Roberts was ideal for Westerns; her grandfather had been a sheriff, her father a town marshal. "Daddy put me on a horse before I knew how to walk," she would tell Tina Daniell. "I was weaned on stories about gunfighters and their doings, and I know all the lingo, too." She'd scripted pictures for Gable, Peck, Mitchum, and Tracy, but for a decade, she hadn't written anything that reached the screen. She'd joined the Communist Party in the 1930s, quit in the 1940s, but when questioned by the House Committee on Un-American Activities, she refused to name names and was blacklisted. Would Wayne, who'd supported the blacklist, even read her script? Yes; and often thereafter he'd say it was the best screenplay he'd ever read. Portis, who visited the set, notes, "The screenplay stayed pretty close to the book. I noticed that . . . Hathaway used the book itself, with the pages much underlined, when he was setting up scenes."

Hathaway began as a child actor in Allan Dwan Westerns in 1909. By age fourteen he was a propboy at Universal, and after serving in the Army in World War I was back in Hollywood, assisting masters like Victor Fleming, Joseph von Sternberg, and Ernst Lubitsch. Between 1932 and 1933 he directed seven Zane Grey Westerns for Paramount starring Randolph Scott.

Hathaway had known Wayne since they were both silent-movie propmen, and he'd already directed Wayne in five movies. But, as Hathaway himself explained it, "To be a good director, you've got to be a bastard. I'm a bastard and I know it." Stuntman Gary Combs, who'd come to *True Grit* straight from *The Wild Bunch*, explains it more generously. "Henry knew everybody's job on the set just as well as he did his own, 'cause he'd been around for so long." He had no patience and screamed at actors.

Rosemary's Baby star Mia Farrow had agreed to play Mattie, but Robert Mitchum, who'd made *5 Card Stud* with Hathaway, warned Farrow against working with him. Farrow asked Wallis to replace Hathaway with *Rosemary's Baby* director Roman Polanski. That was the end for Mia, who years later would tell *The Independent* that turning down the roll of Mattie "was the worst career choice I ever made." Wayne asked Katharine Ross, his co-star in *The Hellfighters*, about the role. She recalls: "I read the book, and she was fourteen, and I thought that I was too old, so I didn't do it. What an idiot." She made *Butch Cassidy* instead.

Then Wallis saw Kim Darby in an episode of *Run for Your Life*, and knew he'd found Mattie Ross. Although age twenty-two, with a newborn baby, and divorcing James Stacy, she gave a convincing performance as the feisty fourteen-year-old.

For the role of Le Boeuf, Wallis cast Elvis Presley, who'd shown his acting talent in the Western *Flaming Star*. All that Col. Tom Parker, Elvis' Svengali, demanded was that Elvis be billed above Wayne. Elvis was out, and in was country singer and first-time actor Glen Campbell.

Puzzlingly, Jay Silverheels, *The Lone Ranger*'s Tonto, has a no-lines role as one of three men hanged when Mattie first arrives at Fort Smith. A look at the novel and screenplay reveals that originally each man had a speech, drawn from newspaper accounts, but all were cut from the film. It was a memorable scene for Combs, who doubled for Campbell and Robert Duvall, and was also up on the scaffold. "[We wore] leggings with cables that went under your instep, and up to a harness on your hip, so when you drop, you hit on your insteps, not your neck." They wore hoods. "The trapdoor was pretty small, and when you drop, you don't want to hit your head. I'd pulled the hood out in front so I could see the floor. Henry's rolling camera, and as hangman Guy Wilkerson comes by me, he jerks my hood down! My hands were tied behind my back, but they just had these little [fake] things wrapped around. So I snuck my hand out, pulled the hood out, and nobody saw it. Because I didn't want to go through that hole off-center and catch my nose on the edge."

The story was set in Arkansas, but Portis learned that during the making of *How the West Was Won* Hathaway had "marked down that stand of yellow aspens in the mountains near Montrose, and was determined to make [a] Western there." It was shot largely in the tiny town of Ridgway, Colorado, where Portis got to meet Duke. "Wayne was no letdown. He was actually bigger than his image on the screen, both in stature and presence." Wayne was, in fact, so big that casting notices for extras said they had to be at least 5'10", so they wouldn't look like munchkins next to him.

For Luster Bayless, wardrobe man on a dozen Wayne movies, the smallest item was his biggest challenge: the eye patch. Wayne insisted on being able to see through the patch, and after much experimentation, Bayless concocted a patch using window-screen mesh and gauze. There are always duplicates for key wardrobe items, but, he recalled, "John wanted a fresh patch every day, because they got dirty." Also, Wayne had put on weight. "He had some trouble getting on and off the horse. I had a stretchy fabric for his pants, that made it easier."

One unanticipated problem was just how scared Darby was of horses. Something as simple as leading her horse in a natural way was so difficult for her that, Combs remembers, "Henry went nuts. He got a fire hose—he was gonna hose her down, and the assistants came and calmed him down, and finally we got the shot." Nearly all of her riding was done by stuntwoman Polly Burson. "They made a mask of my face out of clay," Darby told the *L.A. Times*, "and she would wear that."

Glen Campbell was also not too experienced on a horse, "so they gave me a Shetland pony," he'd said. It wasn't quite that, but it did, purposely, look silly next to Wayne's steed. Campbell wasn't an experienced actor, "but The Duke promised that he could drag me through it alright." The modest Campbell often joked that his own poor acting made Wayne look so good that he won an Oscar.

Western film icon Wayne and ingenue co-star Kim Darby developed a great rapport on the set of *True Grit*. According to an interview by Susan King in the *Los Angeles Times* in 2011, Darby "fondly recall[ed] working with Wayne. 'He was there on the set before anyone else and knew every line perfectly.'" Among the powerful supporting performances were Robert Duvall as Ned Pepper. "John Wayne, he was a wonderful man," Duvall remembers. "But Henry Hathaway—we won't talk about him." And in a single scene, as a rustler who gets his fingers cut off, Dennis Hopper makes an indelible impression. He and Hathaway had clashed so famously on *From Hell to Texas* that Hopper became unemployable in features for years, until Hathaway hired him for *The Sons of Katie Elder*.

They'd shot most of the final scene, with Mattie offering Rooster a place in her family's cemetery, but when they returned the next morning, there were four inches of snow on the ground. It looked so beautiful that Hathaway scrapped the previous day's footage and shot it all over again. "Wayne wanted to jump the horse over the fence," remembers Combs. "So we took [stuntman] Chuck Hayward's falling horse, Twinkle Toes. He looked just like the horse that Duke was riding. Hayward and I were on either side, out of camera range, to protect him, but he jumped over the fence and rode off. He was fine."

John Wayne's granddaughter, Anita La Cava Swift, had seen his movies at home. "But," she said, "the first one I saw in a theater was *True Grit*. My very best friend was Alfred Hitchcock's granddaughter, and I didn't know my grandfather was as famous as he was until he won the Academy Award, and Alfred Hitchcock said, 'Make sure you tell your grandfather that I said congratulations,' I thought, okay, my grandfather *is* big-time!"

John Wayne left the Sonora set of *Undefeated* to attend the Academy Awards and receive his Oscar. When he returned, he was greeted by a strange sight: Bayless had outfitted every member of the cast and crew with an eye patch to welcome him back.

There were attempts to re-create the magic of *True Grit* over the years, including a sequel, *Rooster Cogburn*, co-starring Wayne with Katharine Hepburn, a reworking of her *African Queen*, with Wayne in the Bogart role; and the TV movie *True Grit—A Further Adventure*, starring Warren Oates. They're both watchable, but only the 2010 remake by the Coen brothers holds a candle to the original.

THE WILD BUNCH, AND BUTCH CASSIDY AND THE SUNDANCE KID—1969

Every period picture, consciously or not, reflects two periods, the time in which the story is set, and the time the film is made. Half a century ago, in the summer of 1969, the tumult of the times was inescapable. The "Summer of Love" of 1967, when hippies and flower-power and LSD were supposed to save the world, had been followed by the ghastly 1968, with the assassinations of Martin Luther King Jr. and Bobby Kennedy, riots at the Chicago Democratic Convention, the seemingly endless Vietnam War and, good or bad, the election of President Richard M. Nixon.

Out of this maelstrom came two Western movies. Each was directed by a TV-trained World War II Marine veteran, each budgeted at the then princely sum of about $6 million, and each fictionally recast and enlarged the legendary story of Butch Cassidy's Hole-in-the-Wall Gang, aka The Wild Bunch. At the box office, *Butch* would earn $102 million, four Oscars, and three more nominations. *Wild Bunch* would earn $638,000, two Oscar nominations, and no awards. Two of the finest films of the 20th century, their popularity today is far greater than when they were made, and their influence on films released since is incalculable.

Although the two stories have remarkably different tones, the historical inspirations for the plots are remarkably alike. In the early 1900s, an

The bounty hunters from *The Wild Bunch*, a remarkable collection of what Strother Martin called "prairie scum." (standing, l.-r.): Strother Martin, Bill Shannon, Robert Ryan, Bill Hart, L. Q. Jones; (kneeling, l.-r.): Buck Holland, Paul Harper, and Robert "Buzz" Henry. *Courtesy Warner Bros.*

outlaw gang learns in the midst of a holdup that they've been set up; a railroad magnate has spent a small fortune to assemble a super-posse to track them down and kill them. The posse in *Butch* is a faceless enemy. In *The Wild Bunch* they are a big part of the story, led by former associate Deke Thornton (Robert Ryan). In both films, the gang flees south of the border. In *Wild Bunch*, the gang stays together, goes as far as Mexico, and becomes involved with revolutionaries. In *Butch*, the gang splits up in the United States, and Butch, Sundance, and Etta flee all the way to Bolivia, and restart their criminal careers.

The longer gestation was for *Butch*. Novelist, playwright, and screenwriter William Goldman started researching the life of Cassidy in the late 1950s. He wrote his first drafts while teaching at Princeton. As he recalls in his book *Adventures in the Screen Trade*, "The Wild Bunch consisted of some of the most murderous figures in Western history. Arrogant, brutal men. And yet, here running things was Cassidy. Why? The answer is incredible but true: People just liked him." Goldman loved that while Sundance was a brooding killer, Butch had never even injured anyone during his outlaw career. Goldman had already had success in Hollywood with 1966's *Harper*, the Paul Newman detective film, when producer Paul Monash bought the *Butch* script for $400,000, the highest price paid for a screenplay at that time. It's frequently been cited as the best screenplay ever written. It won the Oscar.

The Wild Bunch was the brainchild of stuntman and Marlboro Man–model Roy Sickner. While not a writer, he'd worked in many Westerns, including *Nevada Smith* and Peckinpah's ill-fated *Major Dundee*. He had an idea for a Western about some outlaws who move down to Mexico to escape the law, and get into more trouble. Though more about action than plot and characters, Peckinpah was encouraging, as was Sickner's drinking buddy Lee Marvin, a big star since his 1966 Best Actor Oscar for *Cat Ballou*, who attached himself to the project. Katy Haber, who worked with Sam Peckinpah in various production roles on eight movies, says the story really took shape when Sickner teamed up with young screenwriter Walon Green. "It had been a Civil War film, but it was Walon Green who placed it in the Mexican revolution." Green, a Beverly Hills kid, had visited Mexico on a nature program as a teen and fell in love with the country and its people. He went to college in Mexico City and absorbed the nation's history. Though then a writer with no movie credits, he had talent and knowledge, and when he teamed with co-writer Peckinpah, they shaped the screenplay into something magnificent.

Professionally, Sam Peckinpah was on shaky ground when *The Wild Bunch* came along. *Ride the High Country* had been a sleeper hit, especially overseas. But his follow-up, *Major Dundee*, with forty-two minutes slashed from Sam's cut, was not the film he meant it to be, and it bombed. Next, he began directing Steve McQueen in *The Cincinnati Kid* but was fired after a week for filming an unscripted nude scene. He was hired to write and direct *Villa Rides!* but when star Yul Brynner complained that Villa wasn't coming off as heroic enough, Peckinpah was replaced by writer Robert Towne and director Buzz Kulick. He hadn't directed in two years.

George Roy Hill also had his troubles. Robert Crawford Jr., who would produce eight movies for Hill and describes himself as "Sancho Panza to his Man of La Mancha," recalls, "George got fired off *Hawaii* three times. And he was let go in post-production on *Thoroughly Modern Millie*." But unlike Peckinpah's situation, "*Millie* was a terrific success. So was *Hawaii*, and his agent then sent him *Butch Cassidy*." Paul Newman and Steve McQueen had been cast as the leads, but with Newman as Sundance. "George [tells] Newman, 'You're not right for Sundance. You should be playing Butch.' Newman says, 'This is kind of comedy, and I don't do comedy well.' George said, 'No, this is a tragedy, and you'll be terrific as Butch.' He convinced Paul to take Butch.

Chased by a relentless posse, with the only possible escape being a leap from a cliff into a river, Robert Redford (left) as Sundance, is about to tell Paul Newman (right) as Butch that he can't swim, in *Butch Cassidy and the Sundance Kid*. *Courtesy 20th Century Fox*

McQueen said, 'That's great, but I don't want to play Sundance.'" It may seem surprising that Robert Redford wasn't the natural choice for Sundance, but until *Butch* made him a star, he was considered a light comedy actor, not a dramatic lead.

Katharine Ross, who would play Etta Place, recalls, "The first script I got was called *The Sundance Kid and Butch Cassidy*." She was a natural for Westerns. "I started riding when I was seven." One of the last of the contract players at Universal, she'd guested on many Western series, and her first feature-film role was as James Stewart's daughter in the anti-war Western *Shenandoah*. "I really got that because of the *Gunsmoke* I did that Andy McLaglen [who would also direct *Shenandoah*] directed." She got the role of Etta in part because she'd become a star, and an Oscar nominee, for her wonderful performance opposite Dustin Hoffman in *The Graduate*. Also, as Hill noted in his audio commentary on *Butch*, "She came on the picture basically because I thought she was the sexiest girl I'd ever seen . . . just ravishingly beautiful."

As the *Wild Bunch* script evolved, Lee Marvin began to have real doubts. Pike Bishop was becoming more and more like his character in 1966's *The Professionals*, plus same locale, same uniforms; he didn't want to be typed.

When he was offered $1 million to co-star with Clint Eastwood in the musical Western *Paint Your Wagon*, he took it. That gave William Holden the chance to give the performance of his career. Fifty, but looking far more world-weary, Holden had been giving repetitive performances in mediocre films; he'd been convicted of manslaughter after a drunk-driving accident in Italy. He knew Pike Bishop's desperation, when all you have left is pride. He wasn't the studio's first choice, but Peckinpah held firm. "You know, Ernie Borgnine wasn't their first choice either," Haber remembers. After his Oscar for *Marty*, he'd squandered his talent on dross like *McHale's Navy*. "But Sam was emphatic. Proof is in the pudding in the film—that relationship was brilliant."

Most of the rest of the cast was made up of Peckinpah regulars, all doing exceptional work. Among the gang were Warren Oates and Ben Johnson, both on the eve of stardom, as the Gorch brothers. As Paul Seydor, director of the Oscar-nominated *The Wild Bunch: An Album in Montage*, says, "Tell me another movie in which you believe two men are brothers more than in *The Wild Bunch*." New to the Peckinpah fold was Bo Hopkins as Crazy Lee, the first of the Bunch to die, but making a strong impression with his character's affable menace. It was an unforgettable time in his life because, he says, "I got to work with my heroes. Bill Holden got me into two pictures. Ernest Borgnine became like a father to me till the day he died. Robert Ryan helped me do my first interview, because I didn't know what to say." He remembers preparing for the scene where he holds the railroad customers hostage, forcing them to march and sing hymns, "and Dub Taylor stayed up all night with me, helping me sing 'Shall We Gather at the River,' 'cause I hadn't memorized the whole song."

Between TV and movies, L. Q. Jones appeared in practically everything Sam Peckinpah did, here teamed with Strother Martin as bounty hunters who came off like a degenerate Abbott and Costello. Edmond O'Brien, Oscar-winner for *The Barefoot Contessa*, has a delightful turn as Freddy Sykes, a geezer who recalls Walter Huston in *Treasure of the Sierra Madre*, one of Peckinpah's favorite films. L. Q. recalls, "Eddie was so ill all the way through the picture that I spent two weeks at Eddie's place seeing they were feeding him right, that he was doing what the doctor told him to. Sam spaced his shooting out so Eddie didn't have to work two days in a row. He was sweating blood, but he was getting the work done." Remarkably, O'Brien would recover and live another fifteen years.

Another great performance was delivered by Emilio "El Indio" Fernandez as Mapache, the terrifyingly erratic rebel leader. A unique figure in Mexican history, Fernandez was a star actor, director and a convicted killer. L. Q. remembers, "He was also a military hero for Mexico. He came in one day to get me, and I was studying at my Spanish. He loved it, so after that, every day I came to his place so he could teach me some more Spanish. But I was petrified of the man, because the first day on the show, he tried to kill a waiter for giving him the wrong food."

The music from the two films could not have been more different. Jerry Fielding composed the score for *The Wild Bunch* and five other Peckinpah films. W. K. Stratton, author of *The Wild Bunch*, the definitive book on the film, notes, "Jerry went to Mexico and researched the actual music that was being played during the revolution and then wrote his. *The Wild Bunch* has eighty-five minutes of music in it." Fielding's score was Oscar-nominated. Hill wanted a contemporary feel to *Butch Cassidy*, and that included the score by Burt Bacharach, which was focused on three lyrical music sequences. Crawford reveals that when Hill gave them the rough-cut to work with, he'd cut the famous bicycle scene to Simon and Garfunkel's "59th Street Bridge Song," aka "Feeling Groovy." Bacharach would win Oscars for the score and the replacement song, "Raindrops Keep Falling on My Head."

Katherine Ross reflects, "[One] of the most memorable parts, for me, is the bicycle ride. [It] was done with a very long lens, and the only direction we got was whether we were going left to right or right to left across frame. So we were left to our own devices; it was very improvisational. It is very uncomfortable riding in an orchard on the handlebars of a bicycle."

That wasn't the only uncomfortable situation for Ross on the shoot. She was watching cinematographer Conrad Hall, who would win the Oscar for *Butch*, shooting the sequence where the super-posse bursts from the train. "I was going with Conrad at that time." He invited her to operate one of the cameras. "It was the last shot of the day. There were six cameras, and I was on camera six, an Arriflex on a McConnell head, just panning along. George Roy Hill decided to sit near the camera I was operating, but he never said anything. Back at the motel, the production manager said, you have a very angry director on your hands. I got banned from the set except when I was working." Considering how male-dominated the Camera Union was at that time, Katharine Ross may very well have been the first woman to be a camera operator on a Hollywood movie.

Lucien Ballard was Peckinpah's cinematographer on *The Wild Bunch* and eight other shows, and his work was phenomenal. Notes Seydor, "He would set up four cameras and they would often be shooting at four different speeds." This was particularly crucial for the elaborate shoot-outs at the beginning and end of the film, for which Peckinpah and editor Lou Lombardo masterfully alternated between standard speed and various degrees of slow motion, to make the viewer hyperaware of the destruction and slaughter. No action film since *The Wild Bunch* has *not* been influenced by Ballard's photography and Lombardo's editing.

While the leads in both films die in the end, the filmmakers deal with it very differently. Peckinpah showed it in brutal detail. Hill did not want to see his heroes torn with bullets and decided on a freeze-frame, with the audio of gunfire continuing. While the Wild Bunch's last few speeches were dramatically terse, Butch and Sundance, even when mortally wounded, kid each other rather than talking about their dire situation.

Crawford remembers the first preview of *Butch Cassidy and the Sundance Kid* in San Francisco. "People were laughing right up to the end of the movie, when they were all shot up, and about to charge out. Everybody was elated, all the applause, all the executives saying, 'It's a winner! It's wonderful!' And George was that little guy with a cloud over his head. And he looked at me, and said, 'They laughed at my tragedy.'"

MONTE WALSH—1970

The film *Monte Walsh* was made in 1970, and like so many fine Westerns of its time, it was about the end of the Western era, but unlike most, it wasn't about outlaws, like *The Wild Bunch*, or gunfighters, like *The Shootist*. It was about hardworking, honest cowboys, typified by Monte (Lee Marvin) and Chet (Jack Palance), whose world was disappearing before their eyes as ranches merged into vast tracts controlled by faceless syndicates, their assets to be stripped. Its relevance has only grown with the years.

Critic Roger Ebert gave it four stars but cautioned, "This may be the first three-handkerchief Western." It is by turns uproarious, sweet, wistful, contemplative, exciting, tragic, and suspenseful. *Monte Walsh* got made because producer Bobby Roberts wanted to make a movie with his Malibu neighbor Lee Marvin. Marvin, a decorated World Wat II Marine, a star "heavy" since 1962's *The Man Who Shot Liberty Valance*, had become a leading man with his Oscar-winning comedy performance in 1965's *Cat Ballou*. Roberts asked Marvin's girlfriend Michelle Triola for a suggestion, and she said *Monte Walsh*.

The rambling *Monte Walsh* novel was not the obvious Hollywood home run that author Jack Schaefer's previous tight and taut *Shane* had been. It's more a collection of character sketches than a story, and screenwriters Lucas Heller and David Zelag Goodman surgically isolated the best vignettes to create a plot.

Everyone in the production was stretching their talents in some way. William Fraker was a great cameraman with deep Western roots—he'd started as assistant cameraman on *The Lone Ranger* TV series—but he was directing for the first time. Cinematographer David Walsh was promoted from camera operator; his photography was often heartbreakingly beautiful. Palance was a great villain but was daringly cast as a nice guy. Mitch Ryan, best known for the vampire soap opera *Dark Shadows*, was cast as Shorty, who goes to the dark side when his horse-breaking job is eliminated. "Jack [Palance] and I talked about the complexities of Shorty," Ryan recalls, "about how much of a challenge both our parts were, because his was a very sweet, shy kind of a guy. He said it was much more complicated than it looks like."

The film's cast was a perfect mix of seasoned hands like growling Jim Davis as the Slash-Y range manager and youngster cowhand Bo Hopkins, fresh from *The Wild Bunch*. "I was thrilled to death, even though it was a small part, just to work with Lee and Jack Palance," recalled Hopkins.

Perhaps the finest stroke of casting was international film star Jeanne Moreau in her only American film appearance; she's luminous as Martine, the prostitute who loves Monte. Their mutual admiration blossomed on and off the set into a screen romance, which makes their scenes some of the best—and most believable—of the film.

Memorable set pieces include a mustang drive and a familiar bunkhouse brawl, made special with touches like a cowpoke removing his dentures before joining in. The most copied is the sequence in which the cowboys, unable to enjoy the cook's good food because of his foul odor, drag him to a water tank and scrub him, followed by his revenge.

The film succeeds largely on Marvin's portrayal of Monte, and his behind-the-scenes involvement. "He was a meticulous actor, down to the barbwire cuts on his arm, things that make a performance marvelous," Ryan remembers. "He helped me pick my wardrobe." The wonderfully weaselly Matt Clark, as a cowhand and occasional bank robber who leads Shorty astray, recalls, "Lee said, 'I'm gonna tell you a secret. I do half of my performance in the wardrobe fitting.'"

When Chet quits cowboying and marries The Hardware Widow, Monte begins to rethink his own future. He asks Martine why they never married. "Because you never asked me." He asks her then, and although she says an immediate yes, it turns out to be too late to make it work.

A saloon scene in which a lawman draws on Clark while he's with Billy Green Bush and Ryan, leading to Ryan killing him, was simple on the page but a logistical nightmare. Clark remembers riding to the set with the other actors and "Lee is drunker than Cooter Brown. I said, 'This doesn't make sense. I'm not going to pull a gun when he's standing there with a gun on us!' So Lee said, 'What if you have your arm on the bar—'" And Marvin choreographed the scene, positioning the three outlaws so that Bush could slip a gun to Clark that the lawman couldn't see. "If Lee'd been interested in anything other than catching blue Marlin and drinking, he could have been one of the best directors going."

Fraker went on to direct the infamous *Legend of the Lone Ranger* but redeemed himself when he returned to cinematography for *Tombstone*. Palance would win his Oscar twenty-two years later, like Marvin did, for a comedy, *City Slickers*. Marvin would go on to many more great performances, but *Monte Walsh* would be the last straw with him and Michelle Triola, who sued the producers, claiming partial ownership of the film. She also sued Marvin, and lost both cases, but introduced the word *palimony* to the English language.

THE COWBOYS—1972

Who would've guessed that, in the last decade of his life, a lung lost to cancer, John "Duke" Wayne would star in a dozen films, three of them—1969's *True Grit*, 1972's *The Cowboys*, and 1976's *The Shootist*—among the best of his career?

The premise of *The Cowboys* was refreshingly original: with all the able-bodied cowhands chasing a gold strike, an aging rancher (played by Wayne) hires a schoolhouse-full of boys to move his cattle to market.

Actor-turned-director Mark Rydell, of Lee Strasberg's famed Actors Studio, wasn't known as a Western filmmaker, but he'd already directed ten *Gunsmoke* episodes for CBS. Fresh from the success of the 1969 Steve McQueen comedy *The Reivers*, he began reading an as-yet-unpublished novel, *The Cowboys*, by William Dale Jennings. Forty pages in, Rydell knew he wanted to film it.

Jennings was an unconventional Western author to say the least. Raised in Denver, Colorado, the playwright, novelist, and decorated WWII soldier gained fame in 1952 by refusing to plead guilty to homosexual solicitation in a Los Angeles park; he's frequently cited as the "gay Rosa Parks."

John Wayne and the eleven boys he hires to drive his cattle in 1972's *The Cowboys* (from left): A Martinez, Stephen Hudis, Mike Pyeatt, Norman Howell, Steve Benedict, Nicolas Beauvy, Sam O'Brien, Bob Carradine, Al Barker Jr., Sean Kelly, John Wayne, and Clay O'Brien. *Courtesy Warner Bros.*

When Rydell brought the property to Warner Bros., his heart was set on George C. Scott as rancher Wil Andersen, but the studio heads pleaded with him to consider Wayne. Rydell reluctantly flew to Durango, Mexico, to meet with Wayne on the set of 1971's *Big Jake.*

"He was very conservative politically," Rydell says of Wayne, "and I was a liberal Jewish kid from the Bronx. We couldn't have been more polar opposites. But I found him to be one of the nicest guys I ever met."

For the screenplay, Rydell matched Jennings with Irving Ravetch and Harriet Frank Jr., the legendary husband-and-wife writing team from *The Reivers.* He also brought along *Reivers* composer John Williams and hired three-time Oscar-winning cinematographer Robert Surtees.

All the bad guys except the lead were stuntmen who knew how to ride, fight, and die on camera. To keep Wayne out of his comfort zone, Rydell did not cast characters from Wayne's stock company (with the exception of Duke's friend Slim Pickens, with whom he'd never actually acted), but from the Actors Studio: Roscoe Lee Browne as the cook, Colleen Dewhurst as the madam, blacklist-victim Sarah Cunningham as Wil's wife.

For the lead villain, Bruce Dern was ideal—except he was acting for Douglas Trumbull's sci-fi film *Silent Running.* "My first starring role," Dern remembers. "My agent called me: 'You've got to have two days off next week because I have a role you must do. No one can know this. They're doing a movie where John Wayne's going to be killed, and you're going to be the guy that does it!'" Trumbull shot miniatures for two days so Dern could get away to act in *The Cowboys*.

The biggest casting challenge was finding eleven boys to play the cowboys. In a stroke of genius, Rydell cast half actors and half rodeo kids. Actor-turned-stuntman Stephen Hudis, who played Charlie Schwartz, remembers, "Before we set foot on location, we had eight weeks of intense riding training. They would have acting classes, and we would help them out with that, and they would help us with the horseback."

Dern remembers Clay O'Brien, the smallest boy of the group, almost didn't make it into the film. "John Wayne said, 'Well, you're too small, son,'" Dern recalls. "Clay, in that little voice, piped up, 'I can drop you, you big son of a bitch.' The kid twirled a rope three times, hooked his boots and dropped Wayne on his ass. 'Who's too small now?'"

Since then, O'Brien has won seven World Champion rodeo titles.

Stuntman Walter Scott was thrilled to act with Wayne, playing one of the cowhands who abandons him: "When [Wayne] says his line, I say, 'What do you expect? You work us like dogs, night and day and Christmas too.' He looks at the director, says, 'Is he gonna read that line that way?' I'm thinking, aw hell, he hates my acting. 'Because if he does, I'd hit him. You'd better move him over there.' And I just jumped across to where he was pointing, and we did the scene again."

The kids adored Wayne; Dern, not so much. But that was by design.

"When I got there," Dern says, "John Wayne said, 'I want you to do yourself and me a favor. Around the set, I want you to kick my ass in front of these little kids, so they're absolutely terrified of you.' He gave me the license to do that.

"The day we come to the scene where I shoot him, [Wayne] said to me, 'Ooh, are they going to hate you for this!' I said, 'Maybe, but in Berkeley, I'm a hero.'"

Ironically, Dern, the bully who terrorizes and almost drowns the kid with glasses played by Nicolas Beauvy in the movie, made friends with the actor. Beauvy, now a realtor, remembers, "I was a big sports fan and so was he, so even after the movie was finished, he'd invite me to Lakers games in Los Angeles. He is a great guy."

Looking back, men and boys-turned-men talk with amazement at how hard Wayne pushed himself, doing nearly all his own stunts, his own riding. Rydell and Wayne set the bar awfully high, and in grasping it, cast and crew did some of the finest work of their careers.

The Cowboys premiered at the tail end of the Western movie cycle that had continued uninterrupted since 1903's *The Great Train Robbery*. Dern concedes, "A lot of people will tell you that the reason they don't make them anymore is because *Star Wars* and *Lord of the Rings*, those are the Westerns to the kids now. But you and I know there's always a place for a Western. The stories are great, the times are great and, for the most part, it really happened."

THE OUTLAW JOSEY WALES—1976

In the latter quarter of the 20th century, the only person indispensable to Western film was Clint Eastwood. Losing a Peckinpah or a Leone would have been bad, but without Eastwood, the genre would have been deader than the Daltons. It's been nearly half a century since Clint Eastwood made one of his finest Westerns, *The Outlaw Josey Wales*. Many consider the 1976 film one of the best Western movies ever made.

When Forrest Carter's first novel was published—an initial press run of seventy-five copies—he was unaware that Eastwood's Malpaso Company did not accept unsolicited material. But producer Robert Daley was so moved by the cover letter accompanying *The Rebel Outlaw: Josey Wales* that he read the book. He then told Eastwood, "This thing has so much soul to it that it's really one of the nicest things I've read."

The actor-director agreed. He bought the film rights.

The movie is an unconventional Civil War and post-war story, focusing not on generals and battles but on the aftermath of the guerilla war between the North's Red Legs and the South's Bushwhackers, and the abuse of Indians who had sided with the South. Josey Wales, Eastwood's character, is a farmer who joins the Bushwhackers after his wife and son are murdered by Red Legs. When the Civil War ends, he refuses to sign a loyalty oath. He and Jamie (played by Sam Bottoms) set out, tracked relentlessly by the Red Leg commander (Bill McKinney) and a Judas (John Vernon).

The story contains not only grim elements and action but also humor and beauty and endearing characters. Eastwood's co-star, Oscar-nominee Sondra Locke, shares why the film is special to her: "It had a great story, a great hero too, and Clint was perfect for it. [In his] Spaghetti [Western] films, he had no attachment to anybody. He was a loner out for himself. In *The Outlaw Josey Wales*, he'd been victimized; he had a family that he'd lost. He was a man who responded to humanity, to other human beings. *The Outlaw Josey Wales* had a traveling band of colorful characters—all struggling for a dream. I think it was that soul in the film that made it special."

Walter Scott, who began doubling Eastwood on CBS's *Rawhide* series, was double and stunt coordinator on *The Outlaw Josey Wales*. He says scenes were shot all over the West: "We were in Utah first, for all the Indian stuff. Then down to Old Tucson [Arizona], then to Marysville, up by Sacramento [California] for all the stuff with the raft."

There, the Red Legs are on a ferry, trying to catch up to Wales, when he shoots the ferry rope, sending the raft spinning down the river. "I had seven or eight stuntmen and horses on it," Scott says. "We thought it would twist and turn, but that raft was so good, it didn't move! They had to push the horses off, and I'm yelling at them, 'Get off! Someone go into the water!'"

Eastwood had already directed five features by that time, including 1973's *High Plains Drifter*, but he had not intended to direct this one. He hired Philip Kaufman, who had written and directed 1972's *The Great Northfield Minnesota Raid*. Then problems developed between them on the set. Locke remembers, "Kaufman's a good writer, and it was a really well-written script. [As a director] he was unbelievably slow; he would intellectualize everything. Clint was just the opposite. Clint just would run on his gut. He knew what he wanted, and he just grabbed it."

"Clint fired him after two weeks and took over," Scott recalled. "The Directors Guild passed a law after that and said an actor couldn't do that; it's called the Eastwood Rule. Clint started all over again, and we still finished two weeks under schedule."

Scott remembers the big shoot-out at the end, with Wales and his friends in the cabin, being attacked on all sides by the Red Legs, a sequence that would normally take several days to film. "Clint gave me a day with the stunt-men to rehearse and lay out every piece," Scott says. "He said, 'Tell me what you've got.' 'I've got some guys going around the hill; they'll fall the horses down. The guy up on top, he's going to cave the roof in. Other guys are riding by—we've got a jerk wire on one guy.' We filmed it all in half a day. End of the day, I'm [paying off] the stuntmen, Clint walks by, and says, 'Hey boys, whatever he gives you, just double it, because it was a helluvah day!'"

If the characters in *The Outlaw Josey Wales* dreamed of changing their lives, so did the author of the book that inspired the movie. But Forrest Carter's success was his undoing. He was exposed as Asa Carter, a once powerful leader of the Ku Klux Klan. Although he, unlike Wales, did not succeed in leaving his past behind, he did leave a heartfelt literary legacy. It includes *The Education of Little Tree*, the story of a Cherokee boy growing up during the Great Depression—Carter claimed that it was his autobiography, rather than a work of fiction, but it is much-beloved and often read in schools.

Locke cherished her memories of cast members, from character actors Sheb Wooley and Royal Dano, to seventy-nine-year-old Paula Trueman, "who would do somersaults to make Clint laugh," to Chief Dan George and despicable Bill McKinney. "Chief Dan was just the way he was on-screen," Locke says, "and Bill McKinney was just the opposite; a funny, funny guy."

THE LONG RIDERS—1980

In 1980, an audacious casting inspiration—real acting brothers portraying the outlaw brothers who made up the James–Younger gang—triggered the making of a classic Western, *The Long Riders*. Surprisingly, the brothers who thought of it, Stacy and James Keach, credit another pair of brothers with inspiring it. In 1972, they'd co-starred in a TV movie called *Orville and Wilbur* and, Stacy recalls, "We said, well, we've done the Wright brothers. Now let's do the wrong brothers: the James brothers." The sons of actor and *Tales of the Texas Rangers* creator Stacy Keach Sr., they were no strangers to the genre: Stacy had been nominated for a Tony in 1969 for playing Buffalo Bill in *Indians* and starred as the consumptive dentist John Henry Holliday in *Doc*. James remembers, "I wrote a show called *The Bandit Kings*, a musical about Frank and Jesse James. We did it off Broadway."

"It was not very good," Stacy admits, "but it was spirited, and we decided we should do it as a movie rather than a play." They headed for California, dropped the songs, rewrote it as a screenplay, and tried for nearly nine years to get it made. Then came the Keaches' stroke of genius, the casting: the Keaches as the James boys; David, Keith, and Robert Carradine as the Youngers; Randy and the then-unknown Dennis Quaid as the Millers; and Beau and Jeff Bridges as the dirty little cowards, the Fords. When the studios wouldn't believe they were all on board, James remembers, "We got all the brothers together, and we took a picture. And that was our calling card for anybody who couldn't believe we could get all these guys together."

While James was in Bora Bora, acting in *Hurricane*, producer Tim Zinneman (son of *High Noon* director Fred Zinneman) read his script. A friend of Walter Hill's since they'd been assistant directors on *Bullitt*, Tim told James, "I've got to give this to Walter. He's going to love this."

Hill, a big-time screenwriter since writing Sam Peckinpah's *The Getaway*, had made a splash as an action director with the hit gang drama *The Warriors*. Zinneman set up *The Long Riders* at United Artists. Hill says with a laugh, "They thought they were getting a 'catch' in me. The truth is, it was my first Western, and I'd have crawled through fire and broken glass to do it. So they

The Keach boys are the James boys, and the Carradines are the Youngers in Walter Hill's *The Long Riders*. (l.-r.): Robert Carradine, David Carradine, Randy Quaid, Dennis Quaid (partially blocked), Stacy Keach, James Keach, and Keith Carradine. *Courtesy United Artists*

had me at a bargain, and all the brothers worked at a bargain too, [even] those who were in more of a commanding position for salaries, David [Carradine] and Stacy [Keach]."

There was more casting to be done. The Quaids were added, then the Guests, Robert Carradine remembers, because, "the Bridges backed out. They didn't want to be the guys who shot Jesse James in the back." Pamela Reed, who played Belle Starr to David Carradine's Cole Younger, had very little film experience, but Hill remembers, "She came in and read and I just thought she was perfect."

Reed had her doubts. "There was the scene in the bathtub with no clothes on, something I swore I'd never do. Hill said, 'I will not embarrass you, and I will give you the respect that an actor deserves.'" She agreed. "David was just a consummate professional: wry, dry, charming, sexy, smart, really sensitive. On the first take, he just looked at me. He started with my toes and went up to my head, and by the time he finished looking at me, I felt like I was Simone Signoret in her prime. I stood up out of that tub and I said, 'Well, here I am.' And I guess I meant it in every sense of the word."

James Keach says the film was shot in Georgia because "Missouri [had] too many Fosters Freezes and telephone poles; the first day of shooting was nearly a terrible disaster." James and Stacy were riding across a river when, Carradine remembers, "Stacy's horse caught a foot in the rear cinch on his saddle, was going to drown." The horse kept coming up, gulping air and going down again. "The head wrangler timed it for the next time he came up, threw a rope around that horse's neck and they were able to pull him out."

There were other occasional problems along the way. In the barn shoot-out, James got too close to a squib, "and it blew a hole in my back." The crew went to Texas to shoot a scene with a train that the *Heaven's Gate* crew had been using, "And when they gave it to us, they'd painted [it] red, so they would fuck us up. We did the train robbery in Northern California."

Despite outside predictions, the brothers got along well. James suggests one reason: "We were all musicians, so we would play music all the time. Keith won an Academy Award. Bobby's an incredible guitar player."

Stacy's only complaint is that they changed his ending. "We felt that Jesse shouldn't die at the hands of Bob and Charlie Ford, hanging a picture on the wall." In the Keach version, they faked Jesse's death, the Fords took the credit, "and Jesse went off and lived in obscurity. Walter thought it was too gimmicky; but my brother and I still would love to tell that story." Why not in *The Long Riders II*?

LONESOME DOVE—1989

Making the film should have been easy. Movies from Larry McMurtry's novels—1963's *Hud* and 1971's *The Last Picture Show*—had already earned five Oscars when, in 1972, *The Last Picture Show* director Peter Bogdanovich tried to package McMurtry's new Western screenplay. The story of retired Texas Rangers on a cattle drive was then titled *Streets of Laredo* (a title McMurtry would reuse). They had signed James Stewart as Gus and Henry Fonda as Jake Spoon. But when John Wayne turned down the part of Woodrow Call, the deal fell through.

More than a decade—and five Oscars (for 1983's *Terms of Endearment*)—later, McMurtry bought back his script from the studio, expanded the story into a novel and, this time, all of the stars aligned properly. Motown Productions was best known for shows with a black music core, like 1975's *Mahogany* and 1978's *The Wiz*, but production head Suzanne De Passe read the pre-publication (and pre-Pulitzer) galleys and amazed everyone by purchasing the rights.

The cowboys of *Lonesome Dove* left to right: Robert Urich (back to the camera), Timothy Scott, Tommy Lee Jones, D. B. Sweeney, Robert Duvall, Danny Glover, and Ricky Schroder. *Credit: Bill Wittliff, courtesy of Wittliff Collections, Texas State University*

She hired Texas-centric writer and director William Wittliff, who had made three Westerns with Willie Nelson, 1980's *Honeysuckle Rose*, 1982's *Barbarosa*, and 1986's *Red Headed Stranger*, to adapt the novel into a miniseries. Sydney-born Australian Simon Wincer, who had shown a penchant for frontier-based movies and would become a Westerns specialist—witness the excellent 1990 Western *Quigley Down Under*—was signed to direct. A rich supporting cast was bolstered by the leads, Robert Duvall and Tommy Lee Jones.

Today, *Lonesome Dove* is widely recognized as the best Western ever made for television. Many count it among the half-dozen best Westerns of any medium. While *Lonesome Dove* never played on the big screen, its astonishing ratings and video sales revitalized Westerns. Without this miniseries, would we have had 1990's *Dances with Wolves*, 1992's *Unforgiven*, and 1993's *Tombstone*?

Lonesome Dove was a high-water mark in the careers of most of the folks involved. Ricky Schroder was just coming off five seasons on the sitcom *Silver Spoons* when he landed the role of Newt, the illegitimate son of Tommy Lee Jones's character, Call.

"I was seventeen, and I turned eighteen making *Lonesome Dove*," Schroder says. "Newt was a career-changing role. It helped me grow from a teen-aged—'heartthrob' was your word—into part of an iconic Western piece of history. It helped me immensely. It is, in my opinion, one of the best five Westerns ever made." His relationships with the two leads were quite different. "Duvall would always have a gathering, whenever he could get people together to go to this little local Mexican restaurant where they had live music. And he would dance—he loved to tango. He was always the life of the party. He was fun to be around. He was Gus. Tommy Lee I don't think said two words to me besides what was in the script. He didn't interact like that with me. Maybe he was just playing it the way (his character) Call played it, which was he didn't acknowledge Newt. So I didn't get to know him at all.

"The genius behind *Lonesome Dove* was the script (by Larry McMurtry and William D. Wittliff), and it was Duvall, and the source material (the novel by Larry McMurtry). That was the genius."

Why has *Lonesome Dove* lasted? De Passe gave the reason when she spoke at Rob Word's luncheon marking *Lonesome Dove*'s 25th anniversary: "I was always fighting the guys, Simon Wincer and [producer] Dyson Lovell, saying you can't take out the two little pigs following the wagon, you can't take out Clara begging Gus to stay, because that was the romance of the piece. And if I was anything, I was the romance cop when it came to editing. *Lonesome Dove* appealed to women and men in equal measure, and that is why it stood the test of time."

DANCES WITH WOLVES—1990 (A QUARTER-CENTURY TRIBUTE)

Dances with Wolves, released in 1990, garnered Kevin Costner both Best Picture and Best Director Oscars. The film also won Best Screenplay, Score, Editing, Cinematography, and Sound. Aside from these well-deserved awards, Costner did something else remarkable: he made an epic Western that was both a critical and popular success, taking in more than $184 million.

The excesses and financial disaster of 1980's *Heaven's Gate* had nearly killed the Western. Costner proved the genre still had plenty of life and artistic value, and that huge audiences, male and female, would come out to see a good one. Arguably, without the success of *Dances with Wolves*, we might not have gotten 1992's *Unforgiven*, 1993's *Tombstone*, or 1994's *Wyatt Earp*.

Costner's equal partner in this great success was Michael Blake. They met on the set of 1983's *Stacy's Knights*, written by Blake and starring Costner. The writer told the actor a story he had been toying with concerning Lt. John Dunbar, an inadvertent Civil War hero assigned by a madman to the farthest fort on the American West frontier. There, he learns about himself through hardship and brutal danger, and learns about the American Indians who have been dismissed as "thieves and beggars." His life is forever changed.

Blake, who passed away in 2015, at age sixty-nine, left not only *Dances with Wolves* as his legacy but also other Western stories to come.

We, the audience, have our own special memories of the film: the buffalo hunt, the opening battle, the beautiful South Dakota vistas, Dunbar's romance with Stands With A Fist.

Those lucky enough to have worked on the film will never forget the experience. Bill Markley authored *Dakota Epic*, his day-to-day account of being a reenactor on *Dances with Wolves*. He later shouldered a musket in 1991's *Son of the Morning Star*, 1992's *Far and Away*, and 1993's *Gettysburg*.

"It really was kind of a family; Kevin and Michael and [producer] Jim Wilson were close friends, and that esprit de corps really rubbed off on everybody. I didn't experience that comradeship, that friendliness, on any other movie sets," Markley says. "There was one where, if you tried to talk to the actors, you'd be fired immediately. To have the opposite kind of experience first spoils you for everyone else.

"Michael Blake was a really nice guy. He'd stand with three sweaty, grubby guys to have his picture taken. Blake said he had Kevin in mind when he wrote the book. He was going through a divorce and living out of his car. He'd go over to the Costners' house to take showers when he was writing it."

Daniel Ostroff, who produced 2003's *The Missing*, was Blake's agent during *Dances with Wolves* and had been his producing partner afterwards. "Michael was there for about half of the shooting, when he had to come home," Ostroff says. "Kevin had invested his own salary in the movie; he wasn't getting paid. It was costing $1,000 a week to keep Michael there, and they just couldn't afford it. Kevin was committed to shooting every single word [of the script]. A few months after principal photography, we watched Kevin's first cut. We were blown away—Michael's vision was all there on-screen, and that's 100 percent owing to Kevin."

One of the most recognized of American Indian actors, Wes Studi, gained lasting fame as Magua in 1992's *The Last of the Mohicans*, starred as Geronimo in 1993's *Geronimo*, and is Chief Levi Gall in the Sundance Channel series *The Red Road*. Of his chilling role as Toughest Pawnee in *Dances with Wolves*, Studi reflects, "After twenty-five years, I readily admit it was the firecracker that got my career started.

"There'd been a feeling, certainly amongst the Indian cast, that this was going to be a breakthrough film. There were a lot of aspects that hadn't been done in a good long while. Like the languages, and that we got inside the head of Graham Greene's character, and Wind In His Hair, and got to see a lot of real life happening in the Lakota camps. There was a feeling that this was going to be a successful film, but certainly not to the extent that it came to be successful."

Studi's most vivid memory of the filming? "Maybe my death scene," he says. "When they all surround me and fire away, and I roll off the back of the horse—into very cold water. I kid my Lakota friends about how it took that many Sioux to kill one Pawnee—and they all had guns."

CHAPTER 2
THE STARS—MAINLY FILM

ROBERT DUVALL

With seven Emmys won, *Lonesome Dove* is unquestionably television's most respected Western achievement. The roles were so good, the nominations of Robert Duvall and Tommy Lee Jones as Best Actor, and Diane Lane and Anjelica Huston as Best Actress, may have split the vote and cancelled each other out.

The miniseries had such a profound effect on the filmmakers and actors that many careers are now seen as pre–*Lonesome Dove* and post–*Lonesome Dove*. Jones had been a respected film and TV actor for nearly two decades, but *Lonesome Dove* made him a star. Lane's performance solidified her transition to adult roles, as was true for Ricky Schroder, who went from teen heartthrob to leading man. With his Emmy win, Simon Wincer went from being an obscure director of Aussie TV episodes to perhaps the most in-demand Westerns director since John Ford.

Duvall, on the other hand, was already a star. Famous for his portrayal of Tom Hagen, the adopted son of Don Corleone, in 1972's *The Godfather* and 1974's *The Godfather: Part II*, Duvall had been nominated for Oscars for *The Godfather*, 1979's *Apocalypse Now*, and *The Great Santini*, and won the statue for 1983's *Tender Mercies*. Millions of schoolkids knew him—and generations of them still do—as Boo Radley in 1962's *To Kill a Mockingbird*. He had hardly stepped before a TV camera in twenty years, but he knew this would be no ordinary miniseries. "In fact," he says, "on *Lonesome Dove*, I walked into the dressing room and said, 'Boys, we're making the *Godfather* of Westerns.'"

He spoke from his home in Virginia on January 5, 2016, his 85th birthday.

Do you still feel that Gus McCrea in Lonesome Dove was the best role you ever had?
Probably. There are other parts I liked. I played a Cuban barber [in 1993's *Wrestling Ernest Hemingway*], with Richard Harris, which was one of my favorite parts. Man, I worked on that accent. Another one of my performances I liked was when I played Stalin [1992's *Stalin*]. I try to do different things.

But I would say *Lonesome Dove* was like my *Hamlet* or my *Henry V*, so to speak. When it was over, I felt like I could retire; I felt I'd done something fully and completely. He was a very complex guy. He said, we killed off all the people that were interesting. That was years ago, but it was a fine character to be able to play.

How much are you like Gus McCrae?
McMurtry still thinks we [me and Tommy Lee Jones] should have switched parts, and I totally disagree with the guy.

Way back, my second wife—and I thank her eternally for this—said, 'I read a book I like better, maybe, than Dostoyevsky: *Lonesome Dove*.' She said, 'They're going to offer you the other part, but you have to play Augustus McCrea, because it's the most like you.'

You always try to find in yourself what the character calls for. They had offered the part to James Garner. I said to my agent, 'If you can get him to change parts, I'll do it.' He called back four hours later, said Garner's got a bad back. He can't go horseback for sixteen weeks. I said, 'Now go after that part.'

It was so well-written, the adaptation by [William] Wittliff. It was something that just drew me along. I was riding a lot of horses then, so I was very comfortable; I felt ready when we went. I had a little leverage; I wish I'd had more.

They asked, 'Who do you want for Call?' I said, 'Tommy Lee Jones.' We had a true Comanche Indian to play Blue Duck, but they wouldn't go for that. We went to [Jones's] ranch in San Saba; we herded cattle riding Argentine polo saddles. He was a very open guy.

I'm told you designed the Gus McCrae hat.
They insisted, some of the powers that be, that I wear a Mexican sombrero to play Gus. I said, 'I will not play the part if that's the case.'

I had to go to the producers. I showed them pictures of Texas Rangers on the border, and they all wore the kind of hats I wore in the movie. I said, 'Let me pick my own hat,' which, finally, they allowed.

How did starring in Lonesome Dove *affect your career?*
It's a lot like when I got an Oscar [1984's *Tender Mercies*]; a lot more recognition in airports. Wherever I go, people refer to that.

When I was made an honorary Texas Ranger, a woman came up to me. 'Mr. Duvall, we watch this once a year. I wouldn't let my daughter's fiancé marry into the family until he'd seen *Lonesome Dove.*'

In other places I go, too, but especially in Texas. It's kind of a landmark for people.

What were the other actors like to work with?
Diane Lane was fine; wonderful to work with. And Ricky Schroder. It's interesting, because her husband, I think they're divorced now, Josh Brolin, was up for the part [of Newt], but he was a week late, because Ricky Schroder got it a week prior.

Originally, we wanted Freddy Forrest for [Robert Urich's role], but then Freddy ended up playing Blue Duck. Robert was very nice to work with.

Anjelica Huston was great to work with. And she'd grown up riding horseback; riding on hunts with her father in Ireland.

Did you have any doubts about a non-American director for your Western?
No, Simon Wincer had done stuff. He came in well-prepared, and we went to work. And Dougie Milsom—the cinematographer—was terrific: he'd done *Full Metal Jacket.*

We had sixteen weeks to work, and it was nice; it was concentrated. First ten days around Austin. Then down around Del Rio, Texas, near the border. Then up to New Mexico. Then up to Angel Fire Mountains farther up in New Mexico, to suffice for Montana's Rockies, because we couldn't afford to go there.

I was fortunate to be in, what I think I'm correct in saying, the two biggest film epics of the 20th century: *The Godfather I* and *II,* and *Lonesome Dove.*

Earlier in your career, you played villain Ned Pepper in True Grit, *working with two legends, director Henry Hathaway and John Wayne.*
Henry Hathaway—we won't talk about him. But we'll talk about John Wayne, definitely. He was a wonderful man. Good actor, good guy. So good in *The Shootist* at the end of his career.

Back to Hathaway. I don't want to badmouth him, but he's the guy who said, 'When I say action, tense up, Goddamnit!' There's a difference between intensity and tenseness. I didn't enjoy working with him, and I didn't think he treated Kim Darby so well.

You played Jesse James in The Great Northfield Minnesota Raid.
Right. I said, 'Let's get Gene Hackman to play my brother, Frank.' They said he wasn't well known enough back then. Now he's retired. Retired! Jesus, it's funny.

How does playing villains compare with heroes?
You try to find the human being in yourself that will parallel what the script calls for. I call it the journey from ink to behavior; you find the behavior that the character calls for. I always try to find the contradictions. Even when I played Stalin, I tried to find the contradictions, some kind of vulnerability in the guy, whoever it is. I could find it with Gus McCrea because he was a romantic anyway.

What does the American West mean to you?
It's an elusive thing. Like when you go to England or wherever, they want to know about the West. That thing of pushing forward; pushing outward. The frontier.

What's your next project?
I'm trying to get two Elmer Kelton things that have fallen through. Can't get 'em done—Netflix or anybody.

You know, they can be Westerns, but you have to find the human thing in them, aside from horses and hats and spurs and Indian fighting. You have to find the humanness in the characters. For good and for bad, I think the Western kind of defines us. The English have Shakespeare; the French, Moliere; the Russians have Chekov. But the Western is ours, from Canada down.

FRANCO NERO

The term "Spaghetti Western" creates a specific image in most American minds: Clint Eastwood in a serape, gunning down a sea of bearded bandits. But in much of the rest of the world, Spaghetti Western doesn't mean Eastwood; it means Franco Nero. In 1965, the Italian-born international star was spotted by director John Huston while working as set photographer on *The Bible* and was quickly cast in the role of Abel. The rest is cinema history: the star of more than two hundred movies and TV shows, Nero has appeared in

Franco Nero takes aim in the first of his collaborations with director Sergio Corbucci, *Django.* ***Courtesy B.R.C. Produzione S.r.l.***

every genre, and from 1990's *Die Hard 2* to 2017's *John Wick: Chapter Two*, has played every sort of suave villain and hero imaginable. Notes Nero, "I think I'm the only actor in the world that played characters of thirty different nationalities."

Before *Django*, and his career-making performance as the gunman who walks from one mud-drenched town to the next, dragging a coffin behind him, Nero had played only small roles in a fistful of films. But suddenly he was popular, he said, "because I was the discovery of John Huston." Sergio Corbucci, known in Spaghetti Western circles as, "the other Sergio," had already directed twenty-five movies when he offered Nero the role in *Django*. Nero said yes, but that wasn't the end of it. "Corbucci wanted me, but one producer wanted Mark Damon, another one wanted Peter Martell." Finally, they went to Fulvio Frizza, the distributor, with three photos, "and he looked at the three faces and he pointed his finger on my face. That's how it happened."

They got right to work, but not for long. "We did one scene before Christmas, but there was not a proper script. During the holidays, Sergio and his brother Bruno managed to do a *scaletta*, a treatment. After Christmas we managed to finish the film, but nobody thought it was going to be successful."

They were wrong: "It was an incredible success all over the world." To boost ticket sales, the name Django was added to many Nero movies. "I did a [gangster] movie in Sicily, and they called it *Django with the Mafia*. I did a movie called *The Shark Hunter* and the Germans called it *Jungle Django*."

Because of the rapid pace of production in Europe versus the United States, by the time *The Bible* opened, Nero had starred not only in *Django* but also in two more Westerns, two sci-fi movies, and was in the United States playing Lancelot to Vanessa Redgrave's Guinevere in the musical *Camelot*. Appropriately, Nero and Redgrave would marry, although not until 2006.

Meanwhile, without strict copyright laws, anyone could put *Django* in their title, spawning easily a hundred imitators. Nero was not interested in returning to that role. "Laurence Olivier said to me, 'Do you want to be a star or a good actor? To be a star you have to do one movie a year, like Americans do, and the movie has to be a commercial success, and they always do the same role. Or do you want to be an actor? Your long career will be up and down, but you get the fruits.' I followed his advice." Throughout the 1960s, 1970s, and 1980s, Nero would average three to five films per year, maybe a Western every couple of years. Nero would finally return to the character two decades later, in *Django Strikes Again*, filmed not in Spain but in Colombia.

Although usually working with a largely European cast, Nero has enjoyed working with many American actors. "My favorite was Eli Wallach. I put him in six or seven of my movies in Europe. Another one was Tony Quinn. When my real father died in 1984, he said, 'Don't worry, from today on, I will be your dad.' From that day I called him dad and he called me son. It was a great relationship."

It was while making *Deaf Smith & Johnny Ears*, a film about the Texas Republic, that Nero connected with director Enzo Castellari. "He wanted to offer me a movie. But he looked like a boxer with muscles. I said to myself, I will never work with this guy." Nero was in negotiations to co-star with Joanne Woodward in another film, but the director wanted a different actress. "I said no way; I don't feel like doing the movie. He said, 'I know why, I heard that Enzo Castellari just offered you a movie. Castellari is nobody; he is nothing.' He said such terrible things about him that, the next day, I accepted Castellari's movie." They've collaborated on more than a dozen films since then.

Franco Nero finally became a Western star in the United States in the 1980s, when many of the six-hundred-plus Spaghetti Westerns made between the mid-1960s and mid-1970s were suddenly released with the explosion of home video. *Jonathan of the Bears*, which Nero and Castellari shot in Russia in 1994, would be his last Western until Quentin Tarantino featured him in 2010's *Django Unchained*.

And now there's more to look forward to, with a sequel to *Django* in the offing. "*Django Lives* is a great script from John Sayles," the Oscar-nominated writer/director of *Lone Star*. "Django is old now, but he managed to survive. He's even stronger, you understand? Cross your fingers, maybe we'll do it this year."

TOM SELLECK—THE LAST OF THE BREED

A 1969 episode of the Western series *Lancer* opened with an un-mustachioed but unmistakable Tom Selleck cheerfully harassing a one-handed lawman. It was just a bit, but it was a start for an actor who would become nearly the lone standard-bearer for Westerns in the 1990s and 2000s, much as Clint Eastwood had been in the decades before, and John Wayne had before him. Coincidentally, later a clean-shaven Sam Elliot appears just long enough to have his horse stolen. "Sam and I were already good friends," Selleck says. "Fox had a new talent program, like the old studio system; we were in it. I've always said Sam was more formed in those days, [knowing] exactly what he wanted. I was still learning the craft.

"Other than a Muriel Cigar commercial, where I got on a horse for about three seconds," it would be a busy but Westernless decade before Selleck would saddle up again. A miniseries based on Louis L'Amour's *The Sacketts* was in preparation, about three brothers uniting after the Civil War. Two brothers had already been cast: Sam Elliot and Jeff Osterhage. Writer/producer Jim Byrnes recalls, "Director Robert Totten wanted Buck Taylor for the part. Tom came in five times to read, and Bob still wanted Buck. I said to Bob, 'This guy is going to be a star.'"

"I'm glad I was honest with Bob because most actors lie," admits Selleck. "He asked, can I ride a horse? I told him, 'No, but I'm not afraid of them. I'm a good athlete, and I can learn.' All of us finalists had our audition at the Randall Ranch. He had us get on a horse and ride over to the grandstand. And in the grandstand were Glenn Ford, Ben Johnson, Sam Elliott, Jeff Osterhage, and Bob Totten." Selleck won the role, and Taylor played a cowboy who made plans to kill Selleck's character the moment they met.

"Bob Totten left a big impression on me. He commanded a lot of respect. He'd done more *Gunsmoke*s than almost anybody. Totten assembled a Western stock company like John Ford had, people who did one-day bit parts: Slim Pickens, Pat Buttram, and Jack Elam." And then there were the stars. "Glenn

Ford was an actor ahead of his time; his acting style was very naturalistic, like early Brando. Ben Johnson would be embarrassed if I called him a mentor, but he was—everybody looked up to Uncle Ben. He spent a lot of time with us, taught Jeff and me how to rope—and he was a world champion roper. I got to know Louis L'Amour well. Louie was on the set every day. I got hooked on Westerns with *The Sacketts*."

The wrap party was memorable. Totten took off one of his boots, "poured Jack Daniel's in it, said, 'This is tradition: you need to drink out of this.' But the big thing out of that party was Sam, Jeff, Ben, and I all said if we ever get a chance to do this again, we're there. And that was the germination of *Shadow Riders*." In 1980, Selleck was cast in *Magnum P.I.* and became a major star, playing the Hawaii-based detective for eight seasons. But he always made movies on hiatus, and in 1982, the three brothers and Ben were back, now called the Travens rather than the Sacketts, to avoid litigation. "Louis created a new book for us, *The Travens*, and it was such a thrill when the book came out, to see us—Sam, Jeff, and I—pictured on the back."

Magnum ended in 1988. "The script by John Hill, *Quigley Down Under*, had a bunch of fingerprints on it—Steve McQueen, Sean Connery—but it didn't get made, and I absolutely loved it."

Quigley is the story of an American cowboy, maybe the best long-range shot in the world, who comes to Australia to work for a rancher named Elliott Marston (Alan Rickman). Quigley rebels when Marston wants him to slaughter Aboriginal people, takes their side, and declares war on Marston. Helping him is Crazy Cora (Laura San Giacomo), who has some issues, hence her name, but rises powerfully to the occasion. San Giacomo recalls that it was her first Western, "a genre I'm not familiar with, but I'm going to dive in and do my best, and shoot guns and ride horses; things that I have never done before."

Selleck already knew Australian director Simon Wincer. "[When] Simon was directing *Lonesome Dove*, I was offered the part that my dear friend, the late Robert Urich, did.

"I was doing *Magnum*, and I couldn't get released." *Quigley* was not an easy shoot. Wincer explains, "Where we filmed was very much the Outback, that sort of landscape." It was particularly demanding of San Giacomo. She remembers, "The wardrobe designers in Australia said, you're not going to survive in this corset, in the terrain where we're going. So they had to strip the corset down several layers of fabric and bone."

"She was absolutely wonderful," recalls Wincer. "A real pro, and filming with the flies and that heat is challenging. That sad speech, when she tells how she smothered the baby unknowingly—just wonderful." For her part, San Giacomo loved working with the Aboriginals, "And just the magic and the mystique of being in the Outback was pretty great," she says. "Tom is a real gentleman, real considerate. I remember him being so proud of the detail that was in all the props and the guns. He loved that project, and he brought all of that with him."

Wincer concurs. "Tom's fantastic with all that, because he loves the detail, the minutia. And his Sharps rifle, when he first reveals it, that's a favorite scene of mine. And when he demonstrates with the bucket on top of the hill, telling the rider to keep going. Then the wonderful delay when you hear the almighty crack of the gun and eventually the bucket goes hurtling up in the air!"

"That would have been a great John Wayne movie," Selleck notes. "When you realize John Wayne could have done a better job, it's a little intimidating. But every good part should scare you; put it that way. It was iconic; this guy was bigger than life. I worked very hard on it. I'm very, very proud of *Quigley*." He also developed a great rapport with Spike, his horse in *Quigley*, who was big enough to look good with the tall actor astride. Given to Selleck after filming, Spike would co-star with him in *Last Stand at Saber River* and spend the rest of his thirty years at Selleck's ranch.

"Tom's always such a stickler for having the right saddle, the right gun, the right horse," recalls stuntman Walter Scott, who started doubling Selleck for a *Rockford Files* and continued with *The Sacketts* and many more. "We got along great, and when I quit doing stunts, he would call me to coordinate his stuff." Selleck's next Western was *Ruby Jean and Joe*. Selleck explains, "It was a low budget movie about a washed-up rodeo cowboy," who befriends Ruby Jean, a black teenaged hitchhiker. "It's a nice, simple movie about redemption. My character has a problem with the bottle. His horse is lame; he puts it out to pasture, which is symbolic of himself, and he does it at his mentor's ranch. I said, that has to be Ben Johnson. They say, we can't afford Ben. I paid his salary out of my salary, because it wouldn't have been the same."

They shot Selleck's rodeo sequence during a real Tucson rodeo. "There were eighteen thousand people in the audience," Scott remembers. "He just wasn't afraid of doing anything. I had a bulldogging sequence. I put Tom on a real bulldogging horse—he slid off the horse, he did it three or four times; it was great."

Selleck remembers, "I used to bump into Ted Turner, and he'd say, 'Let's do a Western!' Ted was very big on it." Starting in 1997, Selleck would make three elegant theatrical-quality Westerns for TNT, each with a strong literary background: *Last Stand at Saber River* by Elmore Leonard, *Crossfire Trail* by Louis L'Amour, and *Monte Walsh* by Jack Schaefer. "That was very intimidating; they're all different to adapt. Louis' stories, to make them filmic, you need to capture the spirit, but you had to make some changes. With Elmore Leonard, you could literally lift his dialogue off the page. And Jack Schaefer was just a great storyteller. *Monte Walsh*, I always wanted to do a sequel, because there's so much more to it. He wrote *Shane*, but *Shane* was a short story. *Monte Walsh* was a great piece of work, but very intimidating to adapt."

A spectacular moment in *Saber River* is when Cable, Selleck's character, riding after a runaway wagon with his daughter aboard, snatches her to safety just as the wagon flies over a cliff. They'd filmed it a couple of times, with Scott's brother, Ben, doubling for Selleck, catching the small stuntwoman standing in for the daughter. "And now we're getting ready to send the wagon over, with the team breaking loose," Scott remembers, "and the director [Dick Lowry] said, 'Wouldn't it be great if you could get Tom to do it?'" Selleck saw them walking his way, and he knew. "They're going to ask me to do this. And sure enough, Walter says, 'What do you think? One time.' I said, 'You think I can do this?' And Walter said yes. And I trust Walter. I've trusted him with my life many times." You can see it's really Selleck, in close, as the girl jumps to his arms just before the wagon goes airborne.

"Tom would say, 'Walter, why are you making me do this?' 'Because you can do it, and you know it always looks better if you have the actor doing the fight and everything.' He threw good punches and did good fights."

The third TNT Western was *Monte Walsh*. "You know, Monte Walsh wasn't a gunslinger," Selleck points out. "He was a cowboy in an era where the life is going away. And I just loved that. I have no problem bringing up the original with Lee Marvin; that movie really moved me." Scott, who had worked on the original, had his doubts. "I said, how do you remake *Monte Walsh*? He said, 'Well, I'll put my twist on it.' I didn't think anybody could do *Monte Walsh* justice like Lee Marvin, but Tom Selleck damn sure pulled it off—he did a hell of a job."

Monte Walsh got off to a shaky start. Robert Carradine, who played one of the Slash-Y cowboys, remembers, "It was our third day, and all the hands and Tom and Keith [Carradine] are gathered on this hilltop looking down on a group of maybe twenty mustangs, and every time we fire this shot, the

Tom Selleck, Sam Elliot, and Jeff Osterhage would play brothers twice, first here in *The Sacketts*, and again in *The Shadow Riders. Courtesy NBC*

mustangs scattered, and we have to spend half an hour gathering them all. So we're all set up to do another take and the director says, 'Can we move that herd about five feet to the left?' And Tom Selleck says, 'Why don't you move the camera one inch to the right?'" They were already behind schedule and needed a new director fast. Wincer was suddenly available, and he took over immediately. "Half the locations chosen for the film, I'd never seen. I'd just have to turn up on the day and do it. *Monte Walsh*, it's a real favorite of mine because it's about the coming of wire, the end of the cowboy era, and how it affects these different characters in many different ways."

Robert Carradine contributed much more than a fine performance. Selleck remembers, "Bobby is the guy who said day one, in front of all the Slash-Y cowboys, 'The set's where it's at. Nobody goes to the trailer.' And he set that ethic."

Carradine elaborates, "We're not in every scene, the cowhands, and I said, 'Look, why don't we get these guys to come out every day, get into wardrobe, and just ride around and do sh*t in the background like they would be doing in the real deal? Why use extras when we have the real guys here just sitting around?'"

Little did anyone guess that *Monte Walsh* would be the end of an era for the filmmakers as well as the characters. Selleck explains, "We had another one planned for TNT, *Empty Land*, by Louis L'Amour. And a new management came in at Turner, and it just went away." Certainly, Selleck has been busy. He's currently shooting season eleven of *Blue Bloods* and developing the next of his annual Jesse Stone movies, but, he says, "Nobody's ringing my doorbell or phone, offering me all sorts of Westerns."

Walter Scott opines, "I wish Tom and Sam Elliott would do one more Western. We got one more in us. There's a great one called *Ride the High Country*, that Joel McCrea and Randolph Scott did. I say, you two guys would be perfect in that."

KEVIN COSTNER

Back in 1989, when *Life Magazine* asked Hollywood legends like James Stewart, Bette Davis, and Olivia de Havilland to pick their favorite young stars of the day, Joel McCrea selected Kevin Costner. He described the *Field of Dreams* star as "a little Clark Gable, a little Gary Cooper, a little Jimmy Cagney. A boy like that is ideal for a colorful Western." McCrea was right, although at that time Costner had played only a supporting role in Lawrence Kasdan's very colorful Western epic, *Silverado*. The similarity in McCrea's stoic appeal and his own wasn't lost on Costner, who'd replied, "Joel and I are the kind of leading men who say, 'Yup,' and 'Nope' and 'Where's the horse?'"

Costner liked hearing McCrea's words again, three decades later. "I remember enjoying Joel McCrea a lot. He was a really humble guy. Joel was constantly trying to give his roles away to Jimmy and to Gary and to other people, saying that they'd be just right for that. I'm pleased that he would say something like that about me."

Does he still see himself as a "yup" and "nope" leading man?

Costner laughed. "Sometimes Westerns get reduced to that. In fact, the Westerns that I depend on are really dependent on the word, but the reality of the 'yup, nope' is there's a level of economy that comes with language that has weight. They're very literate. I mean, it's our Shakespeare. Sometimes a couple lines can leave no doubt as to what someone's intention was. I like classic, so I respond to a *Liberty Valance*, *Searchers*, and certain things that occur in the [John Ford *Cavalry*] trilogy."

Of course, Costner entered the Western film in an era when the genre had been declared legally dead.

"There were a lot of Westerns that I didn't enjoy back then, and there were ones that stayed with me forever. And it's the same way now. A lot of times they missed the mark for me personally, because they're rushing to get to the gunfight. Whenever Westerns start out with a big slaughter, and then one man has to go on some vindictive hunt . . . I mean, that's true, but I think it's a convenient and too easy way to start Westerns. In the right hands, something like that can be dramatic, and in other hands, they miss the point."

What was it like to get *Silverado*, his first Western role?

"Imagine standing in the best spot in a river on a really firm rock, and knowing you're just going to fish there all day. This is everything I need right here. It was a blessing."

Not that it wasn't a challenge playing Jake, a loud and rambunctious cowboy who is the antithesis of his more familiar, thoughtful, soft-spoken heroes.

"Jake was just so full of juice that it was difficult to figure out who he was relating to in the scene, because he was talking at one pitch level. I remember thinking, I know exactly how to play those *other* parts, but how am I going to play *this* guy? And I found a way: I basically tried to compete with the horizon," he said with a laugh, "the outdoors itself, and have a sense of fun. I was really lucky to be able to play that part. It did a lot for me."

In 1990, Costner would become a producer and director as well as star in the most Oscar-honored and financially successful Western of all time, *Dances with Wolves*. It's a wonderful film that helped rejuvenate the genre, and brought women back into the audience.

"I was prepared for people to like the movie because I liked it. I wouldn't have put my money in, I wouldn't have put my time in, if I didn't think that if I made it correctly, people would relate to it. The surprise is that something can be a runaway hit, that it catches that kind of air, that it has that level of momentum."

Nine years after *Silverado*, Costner would act again for director Lawrence Kasdan, as Wyatt Earp.

"Larry's a real thoughtful writer. *Silverado* was a matinee type of movie; *Wyatt Earp* was a darker look at a person's life, and really thoughtful writers get past the gunfight and understand the makeup of what kind of guy actually survives, versus the kind of people that don't survive. Even capable people don't survive because of the randomness of violence; the wrong place at the wrong time. People that look carefully are always interested in why the Wyatt Earps never got hit by a bullet."

In 2003, Costner directed his second classic, *Open Range*, which starts with a look at the day-to-day hazardous life of four cattle drovers.

"The plot is simply: a storm came, and it sunk their wagon, it scattered their cattle. To go on, they have to re-provision and gather their cattle. So they almost escaped danger. That danger was always there, in the town. But the moment it rained on them, they were stuck. I love that plots can come out of that. The idea of friends knowing each other a long time and not communicating intimate information amused people, but we both know it to be true. People were very guarded, [going] back to the Civil War. People fished for information because some carry these grudges, these vendettas for the next fifty years. You'll see that as a theme in all my work."

To put it mildly, grudges and vendettas were a theme of his next Western project, 2012's *Hatfields & McCoys*, for which Costner's performance as Devil Anse Hatfield won him an Emmy and Golden Globe for Best Actor.

Did Costner mind that, while clearly the protagonist, he wasn't a hero?

"I've played a lot of things; I played serial killers. But those characters [in *Hatfields*] that survived out there, in this case, are authentic, real. They are dark; they're hard. They're men of their time period. And I enjoy that. I don't flinch from any of it."

In 2018 Costner began starring in the contemporary Western series *Yellowstone* for Paramount Television, a phenomenal success that he would stay with for five seasons. Costner's character, John Dutton, runs the largest family-owned ranch in America, bumping up against Yellowstone National Park, and is besieged by the government, an adjacent Indian reservation, and land developers.

Would Costner call rancher John Dutton a man out of his time?

"Well, a man out of his time, and time catching up with a way of life. He's having to act like a current-day CEO, but he's mired in the way that he would hope that it could be. It's a critical moment in his life, as a lot of different forces are coming for the property. And the biggest blow to this character is that the family's really dysfunctional as he faces all these things coming at them. So it's a boiling pot when you come in, when we start the series."

While Dutton is a strong character, he's also vulnerable, even frail at times.

"Well, as you play somebody that's at that particular age, those things are always looming. We don't know when they're gonna come. I think that you see how he actually deals with those issues in a very straight-up way."

In 2019 Costner starred for Netflix in the movie *The Highwaymen*, in which he and Woody Harrelson played real-life Texas Rangers Frank Hamer and Maney Gault, who came out of retirement to track down Bonnie and Clyde. The truth was much different from the Warren Beatty film version.

"Hamer's wife sued for defamation, said, 'My husband's a hero. You have no business creating him out of two characters.' And knowing that she was in two shoot-outs with him, Warner Brothers settled."

What attracted him to the project?

"It's always the writing. I thought it captured this guy and that time, and it was interesting to try to understand the men that were chasing these legendary bandits. It was just a whole other side of it, to see the man-hunters without radios, without cooperation state-to-state. You know, Rangers were almost like Spartans—they'd send a single Ranger to towns to take ahold of the situation. Seeing the Rangers evolve from on horse to automobile, knowing they're filling out expense reports, going to chase somebody down and they have their own way of doing it . . . I just thought to myself, this was a moment, this was a man that I could play."

Was Frank Hamer a hero in the Wyatt Earp mold?

"Well, I think that they had a unique way of dealing with situations. You can look at whatever their background is and question their techniques and what they had to do in their times. But whenever we do that, and we don't put ourselves back in that time, we do ourselves a disservice as well as them."

Would he like to make another Western?

"I have a Western that I really want to make; I just can't find the rich guys that want to make it—an epic Western. I want to shoot three movies, all about the same story, at the same time, three separate movies coming out like every four months. And probably lead to the fourth one, which was the one that spawned the first one. So it would be four movies. Now, will I get to do it? I don't know, but that's where my heart is. So if anybody wants that same thing, they can come make that movie with me."

As of this writing, Kevin Costner, after five seasons of *Yellowstone*, has found those rich guys he was seeking, and is currently making *Horizon*. It is expected to have multiple parts and will tell the story, over a fifteen-year period both before and after the Civil War, of the settling of the West, seen through several points of view.

SAM SHEPARD

Sam Shepard died July 27, 2017, at the age of seventy-three, after a hard-fought battle with ALS (amyotrophic lateral sclerosis, also known as Lou Gehrig's disease). His understated, natural style recalled actor Gary Cooper—both were movie-star handsome and exuded effortless self-confidence and masculinity.

"He's a great man, a natural man, which is rare. . . . I've had romances with what you'd call famous men, and none compare to Sam in terms of maleness," Shepard's romantic partner for twenty-seven years, Jessica Lange, told *Vanity Fair* in 1991.

His chivalry touched our magazine personally, when Shepard asked the publisher's permission before calling what would become one of his most-performed plays *True West*.

Much admired as an actor, often described as the greatest playwright of his generation, Shepard won the Pulitzer Prize for *The Buried Child* in 1979 and was nominated twice more. As an actor, he was nominated for an Oscar for his performance in 1983's *The Right Stuff* and for an Emmy for 1999's *Dash and Lilly*. In fact, over his career, he won or was nominated for just about every award a playwright or an actor could receive.

His was not the life one might have predicted for a former ranch hand, rodeo cowboy, and rock band drummer who spent his one formal college year studying agriculture at Mt. San Antonio College in Walnut, California. His parents were farmers and teachers in Illinois. His father had been a bomber pilot during WWII, flying numerous raids over Italy. Tragically, his war experiences left him an alcoholic and a broken man. The explosiveness of Shepard's family dynamic fueled his plays. When Shepard turned age thirty, he already had thirty plays produced.

Sam Shepard had "Western" written all over him, and he looked to the American West to inspire him, whether as an actor or a playwright. "There's more drama that goes down in a rodeo than one hundred plays you can go to see. It's a real confrontation, a real thing going on," he told *American Theatre* in April 1984. "I've been in a few rodeos, and the first team roping that I won gave me more of a feeling of accomplishment and pride of achievement than I ever got winning the Pulitzer Prize. At the same time, I'm glad that the plays are successful and that they do something to people."

Best known to Westerns fans as an actor, Shepard did not take that role seriously until he was befriended by fellow farm boy and iconic writer-director of 1973's *Badlands*, Terrence Malick. "I was totally devoted to writing at that point," Shepard said, adding, "I was running a little ranch up in northern California."

Malick was writing *Days of Heaven*, a story set in the early 20th century, about a poor migrant farm worker (played by Richard Gere) who convinces his lady love (Brooke Adams) to marry their wealthy, but dying, employer to inherit his fortune. Malick offered Shepard the role of the doomed rancher.

"I said, 'Why not?' I rented a Ford Mustang and drove to Alberta, Canada, and that was it," Shepard recalled.

One of the most physically beautiful movies ever made, it turned the three leads into stars.

Although modern and sophisticated—Shepard did much of his writing in New York City and London—something about his looks suited historical stories. He would play many characters in many time periods, but he always returned to the American West. His understanding of and respect for that world, and its people, informed all of his work.

"This notion of the cowboy and of the West," he said recently, "and this solitary character, this person who was able to fend for himself, in spite of everything else, to be self-sufficient: it's a very important thing, which gets more and more lost as we move into our idea of civilization. We don't have that quality anymore; we don't have that way of testing ourselves."

Sam Shepard's final Western set in the frontier was *Klondike*, about the Yukon gold rush during the late 1890s, a miniseries that appeared on Discovery Channel in 2014.

Whether in a lead or supporting role, his presence in a Western lent it authenticity. He was endearing as Pea-Eye Parker in the 1995 sequel to *Lonesome Dove*, *Streets of Laredo*. That same year, he played Tarnell, cowhand buddy to Tommy Lee Jones's Hewey Calloway in the Jones written-directed feature *The Good Old Boys*. Five years later, Shepard played the sympathetic lawyer in *All the Pretty Horses*.

In 2006, in the Western action-comedy *Bandidas*, Shepard played Mr. Buck, a retired bank robber coaching two ladies, played by Penélope Cruz and Salma Hayek, in his former trade.

The frontier West even inspired Shepard and wife O-Lan Jones to name their son Jesse, after outlaw Jesse James, in 1970. Shepard went on to play Jesse James's brother Frank in 2007's under-appreciated *The Assassination of Jesse James by the Coward Robert Ford*. Though at age sixty-four, Shepard was twenty-five years older than the real-life Frank, his performance was excellent. His sober distrust of Ford made him easily the smartest guy in the bunkhouse.

In the 1999 fantasy Western *Purgatory*, Shepard is the gunless lawman in the town of Refuge, a waiting place for deceased Westerners whose final destination is not yet determined. His character may be called Sheriff Forrest, but he died holding aces and eights.

His final Western lead was in 2011's *Blackthorn*. Living in Bolivia, where the movie was filmed, James Blackthorn (Shepard) is actually Butch Cassidy, who survived the shoot-out that killed his partner. Now an old man, he decides to head home, with the assistance of a young robber (Eduardo Noriega).

"Sam's voice was very singular. It was very distinctive, like all great writers," recalls Tracy Letts in a PBS interview. Letts wrote the Pulitzer-winning *August: Osage County*, which inspired the 2013 film, in which Shepard played the patriarch. "And he synthesized a lot of different elements—European avant-garde, Rock 'n' Roll, cowboy movies, poetry, and a working-class sensibility. He synthesized all of that, and when it came out in his writing, it was such a new and exciting and individual and true voice."

The voice will live on.

POWERS BOOTHE

On May 14, 2017, actor Powers Boothe died just short of his 69th birthday. A magnetic and commanding presence, he enjoyed simultaneous stardom as villains and heroes in films *noir*, action-adventures, thrillers, and comedies. But he will be best remembered for two characterizations in two classic Westerns: "Curly Bill" Brocius in 1993's *Tombstone* and Cy Tolliver in the HBO series *Deadwood*.

Born in 1948 in Snyder, Texas, Boothe chopped cotton on his father's ranch, played football, and acted in high school plays. The first in his family to attend college, he earned his drama bachelor's degree at Southwest Texas State and his doctorate at Southern Methodist. While in college, he met and married Pamela Cole; they would be together for the rest of his life. He joined the Oregon Shakespeare Festival, which led in 1974 to Boothe's New York debut in Lincoln Center's production of *Richard III*. His Broadway debut was in James McClure's *Lone Star*.

In 1980, he soared to sinister stardom on television, portraying the cult leader in *Guyana Tragedy: The Story of Jim Jones*. "I approached him like I was playing King Lear," he told interviewer Matt Patches. "I made no judgments on him—I don't make judgments on any character I play."

Members of the TV Academy did make a judgment, voting Boothe a Best Actor Emmy. Incredibly, on awards night, Boothe's two unions, S.A.G. and A.F.T.R.A., were on strike. He was the only actor to cross the picket lines and claim his award, noting in his acceptance speech, "This is either the most courageous moment of my career or the stupidest . . . I came here because this is America and one must do what one believes. I believe in the Academy. I also believe in my fellow actors in their stand."

Whether by chance or by blacklisting, the normally busy Boothe made only one film in the next three years. But soon after, he was starring in big films for top directors: 1984's *Red Dawn* for John Milius, 1985's *The Emerald Forest* for John Boorman, and two for Walter Hill, who would dub Boothe the "Hamlet of the prairies," 1981's *Southern Comfort* and 1987's *Extreme Prejudice*.

Then in 1993 came the movie that would turn Boothe from an actor into an icon, *Tombstone*. A classic today, *Tombstone* was originally a $9 million "quickie," which Disney rushed into production to cash in on the hoopla around Kevin Costner's $63 million *Wyatt Earp*. Word got around town about *Tombstone*'s screenplay. "Kevin Jarre wrote a brilliant script," Michael Biehn, who played Johnny Ringo, remembers, "And everyone flocked to it—you can tell by the cast.

"I immediately was interested in who they were going to cast as Curly Bill because we'd be working together. I knew Powers from his Jim Jones performance, which was incredible. Powers was always a real presence on film. There are certain people—like Lee Marvin—who just have character in their face, in them. You just know that they've lived a life and it's been an interesting one.

"Before we went to Tucson, [Boothe and I] went out to dinner. I said, 'I'm going to take my car out there. It's only going to be a seven- or eight-hour drive. Why don't you come along with me?' So, we drove to Tucson together."

Boothe once said, "'Curly Bill' was a guy who . . . everybody liked. He had a lot of dash about him, a lot of panache . . . a tremendous sense of humor. He really lusts for life—he just eats it up. He's certainly got his mean streak and his killer streak, but there was a sympathetic quality to him as well."

Peter Sherayko, who played "Texas Jack" Vermillion, also assembled the riders for both the outlaw gang known as the Cow-boys and the Earp posse. He recalls, "Powers really got into his Curly Bill character. He was in control of the Cow-boys."

The sharp division between the Earps and the Cow-boys remained even after the day's work. "Every night, we'd come back from the set, and when you walked in the bar, there were always two or three tables with the Cow-boys—Powers, Michael Biehn, Thomas Haden Church, all those guys were sitting there. And way at the other end of the room it was Bill Paxton, Sam Elliott, myself, Buck [Taylor]."

"Peter's right," Biehn says. "I'd done a couple of pictures with Bill Paxton, was a great friend of Bill's, but we did not spend time together on that set."

While Jarre was a fine screenwriter, he was a first-time director, and with shooting far behind schedule after four weeks, he was fired. "[Producer] Jim Jacks and Kurt Russell saved the movie, held it together," Biehn believes, "because I think Disney was just going to flush it at that point."

George Cosmatos was hired to direct, with John Fasano trimming the script.

Originally, the story was almost evenly divided between the Earps, who weren't all good, and the Cow-boys, who weren't all bad. But the cuts shifted the focus to the Earps.

"A lot of actors lost scenes—the Cow-boys especially got nailed," Biehn says. "Johnny Ringo [historically] never shot a priest—that's completely a setup that he's a really bad guy from the beginning. After the rewrite came out, Powers and I both knew that the dynamic had changed; some of his best scenes were gone."

The changes also shifted the balance between Curly Bill and Ringo. "Powers could have said, 'I'm the antagonist in the movie. I'm not going to support Michael Biehn—he was signed to support me!' But he was very, very gracious," Biehn says. "Powers's [reactions] made Johnny Ringo—he had a comedic way of complementing my character as being someone he really enjoyed, that impressed him. If everybody around you is walking on eggshells, you don't have to do very much."

But even with his reduced role, whether shrugging off Wyatt Earp's dramatic, "I want you to know that this is over," with an indifferent "Well . . . 'bye," or joyously taking potshots at the moon while his character was high on opium, Boothe gave a performance that is unforgettable.

"There were a lot of great characters in that movie, but Powers—his screen presence just dominates," Biehn says.

Boothe wouldn't return to the Western for a decade, until David Milch offered him the role of Cy Tolliver in HBO's foul-mouthed Western drama *Deadwood*. As the proprietor of the saloon and brothel, the Bella Union, Tolliver was a worthy adversary to Ian McShane's Al Swearengen, proprietor of the Gem Theatre and, like Tolliver, homicidally ambitious.

Boothe told *TV Guide*, "For me, it was almost like doing Shakespeare . . . in that if you had one word out of place, the dialogue just flat didn't work. . . . David explained [the character] to me like this: [Cy] was raised in a whore-house. So you can imagine watching your mother turn tricks and what it does to your thoughts on women."

"I loved being around Powers—he made you laugh all the time," says Leon Rippy, who played Tom Nuttall, manager of the No. 10 Saloon. "And what a gentle soul in comparison to some of the roles he played. He was a man of principle and character. And a lot of that has to do with how you were raised and what your parents instilled in you. I'll miss him; he was a great talent."

Sherayko, who worked with Boothe in *Tombstone*, was in charge of background casting for *Deadwood*. "I used a lot of riders that had been the Cowboys from *Tombstone*," Sherayko says, "and Powers remembered all these guys, remembered the names, even though it was ten years later. He was a consummate actor, fun to work with, and I'm glad I got to work with him twice."

Tanner Beard, also born in Snyder, says that Boothe "was definitely the hometown hero." Beard has directed two Westerns, 2011's *The Legend of Hell's Gate* and 2014's *Six Bullets to Hell*, but he was still in his teens when Boothe hugely influenced his career.

Beard met him when Boothe's daughter, Parisse, answered Beard's casting notice for a stunt-show spoof of *Tombstone*. "We got to do rehearsals at Powers's house! He was everything you hoped he'd be; his voice just rattles your soul.

"The stunt show led to me writing a short film called *The Mouth of Caddo*, which Parisse helped me produce. Powers read the script, talked about the character breakdowns, told us that we needed to focus on a single lead rather than having three. It was amazing guidance coming from someone I already admired so heavily. He even did the narration for us. It starts off, you hear that voice. I think that was a big reason we were able to expand it to a feature, *The Legend of Hell's Gate*."

Boothe would have acted in *The Legend of Hell's Gate*, but he had to go back to do the third season of *Deadwood*.

Unexpectedly, that was the final season. "I, like everyone, was stunned," Boothe told *TV Guide*, "because when we left the third season, it wasn't a matter of, 'Are we going to do a fourth?' They were negotiating a fifth. And then I got the call from [Milch] that it was all over."

Boothe's final Western performance was as the not entirely impartial Judge Valentine Hatfield in 2012's *Hatfields & McCoys* miniseries on the History Channel, co-starring with *Wyatt Earp* star Kevin Costner and *Tombstone*'s Morgan Earp, Bill Paxton.

For a man who acted in a few Westerns, Boothe left a remarkable legacy in the genre.

CHAPTER 3
THE STARS—MAINLY TELEVISION

HUGH O'BRIAN

One role defined Hugh O'Brian's acting career—the title character in *The Life and Legend of Wyatt Earp*.

The adult Western premiered on ABC on September 6—sixty-one years and one day before the actor passed away at the age of ninety-one. Born Hugh Charles Krampe in Rochester, New York, he dropped out of college in 1942, at age nineteen, to join the Marines, where he became their youngest drill sergeant. As ruggedly handsome as any man has the right to be, he embarked on an acting career in Hollywood. In 1950, he appeared in his first Western, *Beyond the Purple Hills*, starring Gene Autry. By his fourth year, he had won the Golden Globe for Most Promising Newcomer, for his performance in *The Man from the Alamo*.

But most people remember him as "The Man from Tombstone."

Many of his friends and his coworkers, on the big screen and the small, have fond memories of Hugh O'Brian. In 1954, Earl Holliman recalls, "We played brothers. Richard Widmark, Hugh O'Brian, and I were the sons of Spencer Tracy in a picture called *Broken Lance*. I'd seen him on the screen; I knew he was a man-about-town and dating all the girls at Fox. I wasn't sure I was going to like him, but we sat together on the plane to Nogales in Arizona, and he laughed at my jokes.

"So we became friends. In those days, when you were a supporting actor, on location, you shared a room with another supporting actor. Hugh and I shared the same room. I liked Hugh; he was easy and fun to work with, had a nice sense of humor.

"He was the most dedicated guy I'd ever seen. He really worked so hard on his career. Every night he would be typing letters to [showbiz columnists]

Hugh O'Brian in his career-making role, as the title character in
The Life and Legend of Wyatt Earp. Courtesy ABC

Hedda Hopper or Louella Parsons or Jimmy Starr. I didn't want to do that much work, but I really admired him for it.

"Later on, he established a college scholarship fund for young actors. That was very generous of him, and one year, he invited me to be one of the judges for the scholarship."

Louis F. Edelman produced *The Life and Legend of Wyatt Earp*. His daughter, Kate Edelman Johnson, recalls, "The first job I ever had was answering Hugh O'Brian's fan mail, when I was twelve. I always said to him, 'Hugh, I can still sign your name better than you can.' He was very, very sweet.

"My dad created *The Life and Legend of Wyatt Earp* from his love of Westerns. He found Hugh, and it was magic. It was such a major hit, because, up until then, you had *The Lone Ranger* or you had *The Cisco Kid*, but they were made-up characters. My father bought the book by Stuart Lake. Stuart Lake had interviewed Wyatt Earp just before the lawman died in 1929. For the first couple of years of the show, Stuart Lake was alive, and he was a consultant.

"Hugh had a great relationship with Stuart Lake. Hugh created that costume, with the flat hat and the brocaded vest and the string tie. Hugh loved the role. He got very into it; he studied it. He was that character for all those years.

"Hugh was always a little bit at war with the producers. And yet, they knew what they had. I remember the time when they called Dad from Washington, DC, to say that Hugh had gone to Congress, and they were about to arrest him. He went on the floor of Congress with his costume and his guns on. They asked, 'What should we do?' And my father actually paused for a few minutes and thought, 'Hmmm, what should I do? Should I let him go to jail? No, we were just picked up for a fifth season. I guess you'd better get him out.'"

From 1958 to 1961, Morgan Woodward played Shotgun Gibbs in eighty-one episodes of *Wyatt Earp*, opposite Hugh O'Brian.

"I was with him for four years. Hugh was an unusual man," Woodward says. "He was not 'hail fellow well met.' When we first got on the show, Hugh let me know that he didn't want to be upstaged, or anything like that. And of course, I'm the sidekick. I let him know that I wanted the show to last as long as possible; wanted to make him look good and make me look good. Once he got to know me, we got along all right.

"He was a good fellow; he had a good heart. Hugh always invited me to his birthday party, and I went to his 91st a couple months ago. I had my 91st birthday last Friday [September 16]. I called to see how he was doing the other day, and he'd just gotten home from the hospital. His kidneys were failing and his liver was failing, and his wife, Virginia, said he's not going to make it. And sure enough, the next morning he died."

In 1993, thirty years after Hugh O'Brian had left the role of Wyatt Earp, producer Rob Word, working with Kate Edelman Johnson, persuaded Hugh to put the costume on again for a CBS movie. The idea was to mix new scenes with colorized footage from the series, to bring the story up to 1918. *Tombstone* had been a surprise Christmas smash, and the Kevin Costner *Wyatt Earp* was coming in the summer.

"I figured if we called our movie, *Wyatt Earp: Return to Tombstone*, and ran it between them, we'd confuse the viewers, and they'd all tune in, which they did," Word says. "We were the first and only Wyatt Earp movie ever to film in Tombstone, Arizona. Working with Hugh O'Brian was not just a thrill for me but for everybody we met in Tombstone. Hugh was sixty-nine, and still so incredibly handsome.

"We had a scene with Harry Carey Jr., who was a little hard of hearing, as was Hugh. In it, Wyatt was walking through Boot Hill, and Digger Phelps, who was Harry Carey Jr., spots him, and calls, 'Wyatt! Wyatt!' And Hugh was going to turn and look at him, walk over and do their scene. But Hugh couldn't hear him, so he kept walking. So we had to set up flags off-screen to let Hugh know when he was being spoken to; and we had to do the same thing for [Carey] and use hand signals to let them know who should be talking. And that's how we got through the scene. It cracked us up and cracked them up."

Bruce Boxleitner, who himself played Wyatt Earp, in 1983's *I Married Wyatt Earp*, played the sheriff of Cochise County in *Wyatt Earp: Return to Tombstone*.

"Hugh O'Brian was quite something else. He fit into that black outfit, and he had that Buntline. I was astounded—I was watching him do a scene. He had to do this shoot-out with Marty Kove and Bo Hopkins. And he beat them to the draw every take, with that gigantic three-foot-long gun!" Boxleitner says with a laugh. "It was quite amazing. I said, 'Man, you haven't lost it at all.' 'No,' he said, 'I practice all the time.'

"We all enjoyed doing it—I know Hugh did. He was pretty flattered. I guess the word is taciturn—he didn't talk a lot, but when he did, everyone listened. He had that kind of voice, and a very commanding presence. I think he felt playing Wyatt Earp was his legacy, and he was very serious about it."

What actor was the most accurate portrayer of Wyatt Earp? Casey Tefertiller, author of *Wyatt Earp: The Life Behind the Legend*, says, "In my opinion, it would be Hugh O'Brian. If you read what people say about him, he was just cat quick. Hugh O'Brian had that kind of quickness, that kind of ability, to grab the gun out of someone's hand as they were drawing it. And Hugh O'Brian had a sternness about him."

Pierre O'Rourke appeared in celebrity events that showcased O'Brian as Earp.

"Appropriately, I met Hugh O'Brian on a Western film set," O'Rourke says. "I came to wonder if Wyatt Earp was much different than the legendary actor who portrayed him in *The Life and Legend of Wyatt Earp*.

"When filming ended, Hugh took me under his wing—introducing me, in and out of costume, as his deputy for more than two decades. As his deputy, I joined him at his Fortune 500 company appearances as Wyatt. His fee went directly to HOBY, his foundation, which, in sixty years, has helped more than 450,000 sophomores around the world learn how to be more conscious in life, and to give back.

"Hugh would share how a two-week stay in Africa cleaning bed pans and washing sheets in Dr. Albert Schweitzer's leper colony, followed by deep discussions with the great man in the evenings, had left him with the challenge of, 'What are you going to do with your fame and success to give back to the world?' It's a lesson Hugh took to heart, and implanted in my heart.

"Hugh was laid to rest at Forest Lawn, in Glendale, California, amidst the family of his one and only wife, Virginia Stumpf O'Brian. He married his lady at this same cemetery, ten years ago, in what was billed as 'The Wedding to Die for.'

"Some of his friends are only a few plots away: Spencer Tracy, Clayton Moore (The Lone Ranger), and Errol Flynn.

"A twenty-one-gun salute honored the man who reportedly held the record as the youngest drill instructor in the history of his beloved Marines Corps.

"Hugh O'Brian will always be a part of me. Sadly, I am a deputy without his marshal. *Semper Amor*, my friend."

Ann Kirschner, author of *Lady at the O.K. Corral*, came to love the Tombstone story through watching O'Brian star as the legendary lawman.

"Really, could he have been any more handsome? I fell in love with all things Earp when I fell in love with Hugh O'Brian," she says. "Tall, rangy, the jet-black hair, the square jaw. . . . I know, I still sound like a kid with a crush. But even as a kid, I appreciated the balance of the clean-cut hero with that roguish look, the slight air of naughtiness, and the always lurking prankster.

"It would be decades before I could assess the similarities and differences between Stuart Lake's largely fictional frontier marshal, historical Wyatt Earp, and real-time Hugh O'Brian. They all had that lanky build and athletic grace, but alas, our Wyatt wasn't always on the right side of the law.

"And while Wyatt cared more about adventure than accumulating wealth, he was neither philosopher nor philanthropist. O'Brian understood that while intelligence and talent are equally distributed, opportunity is not. And so he created the Hugh O'Brian Youth Leadership foundation."

Bob Boze Bell met the actor after taking the reins as executive editor for *True West Magazine*.

"Hugh used to call me here at the magazine about once a week and regale me with stories about Hollywood, Wyatt Earp, all the while bending my ear about doing a story on him. He could be very persuasive, and I must admit, we obliged him more than once.

"The show was billed as 'TV's first adult Western.' Asked to define 'adult Western,' Hugh quipped, 'The cowboy still kisses his horse—but worries about it.'

"'I was one of about twenty people who were up for the lead role,' Hugh remembered in 2014. 'Stuart Lake, the man who wrote Wyatt Earp's biography back in 1929 [published 1931], interviewed me for the part. I think he favored me for a couple of different reasons. First, he felt that there were certain physical similarities such as bone structure and height. I also think he took to me because he had been a Marine and he felt that my background as a Marine drill instructor would add to the character.'

"His drive to keep his portrayal of Wyatt Earp true to form is something he paid for later in life. As he put it, 'In order to preserve authenticity, I insisted on using full loads on the set so that my gun would fire at the proper volume while filming. All rifles and pistols in movies and television use quarter loads, which release only 25 percent of the volume of full loads. The crew let me shoot my authentic guns, and whenever I fired, they wore earplugs to bear the big explosions. I couldn't wear earplugs or put cotton in my ears because I was in front of the camera, and although I'm glad I used full loads, I am now paying for it because I lost a lot of my hearing during those years filming Wyatt Earp.'"

Who did Hugh O'Brian think was the best Wyatt Earp? When I interviewed him a couple of years ago, wanting to be tactful, I asked him who the second-best Earp was.

"The second best? I guess it was me. The best was Wyatt himself. He was a helluva man. He died here, by the way, in 1929, on 17th Street. He lived here in Los Angeles the last three or four years of his life. He made money doing appearances and stuff. The people just west of Newhall, that huge area between there and Las Vegas, like 150 miles by 200, they put up one notice at the upper entrance. It said 'This Property is Guarded by Wyatt Earp.' Nobody ever came on it again," he said, with a chuckle.

Hugh was too modest to admit it, but we all know he was the best Wyatt Earp: brave, courageous, and bold. Long live his fame. Long live his glory. And long may his story be told.

BRUCE BOXLEITNER

In 1976, *Gunsmoke*'s James Arness was about to take on the lead role in the series *How the West Was Won*. He had full cast approval. As he told the Television Academy Archives, "We watched four guys in scenes from other shows. Hands down, there was just one guy that [was] right for it." When the lights went up, ABC president Michael Eisner said he liked the second one. "I knew that it was live or die at that moment, so I just said, 'Well, I'm sorry, but I disagree with you. I want that third guy, Bruce Boxleitner.' Bruce turned out to be a great choice for it; he was just right."

Contemplating his career, Boxleitner says, "I attribute anything I did to Mr. James Arness. I probably would never have gotten to do anything, had he not made that one decision." Although he achieved stardom in the romantic spy series *The Scarecrow and Mrs. King* and has a huge following for his sci-fi career, with the *Tron* films and the *Babylon 5* series, Boxleitner keeps coming back to Westerns.

James Arness was a mentor to Bruce Boxleitner. After co-starring here in the *How the West Was Won* series, they would reteam in a remake of *Red River* and the TV movie *Gunsmoke: One Man's Justice. Courtesy ABC Television*

Born in Elgin, Illinois, Bruce spent summers at his grandparents' farm, where he played cowboy. "In high school, I wasn't the greatest student. I wanted to do something, and I walked in on an audition for the play, Agatha Christie's *10 Little Indians*." He was hooked.

After graduating and joining a repertory company in Chicago, he auditioned for the play *Status Quo Vadis*, "And I ended up taking it to Broadway; it lasted a little more than a week." After touring in a comedy with Paul Lynde, he reluctantly agreed to a tour of *Status Quo Vadis*, "with the stipulation that I have a one-way ticket to Los Angeles. I came out here with a suitcase, twenty-two hundred bucks in cash, and a pocket full of friends' phone numbers, and I slept on couches and living room floors."

It was perhaps prophetic that while his first paying work was on a sitcom, it was shot at the lot that had once been Republic Studios. "My first job was four lines on the *Mary Tyler Moore Show*. At lunch I asked somebody where *Gunsmoke* shot, and I went in to peek. Main Street, Dodge City, was built inside the soundstage! There's the Long Branch! I was pinching myself."

He had reason to: CBS casting director Paula Palifoni then cast him in "The Sharecroppers": after twenty seasons, the final episode of *Gunsmoke*. "And I was so broad in it. I looked at myself, I was mortified." Ironically, he wouldn't meet James Arness during the shoot, because they had no scenes together.

A year later, in 1976, Boxleitner was starring opposite Arness in *How the West Was Won*, the series that established him. "He was my mentor, because I watched how a real television star worked, sick and well, in the day-to-day of a TV series. He led by example." The show was important to Boxleitner personally, as well as professionally. Without it, "I wouldn't have met my wife. I would not have had my sons," adding with a laugh, "and I married my sister," referring to Kathryn Holcomb, his first wife, who *played* his sister in the series.

After two decades as Matt Dillon, Arness loved playing Zeb McCahan, "because he got to cut loose with this rollicking big mountain man all in buckskin." Boxleitner remembers, "His World War II wounds were kicking in, his leg bowed out a bit. So he got to limp, like an old Indian Wars battle wound. He grew his hair long."

After four years, the series ended. Arness would play Jim Bowie in *The Alamo: Thirteen Days to Glory*, and play Matt Dillon again in *Return to Dodge*, the first of five *Gunsmoke* movies. Boxleitner was exceptionally busy, including playing the lawman in *I Married Wyatt Earp*, and most importantly, starring as Billy Montana, exuberant apprentice to Kenny Rogers in *The Gambler*.

Boxleitner and Rogers became fast friends and would do four *Gambler* films together.

Then in 1988, the *Gambler* producers cast Boxleitner in the Montgomery Clift role for their remake of *Red River*. But who could play John Wayne's part? "They had Robert Mitchum and his son Chris," but the deal fell apart. "Then it was Kirk Douglas, [who] would have been a very short—but very intense—Thomas Dunson. James didn't want to do a role that was identified with John Wayne because of his respect for his friend and mentor. I told him, 'There's only one man left who could even go near John Wayne, James. You're the guy. You know that.' 'Well, damn them, send me the script.'"

In 1994, James Arness made his final film, the last *Gunsmoke* movie: *One Man's Justice*. CBS wanted a country singer, "Travis Tritt or Garth Brooks, to play this young outlaw that befriends Matt Dillon, and dies in his arms." Arness snarled at the executives, "'I don't have the time to teach acting to some singer! Get me Boxleitner!' I didn't learn any of this until after he died."

TIM MATHESON

Despite 183 acting credits, 2 Emmy nominations, and no signs of slowing down, the suave and funny actor Tim Matheson will be forever remembered as Otter, the ladies' man in 1978's uproarious *Animal House*. Yet he already occupied a unique position in television: when a Western series needed new blood, Matheson was the transfusion.

"Either that," he concedes modestly, "or you can blame me for killing the Western. I was on *The Virginian* the last year. And then went into *Bonanza* [the last year].

"Then Kurt Russell and I did *The Quest*; it was sort of the last [TV] Western. That era was over, and I was happy to have been a part of it."

Matheson grew up loving Westerns: "*Davy Crockett, The Rifleman, Jim Bowie, Wanted: Dead or Alive*. One of my all-time favorites was *Have Gun—Will Travel*. I mean, any show that would have a star that looked like Richard Boone in that day and age. He was just cold-blooded—he was a killer, but with a heart of gold, you know?"

Matheson learned about horses because in Burbank, the stables and kennels were together. "I used to work in the kennels, and get free riding lessons. People who owned horses would need somebody to exercise them so I'd take them out and ride and ride."

After getting his first acting job when he was in eighth grade, Matheson broke into Westerns via a cop show. "I got a guest-starring role in an episode of *Adam-12*. I played a young Southern boy who was high on LSD and stole a horse because he was going to ride back to Texas. I think I did a credible Southern accent.

"All of a sudden, I got a call saying that they would like me as a regular on *The Virginian*. I had not met anybody, had no audition. They liked what I did.

"I enjoyed working with James Drury, a gentleman and a cut-up. Always hiding in the catwalks above the sets and dropping water balloons on unsuspecting crew members. . . . I got to work with Tim Holt! He was in an episode, as was Joan Crawford."

The disenchantment of Doug McClure, who'd played Trampas since episode one, paid off for Matheson: "He had contract problems; he was grossly underpaid. So if he didn't want to show up, he'd say, 'Let the kid play my part,' and they'd rewrite it for me."

Matheson had made his mark just in time. "We finished shooting the season, and I literally read in the trades that I was no longer in the show," he says.

"Fade out. Two months later my agent gets a call from Universal. He says, they want to put you back under your contract; they realized they had written a pilot for you called *Lock, Stock and Barrel*. It's by Richard Alan Simmons, a wonderful writer who wrote *Skin Game* later on." Matheson and Belinda J. Montgomery played an eloping frontier couple who get mixed up with outlaws and crooked preachers in what would be a TV movie and series pilot. "They liked it but it didn't work out, so they recast Sally Field in it, called it *Hitched*, and we did it again, this time with Slim Pickens, both times with Neville Brand. Oh my God, he was such a character! Neither of them sold, because Westerns were really hitting the tough times." Still, Universal was a great experience for Matheson. "I guest-starred in every series they did. I studied acting, took fencing, took Shakespeare, took voice, took movement. I did my version of the Royal Academy of Dramatic Art. Then in the fourth year of my contract, Universal loaned me out to *Bonanza*."

Bonanza needed help in 1972. Not only had Dan "Hoss" Blocker suddenly died; the show's ratings had fallen and Chevrolet had dropped its sponsorship. Matheson, who played a prison parolee who Pa (Lorne Greene) takes in, got off to a rough start. "I got into a jam with Michael Landon before I'd even started on the show," he says.

TV Guide quoted Matheson as saying, "I don't think either *Gunsmoke* or *Bonanza* can last much longer; their formats are outdated, new concepts are coming up to take their place."

"Not the wisest thing to say as a new actor on a show," Matheson admits ruefully. "He finally forgave me, but those were the kinds of things I learned from doing Westerns; how to comport yourself on a set. When to keep your mouth shut. I must say I learned a lot."

"Michael was great. He wrote 'em, he directed 'em, and he acted in 'em, and he handled it all with tremendous ease. I thought he was underrated. He knew how to shoot a Western, and they were beautiful shots and beautifully composed."

After *Bonanza*, Matheson did an episode of *Kung Fu* and starred as Emmet Dalton in the TV movie *The Last Day*, with Robert Conrad and Richard Jaeckal as his brothers. Then came *The Quest*, a TV take on 1956's *The Searchers*, with Matheson and Kurt Russell as brothers searching for their sister, a hostage held by Cheyennes. Handsomely produced in Arizona in 1976, the movie and its fifteen episodes are among the best Western television nobody watched. Today, you can catch it on YouTube.

"When we started doing the series, Kurt took me aside one day. He asked, 'Mind if I say something? I think you work too hard. Doing fourteen-hour days, and we're in every scene. Just take it easy during rehearsal and save it for when the camera rolls. Otherwise you'll burn yourself out, and you won't have the energy to get through this.'

"He was absolutely right. He's also one of the most fun guys to be around," Matheson says, adding, "We got to be good pals, and still are."

Then came *Animal House*, a comedy hit in which he starred as one of the frat brother misfits. He's acted a variety of roles since, including the one that earned him Emmy nods, Vice President John Hoynes, on NBC's critically acclaimed *West Wing* series.

Would Matheson act in another Western? "Absolutely. My fondness and love of the Western, I think I learned it from Landon. It was a sense of family. It was hanging out with those wranglers," he says.

"It was good for a kid who didn't have a dad. I grew up surrounded by women, who were lovely, but it was good for me that I was surrounded by these crazy, fun, carefree people. They knew how to ride, how to shoot, how to be a cowboy. They knew how to be a man in that way, and it was a good time for me to have that in my life."

TRACE ADKINS

It's been a great time for Trace Adkins, the six-foot six-inch former oil-field roughneck with the voice too deep to classify. The CMA Award-winner has released his 13th studio album, *The Way I Wanna Go*, to mark the 25th anniversary of his first. He continues to host INSP's *Ultimate Cowboy Showdown*. And another accomplishment: Trace Adkins is the first new Western movie star of the 21st century. He's achieved that entirely with direct-to-streaming films.

Gene Autry spearheaded the transition from country singer to Western actor in 1934, when he was hired to do the warbling in a Ken Maynard movie. Soon, Gene was starring in his own Westerns, often backed by The Sons of the Pioneers, featuring Roy Rogers, who would be starring in his own Westerns by 1938. The B-Western musicals' ranks swelled to include Tex Ritter, Eddie Dean, and others. In A-Westerns and TV movies, Vaughn Monroe, Marty Robbins, Travis Tritt, Randy Travis, Reba McEntire, and Naomi Judd all gave it a shot. In 1969, Glen Campbell triumphed, starring in, and singing the theme song for *True Grit*. In 1980, Kenny Rogers parlayed his hit, *The Gambler*, into a five-film series for television.

Then there were The Highwaymen. In 1959, Johnny Cash sang the theme for *The Rebel* and guested on *Wagon Train*, followed by Kris Kristofferson, acting in 1971's *The Last Movie* before starring in *Pat Garrett and Billy the Kid*. In 1979 Willie Nelson saddled up for *The Electric Horseman*, then a string of his own films. In 1986 Waylon Jennings got on board when the four joined forces for the remake of *Stagecoach*.

"I kinda got bit by the acting bug doing plays in high school," Adkins recalls, "but I didn't pursue it. Once I started doing videos, it bit me again." He did cameos, guest appearances, and played The Angel of Death in *An American Carol*. In 2012, he played a dangerous client in *The Lincoln Lawyer*. "Matthew McConaughey knew I was nervous. He rehearsed scenes with me, went out of his way to make sure I was comfortable. That's probably the best movie that I've ever been lucky enough to be in." In terms of Adkins' role, it could have been a Western. "You know, I either ride a horse or a motorcycle in most movies I do."

A year later, he made his first Western. "That just fell in my lap. I was out in L.A., supposed to fly home the next day, and my agent called and said, 'Hey, there's an opportunity for you to do this Western, and you only have to be there two days.'" *Wyatt Earp's Revenge* is the fact-based story of the killing of

Dora Hand by Spike Kenedy. Adkins plays Spike's protective father, rancher Mifflin Kenedy, cofounder of the King Ranch. Surrounded by earnest twenty-somethings as Earp and company, Adkins dominated his every scene.

In his next Western, Adkins played the original man with no name in a very different take on *The Virginian*. "That was nerve-wracking; that was the first time I was the lead in a movie, and I've only done it once more since. Ron Perlman [as Judge Henry] was just incredible fun to work with. I was pretty awestruck by him." And in an elegant example of life imitating art, Adkins married the schoolmarm, or the actress who played her, Victoria Pratt. Next, Adkins portrayed a reformed outlaw who un-reforms when his wife dies, in *Stagecoach—The Texas Jack Story*.

In *Traded*, where would-be Harvey Girls are forced into white slavery, Michael Paré was the good guy and Adkins the villain. "I like playing the bad guy. I may be better suited to it." He also got to act with one of his idols. "I can't put into words what an honor that was, to work with Kris Kristofferson. I've done a few shows with him over the years, but I always wanted to do a movie with him." They've done a second together, *Hickok*, starring Luke Hemsworth and Bruce Dern, who introduced himself with, "'Hey, I'm Bruce Dern. I was the first man who ever killed John Wayne in a movie! How you doin'?' He was great."

Since then, Adkins has been in *Badland* and played a lawman father hunting down his homicidal son in *The Outsider*. "That was the only one that really bothered me as I was doing it, not to mention how I felt when I watched it. I probably would have killed that boy a lot earlier," he says with a laugh. "He was a bad seed."

That hasn't put him off Westerns. "It was the most interesting, romantic time in our history, post–Civil War, the cowboy era. The myth has outgrown the reality, but that's partly why we enjoy Westerns so much." And a good thing: three more, *Old Henry*, *Apache Junction*, and *The Desperate Riders*, have since been released.

CHAPTER 4
THE SECOND GENERATION

PATRICK WAYNE

In the golden years of Hollywood, a star could always get their kid a bit part in their movie, to keep them busy and quiet. That's usually as far as it went, including for most of John Wayne's children. But not for Patrick. "It was an amazing experience; I enjoyed the work. And one of the greatest things about it was that my brothers and sisters had no interest in doing this. So, when I'd go away with my dad and work on a film, I had him all to myself."

Born in July 1939, Patrick can't remember when he started visiting movie sets. "But, about *Rio Grande* (1950), I do have fond memories," he said. Two years later, when he was age twelve, his father was preparing to star in *The Quiet Man*. "I remember flying out of L.A. with my brother Michael. Seven hours to New York on a prop-plane, and another eight or nine hours to Ireland. Where the overhead luggage-racks are now, there were berths; you had beds up there."

It was a long way to travel to be an uncredited boy on a wagon at a horse race. But his roles in John Ford movies would grow more substantial. "I had an ace in the hole, because he was my godfather. In fact, I worked in several films with Ford, without my father: *Mister Roberts*, *The Long Gray Line*, *Cheyenne Autumn* to name a few." Of course, there was Ford's legendary habit of picking on people to contend with. "It was no myth: he would choose you one day and you would be 'in the barrel,' and you would take the wrath of his acerbic wit for the day. I spent my career with him waiting for that shoe to fall. It never did, but I still had the anxiety of everybody who was going through this, waiting for it to happen."

If he played a callow youth well, that was at least in part because when he played Lieutenant Greenhill in *The Searchers*, he was fourteen years old. "I was a big kid. I was a quick study, so I was prepared," but nothing could prepare him for when his father and Ward Bond went playfully off-script. "These

Patrick Wayne, Natalie Wood, and Danny Borzage take a break between takes while filming *The Searchers*, at the film location's headquarters, Goulding's Lodge, near Monument Valley, Utah/Arizona. *Courtesy Warner Bros.*

clowns are ad-libbing the stuff about 'the joint punitive action' that wasn't in the script, putting me off; but actually, it worked perfect for the part."

For all the time Pat spent with his dad, he didn't get a lot of direct advice. "He didn't advise his kids on anything. He led by example; that's where you learned." As for acting, "his big deal was preparation. When you're going to do a part, you've got to know who that character is. And if he has anything physical to do, it has to be second nature to you, because you will never be able to play a scene if you're thinking about getting on a horse or sword fighting. If you're thinking about that, you're not thinking about the part."

Not that The Duke was trying to create an acting dynasty: he wanted Patrick to choose a career for himself. When Patrick had his first lead in 1959's *The Young Land*, playing the sheriff of a once-Mexican town that had become part of the United States, "They wanted to put me under contract, so my dad negotiated a deal: you pay him every week throughout the year, but you can only use him during the summer months when he's out of school." Sadly, the company produced only the one film.

In 1960, Patrick was juggling attending Loyola University with playing Capt. James Bonham in *The Alamo*, observing his father not only starring in but directing the epic. "He was amazing, because this isn't like *Hondo* with a cast and crew of twenty-five people. This is before CGI, so those battle scenes with thousands of Mexicans outside the fort, those were real people. It was a Herculean task; it would've killed an ordinary man, but he was ready to do this, knew what he wanted."

Patrick was not so sure about what *he* wanted. "I graduated with a degree in biology, and I decided that [acting] is something that I wanted do. So of course, all the work stops." Actually, in rapid succession he was soon seen with his dad in *The Comancheros, Donovan's Reef,* and in *McLintock!* where he worked with Bruce Cabot, "An amazing friend, somebody you'd want in your corner if trouble arose," Yvonne DeCarlo, "a wonderful gal," and Maureen O'Hara. "She gave me my first screen kiss, in *The Long Gray Line*. And when my father passed away, she spoke to Congress for my dad to get the Congressional Medal of Freedom."

Soon he was playing the son of one of his father's frequent co-stars, James Stewart, in *Shenandoah*. He's a gunfighter going blind in *An Eye for an Eye*, and his big secret is that he's Pat Garrett Jr. Twenty-two years later he'd portray Garrett Sr. to Emilio Estevez's Billy in *Young Guns*. "So much fun I can't even tell you. My forty-five-year-old son was about fourteen, and I brought him. You come into these sets, when they've been going for a while, and people form cliques, and it's difficult to impose yourself, but everybody was great, and Emilio was especially nice."

In 1973, Patrick began a new, swashbuckling phase of his career as the star of fantasy adventures, beginning with *Beyond Atlantis*, a quest for a lost civilization and a fortune in pearls. "They were looking to make a sea version of *Treasure of Sierra Madre*. In the Philippines, you're in a paradise." This was followed by the far more elegant *Sinbad and the Eye of the Tiger*. Not an experienced swordsman, he was assured that a stuntman in Europe would cover for him. "I put my foot down. I've really got to do it. I'm not going over there unprepared. I made such a fuss that they finally let me work with this fencing guy, Buddy Van Horn, Clint Eastwood's double. I worked with him every day and by the end I could have joined the Olympic team. Our first location was Malta. [Animator] Ray Harryhausen was very involved in the action sequences because he was the one making the little models, all the demons I was fighting, and they get added later. So there're strict parameter you have to work with.

"We were in Malta, Spain, Jordan. We were in London, at Pinewood [Studios]. It was so much fun, and I was working with Jane Seymour and Taryn Power, beautiful women, and my God, getting paid for it!"

While the topic of our interview was Patrick, not John, his last comments were about his father. "You know," Patrick said, "there've been things written about how my dad drank on-set. It's not true. And that he wasn't prepared: wrong. He was always prepared. He could abide a lot of things going wrong on-set, but he could not deal with a person who was not prepared to come to work and do what he was supposed to. That was not acceptable; for that he would read you the riot act."

CHRISTOPHER MITCHUM

"Dad started acting just about the time I was born, in 1943," Christopher Mitchum recalls. "His first fourteen films, he was uncredited; he was a bad guy in *Hopalong Cassidy* movies. Then William Boyd gave him a break, his first line, in *Hoppy Serves a Writ*. He took off from there." While Robert Mitchum's older son Jim had a film career that was blessed and cursed by his startling resemblance to his father, Christopher Mitchum, with blond hair in a bowl cut, had a look distinctly his own.

He grew up at the studios. "Dad'd take us to the set, but he'd usually drop me off in the prop room. I'd be playing with five-foot-long remote-control battleships, and King Kong and things like that. I just thought he worked in a great toy shop."

Robert Mitchum neither encouraged nor discouraged an acting career for Chris. "We never even discussed it. He was something of an anarchist: he believed in finding your own way without authority telling you what to do." Initially, Christopher had different plans. "I had gone to the University of Pennsylvania to study literature, planning on teaching, and in the off-time, writing." Then junior year at Dublin's Trinity College, and he completed his degree at the University of Arizona, while he and his wife worked at Old Tucson Studios, "as extras for $13.80 a day and a free lunch." That was where he got interested in filmmaking, but on the other side of the camera.

When did Christopher decide to become an actor? "I didn't. I ended up as a gopher," on his father's film, *Young Billy Young*, and played his father's murdered son in flashbacks. On *Bigfoot*, "I was second assistant director. They lost their lead; Jody McCrea, Joel's son, wanted $5,000 a week. They said, 'We only have $500. Do you wanna play the part?' I said, 'Sure! I'm making $150 week as second AD (assistant director).' Then I was working in accounting on *Suppose They Gave a War and Nobody Came?* The director told me, 'We have a part for a hippie GI; you'd be perfect. Wanna do it?'" Like it or not, Mitchum was an actor.

Mitchum's big break came when he was cast in John Wayne's *Chisum*, as wingman to Geoff Duel's Billy the Kid. "But I got to wear a gun and shoot, play cowboy. One day, Duke's sitting back, watching the scene—I'm like fourth guy in the back. After, Duke comes up, slaps me on the thigh, and says, 'Yuh know, you should have played Billy the Kid. Howard Hawks is coming down to talk to me about my next film. I'll introduce you.'"

The film was *Rio Lobo*, "And that's probably the job that turned me. Working with Howard Hawks, he really instilled in me a love for being in front of the camera." In *Big Jake*, Mitchum had an even bigger role, as one of Wayne's sons. "I enjoyed that at the end of the movie, everybody else had a bullet wound. I'm the only one not bleeding."

From there he flew to Spain, co-starring with Karl Malden and Olivia Hussey in the crime thriller *Summertime Killer*. But when he returned home, he says he "didn't get an interview for eleven months." When he finally did, the casting director for *Steelyard Blues* recognized him. "She said, 'You starred with John Wayne. I can't interview you.' Flat out told me I was blackballed." His problems were not just one-sided. During an appearance on *The Tonight Show*, following John Wayne, Mitchum told Johnny Carson he'd been campaigning for an anti-pollution bill. "Duke jumped all over me. He couldn't grasp that a conservative could want clean water, too. He'd signed me to a five-picture contract, but basically never spoke to me again.

"Fortunately, *Summertime Killer* was the biggest grossing film in Spain's history. I lived there for three years; worked in Spain, Portugal, Italy, France. Then Thailand, India. I ended up starring in sixty films in fourteen different countries."

After his exile, Mitchum's next stateside film was another Western, 1976's *The Last Hard Men*, starring with friend Charlton Heston, and he reunited with *Chisum* director Andrew V. McLaglen. Mitchum worked pretty steadily after his return, but hadn't done another Western until 1993, when he got a call from Kevin Jarre, who had written and was to direct *Tombstone*, and was a fan of *The Last Hard Men*. "He said, 'We just hired Chuck Heston. I'd love to see you two together again.' It was the most beautiful script I've ever read in my entire life." Sadly, Jarre was fired and Mitchum's footage cut to one line. "The producers set Kevin up to fire him, because he was a first-time director."

Today, Mitchum happily attends events, often with Patrick Wayne and other family members, including the opening of The John Wayne Experience in Fort Worth, Texas, and the John Wayne Birthplace Museum in Winterset, Iowa. "Anything I can do to help Duke's legacy, I'm delighted to do it, because he helped me so much."

Now, at age seventy-eight, he hasn't given up on acting. "If somebody says, we remember your work and we'd like to put you in our film, I'd do it in a New York minute. I grew up in the era when you sit and talk for an hour with Howard Hawks. I just can't go through that process of putting together a video and sending it out and being rejected by people I've never heard of."

ROBERT CARRADINE

Robert Carradine remembers, "After all of us went into [acting]—my brother David, brother Keith, myself, my half-brother Michael Bowen, my daughter Ever, Keith's daughter Martha Plimpton—my father remarked that he'd created a dynasty." Said father was John Carradine, one of America's finest actors, whose Western credits in 1939 alone include *Stagecoach*, *Jesse James*, and *Drums along the Mohawk*.

Robert, whose long career includes at least two classic Westerns, *The Cowboys* and *The Long Riders*, had a classically Western beginning, living in the landmark Leonis Adobe, built in 1844, and one of the oldest buildings in Southern California. "I had the distinct pleasure of crawling off the second-floor balcony when I was two. My dad had been preparing his garden directly below, and he had a big pile of dirt that he'd just sifted. It was a very soft pile, and I landed with a nice thump."

His on-screen entrance would wait another fifteen years. He'd been boarding at the Ojai Valley School, "and at the end of my 10th grade year, my father said, 'Son, I'm going to have you live with your brother David for a while in Laurel Canyon in the Hollywood Hills.' I go to live with David, and one day he says, 'Hey, there's a movie casting over at Warner Brothers called *The Cowboys*. It's a John Wayne movie about these schoolkids that wind up getting hired by John Wayne to herd his cattle to market. You want to go in and meet him?' I said, no. He said, '*No?*' I said I would be frightened to go in there. He said, 'Well, you've got everything to gain and nothing to lose.' And that stopped me. Okay, so I go in, and they have me do the scene where John Wayne has come into the schoolhouse to see if these kids could possibly be cattle hands, and I had to read this ridiculous poem in front of the John Wayne character. I was as nervous as could be in the audition, and it worked perfectly. So that's how I got it."

The dozen boys they cast were an interesting mix. "Half were real cowboys, and half were actors. They spent three months teaching us every day, four hours a day on horseback under the watchful eye of Red Burns. He also taught us how to throw a rope, and it was just such a gift, because that is a talent, a skill, that I've carried with me through many Westerns. And it was all because of that film and our instructor Red Burns."

On the set of *The Cowboys*, John Carradine (far right) visits his Stagecoach co-star John Wayne, and his son Robert Carradine, who was making his film debut. *Courtesy Warner Bros.*

Carradine first worked with Wayne in the scene where each cowboy has to stay on Crazy Alice, the bucking horse, for a count of eight to be hired. A Martinez's character amazes the others with his skill, then contemptuously tells the next boy, "Maybe you can ride him now." Carradine remembers, "The kid comes off the fence and starts going after A Martinez, and I go to help my little buddy. The Duke breaks us up and says to me, 'You get back up on that fence where you belong.' And I stopped him. 'Hold on a second, Mr. Wayne. I'm the head kid. It's okay if you want to tell me to get on the fence, but I don't think that you should say *where you belong*.' He looked at me like I had two heads. Then he lit into me, reduced me to tears by the time he was done. What would possess a seventeen-year-old in his first movie to try to direct John Wayne?"

Carradine says of himself and A Martinez, "We were the old guys. I think he was twenty-one." While they clashed on-screen, in reality, "We got along great. Because I was seventeen, I needed to have a guardian on-set. And we came up with the scheme that A Martinez would be my guardian. That's how David got out of having to be on-set for three months."

At the wrap party, Wayne was signing autographs; the other boys had grabbed 8x10s of The Duke. Carradine took one and got in line. "I hand him the picture, he's about to put pen to paper, and he looks at me. 'Carradine, you stupid son-of-a-bitch, I just made a picture with you!' and gave back the photo unsigned, which I took as a compliment—that we're colleagues.

"Bruce Dern relished that role. He loved scaring the crap out of us." In the scene where Dern catches one boy, and threatens to kill him if he tells Wayne they're being followed, he "takes the kid by the collar, stuffs the kid's head underwater, and pulls him back up. 'You got it, boy?' And he does it again. 'You got it, boy?' And the kid's like, 'Got it! Got it!' That was not planned. That was Bruce."

The next year Carradine played Bob Hatfield in a TV movie. "The thing about *The Hatfields and the McCoys* was hanging out with Jack Palance. The character that he played in *City Slickers*, that was him." Also in the cast was James Keach. "That was the germ for *The Long Riders*. James Keach said, 'How would you feel about doing a story about the James Younger Gang? It's me and [brother] Stacy; you, David, and Keith; Randy and Dennis Quaid; and Jeff and Beau Bridges.' The Bridges backed out because they didn't want to be the guys that shot Jesse James in the back.

"The sum of the three Carradines is bigger than just three guys; there's this undefinable essence, and it was there with the Keaches, the Quaids, and the Guests. You'd see similar mannerisms and quirks and reactions, that you wouldn't have if you had actors playing brothers. It was an incredible dynamic."

Carradine returns to Westerns whenever possible. About *Django Unchained*, he says, "My brother Mike [half-brother Michael Bowen] and I were really glorified extras. I was supposed to be a hunchback, but the outfit looked ridiculous, so we scrapped that and just made me a half-wit."

In 2017, Carradine appeared in *Justice*. "There was no extra money. It had to run like a Swiss watch to get it done, and our director and DP were a great team." Also that year he starred in *Bill Tilghman and the Outlaws*, wherein a company makes a movie about a bank robbery, starring real lawmen and outlaws. Carradine plays Frank James, Darby Hinton plays Cole Younger, and Johnny Crawford, in what would be his final performance, played his idol, William S. Hart. "I thought *Justice* was close to the bone! God, we were doing everything we could to get that sucker done on time. It was a twelve-day shoot, and some days we'd shoot twelve pages!"

Why does he keep at it? He recalls filming *The Big Red One*, surprised to see Lee Marvin on-set on his day off. "I said, 'Lee, what are you doing here?' He said, 'The set is where it's at.' I told that story to Tom Selleck on *Monte Walsh*, and he's been repeating it ever since."

CHAPTER 5
THE CHARACTERS—GOOD AND BAD

THE GOOD

SLIM PICKENS

Going by his accent, many have assumed that Slim Pickens was from the South, but he was born Louis Burton Lindley Jr. in Kingsburg, California, not far from Fresno, on June 29, 1919. His father, Louis Sr., was from Texas, and his mother, Sally Mosher Turk, hailed from Missouri, which altogether explained his drawl.

The Lindleys were a ranching family, and Louis Jr., then called Burt, was at home in the saddle from an early age—he had his own horse when he was four years old. But while Burt was expected to work on the family ranch, by the time he was fifteen, his true passion was for rodeo.

Louis Sr. was not pleased. Daryle Ann Giardino, Slim's daughter, recalls her father's story of his first rodeo: "When he went to register, Dad told the woman behind the desk, 'I don't know what to do. My dad told me if he sees my name on a contestant entry, I'm not gonna have a home to come to.' She said, 'Well, why don't you call yourself Slim Pickins', kid, 'cause that's what it's going to be.' And it stuck: Louis B. Lindley—Slim Pickens."

That day, he won $400, right out of the chute!

"Dad rode bareback horses and saddle broncs," Giardino says. "But he wasn't making a lot of money rodeoing—it was slim pickings. So that's when he started clowning."

While rodeo clowns may wear costumes and makeup similar to circus clowns, their primary job is much more serious and dangerous: to protect bull riders. When a rider is thrown, the clown must distract the angry animal long enough for the rider to make it to safety. Never a cakewalk, the rodeo clown's job became a lot rougher in the 1920s, with the introduction of the mean-natured Brahma bull to the entertainment.

Before Rex Allen became a singing cowboy for the movies, he spent a few years in rodeo. He told a reporter, "Slim was probably the top clown bull-fighter in the business. You talk to any bull rider back in those days, and he would rather have Slim out in that arena to protect him than anybody in the world, because Slim could handle it."

Beyond his protective instincts, Slim also got laughs. "He clowned a lot of rodeos," Giardino says. "Dad made a lot of money, because he was genuinely funny. Most rodeo clowns had those baggy pants and their faces painted, but Dad didn't do that. Dad always wore a matador's outfit. With the bull riding, Dad would walk out there like a matador, and he could really use a cape. Dad had this doctor's outfit, and if somebody got bucked off a bronc, Dad would run out, pull a live skunk out of his doctor's kit, and the cowboy would get off the ground really fast."

He was so at the top of his game that Slim's name was included in rodeo advertisements, probably a first for a rodeo clown.

The reality is, though, rodeo clowning was a rough business. The late actor Andrew Prine remembered: "When I asked Slim how many bones he'd broken over the years, Slim started counting. 'Well, my elbow, this wrist, my knee.' After a while he said, 'Probably sixteen bones.' I said, 'You didn't count your ribs.' Slim looked at me with great disdain and said, 'Andy, I don't count ribs.'"

In 1950, Slim met the love of his life, Margaret Elizabeth Harmon, in what Hollywood would consider a perfect "meet cute." Margaret was galloping her horse at the Madera racetrack when Slim, not looking, stepped out on the track, and she nearly ran him down. He just had to meet that beautiful redhead who was giving him such a dirty look.

Margaret was the sort of human calculator featured in *Hidden Figures*. "Mom worked for Howard Hughes and was a mathematical genius. She figured out things like how much runway a plane needed to land," Giardino says.

It was a good thing that the math whiz, and not the high school dropout, was in charge of the money. "Dad did not care how much he made on a film. All he cared about was the per diem—because Mom took the checks, but they gave him the per diem in cash, so he liked that," Giardino says.

Slim would find himself in a new arena when his career break came in 1950. Director William Keighley had seen his rodeo act and offered him a screen test. Slim had also ridden a bronc in 1946's *Smoky*, but that wasn't an acting gig. Keighley's film was *Rocky Mountain*, starring Errol Flynn as a Confederate officer leading a small band of soldiers whose covert mission is thwarted when they save a stagecoach from an Indian attack. Shot entirely in Gallup, New Mexico, this exceptionally good Western is Flynn's best. Slim's character was introduced in voice-over by Flynn: "Plank, another real plainsman, hard and bitter, with chain-gang scars on his legs at twenty-two."

Republic Pictures saw Slim's potential and signed him up as a sidekick in the Rex Allen Western series, starting with 1952's *Colorado Sundown*, in which Slim played two characters—both Joshua and Joshua's mother! Although filmed at the tail end of the B-Western era, these nine movies were engaging, well-made, and zestfully directed by action master William Witney.

Aside from Margaret, the other great love of Slim's life was one his audiences would recognize—a blue roan Appaloosa, Dear John. Slim spotted the young gelding in a Montana pasture in 1954 and convinced Margaret that he was worth the $150 investment.

"So my mother would let him buy the horse, he said, 'Let's buy him, and he'll be your horse.' Of course, that didn't happen," Giardino says.

After Slim worked with trainer Glenn Randall, Dear John could buck on cue, throw kisses, shake his head yes or no, sit like a dog, and grab a blanket off his back and throw it.

Dear John rode into the Hollywood arena in the Rex Allen pictures and other films, and performed in rodeos between movies. In the 1958 classic *The Big Country*, Dear John played Old Thunder, a horse that tenderfoot Gregory Peck tries to ride. But when Dear John bucked off Peck, Slim doubled for Peck in the long shots. From then on, Slim would only let Dear John work if he could do the riding; their connection was said to border on the psychic.

During the 1950s, Slim appeared in virtually every Western series on TV, as well as features with Joel McCrea and Glenn Ford, and in Disney Westerns *Tonka* and *The Great Locomotive Chase*. But his first truly demanding acting challenge came in 1961. Prine said, "If you ever want to see Slim really act, you look at the film he did with Brando. He was tremendously good in that."

In *One-Eyed Jacks*, the only film Marlon Brando ever directed, Slim's Deputy Lon Dedrick was mean, humorless, and corrupt.

"That was the first film that I couldn't identify with Dad," Giardino says. "He was so into the character, so double-tough and nasty."

Bruce Boxleitner, who later appeared in the *How the West Was Won* series with Slim, recalls Slim telling him, "Everyone made a fortune on that movie but the studio, because we were on it for months."

In addition to his busy acting life, Slim took on a behind-the-scenes role in 1962 as technical advisor, as well as on-camera actor, on the NBC series

Wide Country, starring Earl Holliman as a rodeo star and Prine as his younger brother. Slim even wrote the stories for a pair of episodes.

"Slim was funny, but he was also very straight and sincere," Holliman remembers. "I was not a cowboy, but I wanted to look like one. He showed me how to get on bucking horses, how to cinch up a horse—the little tricks of the trade, getting ready to come out of the chute—he was right on top of it."

Prine also learned plenty from Slim. Brought to California from Broadway, he'd never even seen a rodeo when he walked on-set in his wardrobe, with his jeans cuffs rolled up.

"Slim looked at me a minute, and asked, 'Do you dig ditches in this script?' I said no, and he said, 'Then roll down the cuffs of your jeans. No rodeo rider rolls his cuffs up, the reason being you'd get hooked by a horn on your cuffs.' He looked at me another minute. I had this brand-new Stetson hat on. He said, 'Let me have that a minute.' I gave him my hat, and before I could say a word, he spit tobacco juice all around the hat band and rubbed it in. He said, 'Makes it look like you've been to work.' I realized that I was dealing with a man who knew what he was talking about. I thought the world of Slim," Prine said.

A rodeo arena was built atop Universal, and things started out rough. "The first time they brought the livestock out, they unloaded this big Brahma bull into a holding pen," Prine recalled. "The wooden crossbars on the fence were nailed [on the] wrong side. The bull took one look at it, and went through it like papier-mâché. We all scattered, and the bull took off over the hill, into *The Virginian* set. Doug McClure said he and the crew looked up and saw this monster running down the hill toward them, and they ran like hell and hid. I saw Slim grab his horse, jump on it; he went over the hill, lassoed the bull, and he brought him back to the set."

Prine saw Slim's courage off the set as well. "Slim took me to rodeos with him," he said. "A bull came out and threw the rider, and Slim had to get the bull off the rider. The bull got Slim down in a corner of the fence, he was on his back, and this 1,700-lb. bull was butting him and trying to kill him. I was terrified. I screamed, 'Slim! Slim! Get out of there!' And Slim, while he's down on the ground underneath the bull, smiled and said, 'No horns!' He wasn't worried at all."

The role that made Slim not only a star but also an indelible image in American consciousness was just around the corner. Filming for *Dr. Strangelove,* Stanley Kubrick's black comedy about a demented general leading the United States into nuclear war, was nearly completed when an unforeseen problem shut down production. Star Peter Sellers had already played three roles: a Royal Air Force officer, the US president, and Strangelove. He was all set to play bomber pilot Maj. "King" Kong, when a problem arose.

Widely reported by the media, Sellers was said to have broken his leg or become ill. But when Slim was urgently contacted to play Kong, the explanation was a lot simpler: Sellers couldn't get the accent right.

Having never been out of the country before, Slim didn't realize he needed a passport until after he arrived in London. He had to stay at the airport until one could be rushed to him.

The mishaps didn't end there. Slim rides down one of two bombs, each showing their names painted on them: "Hi There!" and "Dear John." Kubrick let Slim name them, and, of course, Slim meant to ride down Dear John, but a miscommunication put the bombs in the wrong positions, so Slim ended up straddling "Hi There!" while he whooped and waved his hat in grand rodeo fashion.

Slim would later learn from Van Heflin, an acting buddy and lifelong friend, that Slim had come within two votes of an Oscar nomination for 1964's *Dr. Strangelove*.

The 1960s continued to be busy acting years for Slim. He appeared in the first of four films for Sam Peckinpah, *Major Dundee*. Both men particularly enjoyed working on that film together because they'd grown up in the San Joaquin Valley and knew each other long before they'd entered the film business. In 1966, Slim played Buck, the stagecoach driver in the remake of *Stagecoach*. Norman Rockwell, hired to paint the poster, created individual portraits of the cast. The shy artist, intimidated by the stars, insisted on painting Slim first, because he was a regular guy.

In 1972, Slim co-starred with James Coburn in one of the best films ever made about rodeo, *The Honkers*. A real Westerner as well as comedian, Slim was the most authentic element in Mel Brooks' 1974 delightfully flatulent Western farce *Blazing Saddles*, his best-remembered role after *Dr. Strangelove*.

Among Slim's other favorite roles was Sheriff Sam Creedmore, the lawman who reluctantly hangs Tom Horn, played by Steve McQueen in 1980's *Tom Horn*. Giardino reveals why the movie was so personal for her father: "Years before, he actually met the sheriff, and talked to him at length. He knew Horn was not guilty, and he did not want to hang him. But he had to. Dad said, what happens up there on the platform is almost verbatim what the sheriff told him."

Time catches up to even the best of us. Giardino remembers when her father had to retire Dear John, turning him out to pasture at the ranch of a veterinarian friend in Bishop, California. Her mother told her: "Dad sat up in bed one night and said, 'Oh my God, John's dead.' And Mom said, 'C'mon, Slim, you're having a bad dream; just go back to sleep.' And three nights later, Doc Hird called and said, 'I couldn't call you, but John died three nights ago.'"

After a long career in rodeo, and after 172 film and TV roles, Slim fought a long, valiant battle against a brain tumor. Although the cause is unknown, his daughter suspects that all of the punishing blows he received to his head during his rodeo years may have been to blame. Slim died on December 8, 1983, at the age of sixty-four.

Giardino once asked her father, an untrained actor, if he was ever intimidated by working with so many big stars and important directors. He told her, "As long as I had a horse underneath me, and a rifle in my hand, I knew I was gonna be okay."

EARL HOLLIMAN

The Sons of Katie Elder, Gunfight at the O.K. Corral, Giant. With such an extensive resume of classic Westerns, it's easy to forget that Earl Holliman is best-known for playing Angie Dickinson's partner on *Police Woman.* Looking back from age ninety-two with astonishing recall, he admits, "I can't remember ever wanting to be anything other than an actor. I'd say, 'I'm going to Hollywood and be a movie star.' I just fell in love with what I saw up on the picture-show screen in Texas and Louisiana."

It was 1943, in the midst of World War II, and Earl enlisted, then was sent back to high school when the Navy learned he was only fifteen years old. He enlisted again—he was still underage, but closer—and his mother went along with it this time. Stationed in California, he'd visit the Hollywood Canteen where, he recalls, "I'd meet stars I'd seen in the movies, and would work with later, like Ida Lupino, Roddy McDowell, Dane Clark." After discharge he worked at various jobs, attended Pasadena Playhouse on the G.I. Bill, and tried to break into the movie business.

He learned to breach the seemingly impenetrable studio gates at Paramount "by saying I had an appointment with Victor, the barber." He did it monthly, and once inside he'd visit sets and watch stars like Alan Ladd, Kirk Douglas, Laurence Olivier, and directors like Billy Wilder at work. He befriended casting director Paul Nathan, who gave him his first speaking role,

Earl Holliman plays lawman Charles Bassett to Kirk Douglas's Doc Holliday in *Gunfight at the O.K. Corral*, the first of two pictures they'd make together. *Courtesy Paramount Pictures*

a one-line part as an elevator operator in a Dean Martin and Jerry Lewis comedy, *Scared Stiff.*

His first big role wasn't in a Western, but it was shot just outside of Reno, and "*Destination Gobi* was the first time I really got on a horse. I also learned to ride a camel. Not much call for camel riders anymore." Set in 1943 Mongolia, "it was about seven Navy weathermen who get mixed up with the Mongols," and Japanese bombers. Director Robert Wise, "was a very clever guy. He started out as a cutter at R.K.O. He cut *Citizen Kane.*" The lead, Richard Widmark, "was the first movie star that ever took me aside and gave me advice. 'Don't become one of these Hollywood nightclub actors,' hanging out in the bars, trying to get in the movie magazines."

After a brief appearance in *Devil's Canyon*, Holliman had his first solid Western role in 1953 as one of Spencer Tracy's sons—along with Richard Widmark and Hugh O'Brian, all teaming against "half-breed" brother Robert Wagner—in *Broken Lance*. "I was a big fan of Spencer Tracy and [his longtime love] Katharine Hepburn. He was very kind to me."

In *The Burning Hills*, Holliman was the bad guy, opposite Natalie Wood and Tab Hunter, and Stuart Heisler directed a thrilling, no-holds-barred brawl between Holliman and Hunter. Surprisingly, it was physically tougher to work with Wood because "nobody ever told her how you pull your punches. In the first scene, I come onto her, and she hit me so hard on the side of my head, I really saw stars. And we had to do it twice!"

Shane director George Stevens was making his epic film *Giant* and watched *Broken Lance* to check out New Mexico locations. He saw Holliman and cast him as Bob Dace. "I was so excited because, my God, George Stevens was another one of those icons. I read the book from cover to cover; I closed it with disappointment because Bob Dace is only mentioned twice, once when he's four years old, picking up mountain oysters." Happily, Stevens had built up the role.

Holliman was cast as lawman Charlie Bassett in *Gunfight at the O.K. Corral*, his first time working with stars Burt Lancaster and Kirk Douglas, and he soon would play "the greatest part I ever had," the kid brother whose sister (Katharine Hepburn) is mesmerized by Burt Lancaster as *The Rainmaker*. Holliman had to fight for it, because producer Hal Wallis thought at age twenty-seven, Holliman was too old, and the New York office was pushing Elvis Presley for the part. On Tracy's recommendation, Hepburn went to bat for him, and while watching a screen test for another character, the playwright N. Richard Nash "pointed his finger to the screen, said, 'That's the boy I wrote it for.'" It was the role that won him a Golden Globe.

In *Trooper Hook*, Barbara Stanwyck was a rescued white captive with a half-Indian child; Joel McCrea was the soldier detailed to return her to her husband; and Holliman was the charming young drifter who becomes their ally. He became great friends with both stars, even though he'd beaten out McCrea's son, Jody, for the part. "Joel and I went to a sneak preview, the titles came on, it said 'Joel McCrea, Barbara Stanwyck, Earl Holliman in *Trooper Hook*.' I was stunned; it was the first time my name appeared above the title. Joel said, 'Hey, that's good billing!' He hit me so hard with his elbow that he could have knocked me out of my seat."

In *Last Train from Gun Hill*, Holliman's character rapes and murders an Indian woman, not knowing she's the wife of sheriff Kirk Douglas, who is a close friend of Holliman's father, Anthony Quinn. Kirk, who produced, worried, "'I don't think Earl Holliman is a threat to me.' But he learned." The savage fight between the two in a burning hotel room, with Holliman handcuffed to the bed, is legendary. There's a remarkable scene where Quinn humiliates his son, "and I'm so needy and unloved. It was a whole different side of the character." It wasn't in the original script. "That was added by Kirk, and it was really generous of him."

In 1965, Holliman played brother to John Wayne, Dean Martin, and Michael Anderson Jr. in *The Sons of Katie Elder*. "Acting with John Wayne, you would never have known that he'd just come back from having his lung removed, because he gave it his all. He was the same John Wayne that he always was in front of that camera."

He stills remembers when, at age fifteen, he hitchhiked to Hollywood. "I went to Grauman's Chinese Theatre, and looked at all the stars on Hollywood Boulevard, The Walk of Fame. In front was Joel McCrea's star, then a space, then Greta Garbo. Now, between them, is Earl Holliman's star. Every time I have a chance, I tell that story. And I say, hang on to your dreams, because they can come true."

BARRY CORBIN

There are a certain very few actors whose presence lends the Westerns they appear in an instant credibility and gravitas. Ben Johnson and Harry Carey Jr. are the classic examples. Now that mantle rests on the shoulders of Barry Corbin. "That's a huge compliment to me because I was a fan of both of 'em. Matter of fact, my wife's sort of adopted father was Dobe (Harry Jr.) Carey. Dobe was a great guy, and Ben was one of my heroes growing up.

"We were doing one of Ben's rodeos one time; my horse fell on me, so I was in a cast. So, we were sitting up in the bleachers, watching some of the Hollywood folks practicing team penning. I said, 'Look at them riding around; they don't know there's a cow within a hundred miles. All they want to do is wave at the audience.' And Ben said, 'Ain't nobody in Hollywood knows how to ride anymore, except you and me.' And I said, 'Well, man, we don't live in Hollywood.'"

Corbin was interested in acting early on. "I didn't tell anybody at that time, but when I was seven, watching B-westerns at The Majestic in La Mesa, Texas, I thought, I can do that. First, I was looking at guys like Wild Bill Elliot and Allan Rocky Lane, [but] the other guys, sidekicks, seemed to work more and have more fun. I always liked Al "Fuzzy" St. John, Gabby Hayes."

His mother may have been directing him towards a life in the arts—he's named Barry for *Peter Pan* creator James Barrie—but his family didn't embrace his career goals. "My dad, who was a lawyer and a politician, said, 'Acting's a fine hobby, but nobody makes a living doing that.' He finally came around when I started doing movies and television." But when Barry was in *Henry V* on Broadway, "He thought I was doing something illicit, like holding up banks."

After the New York blackout in 1977, "I thought, I've had enough of this, so we loaded up our Ford Pinto and took off for California." He and his wife barely got by, writing and performing short plays on National Public Radio. "I got *Urban Cowboy* right after [our second son] was born, so that worked out real well." It made his career.

That was quickly followed by *Any Which Way You Can*, and later *Honky-tonk Man*. "I think Clint Eastwood is a good actor, but he's a better director because he knows how to say what he needs in very few words. You know, a lot of directors, they expound on things and end up confusing you."

He worked steadily on TV and in film, occasionally in almost-Westerns like *The Ballad of Gregorio Cortez*, or *Davy Crockett: A Natural Man*, and he carried a self-confidence and authority that made him a natural wearing a badge. "Yeah. For about two years I had to say, if the guy's first name is Sheriff, I'm not interested. I was afraid I'd get pigeonholed." Still, the sense of honesty he embodies has made Corbin a master at delivering bad news. In Westerns like *Shadow on the Mesa*, *Redemption: For Robbing the Dead*, and *Conagher*, if someone has to be told that their husband/daughter/son is missing or dead, Corbin is the man to do it.

Unforgettably, in the Coen Brothers' *No Country for Old Men*, he only has one scene, at the end, and his manager wasn't sure he'd do it, even with Tommy Lee Jones. "I read that scene, and I didn't even finish the script. Hell, yes, I'll do it! That scene is the movie: it makes everything clear."

In *Lonesome Dove* he played a deputy, but one with neither confidence nor authority. "That's one of my favorites. I read that book and I thought, I've got to be in this thing. Roscoe Brown was a ten-year-old child in a forty-year-old body. When Blue Duck killed the two kids and me, he killed three children." It was his first time with director Simon Wincer. "I've worked for him three times: *Lonesome Dove*, *Crossfire Trail*, and *Monte Walsh*, and it was a great experience. He's a very good director, not precious about it. He just gets the job done. That's the way Australians do things." Next came six seasons as a retired astronaut in Alaska in *Northern Exposure*.

Then in 1991, Corbin shared the screen for the fourth time, first time in a Western, with Sam Elliott and his wife, Katharine Ross, in *Conagher*. In the film, Ross, husband Billy Green Bush, and their children move onto a ranch, and Bush disappears on a cattle-buying trip. While it's unspoken, there is a poignancy to Corbin's stagecoach driver's feelings toward the widow. "I figured old Charlie was secretly in love with her, and he'd like to marry her, but he had to see Conagher (Elliott) get her."

In 2001, Corbin wore a badge again in his first collaboration with Tom Selleck, *Crossfire Trail*. Memorably, literally under the gun, Corbin performs a marriage between villain Mark Harmon and the desperately resisting Virginia Madsen, with his own character murmuring, "Not my finest hour." Two years later he worked with Selleck again in *Monte Walsh*.

"Tom's a good guy. Tom makes sure all his equipment is right, and every time he makes a Western, he has a saddle made for it." For *Monte Walsh*, "his spurs had a bar across it so that the rowel wouldn't turn, but just half a turn. 'Cause that's what the bronc stompers used to use." The actor, who recently turned eighty-two, adds, "I'd love to see him do another Western. I think he'd hire me back."

THE BAD

BRUCE DERN

It's no surprise that INSP, a TV network specializing in Westerns, has occasional John Wayne festivals. But when, in June, they celebrated Bruce Dern's birthday with a "That Dern Villain" marathon, it gave one pause. Has any other screen villain received such an honor? Of course, Dern hasn't played only villains. He's been Oscar-nominated twice, as a troubled officer returned from Vietnam in *Coming Home* (1978), and as an addle-brained senior who believes he's won a sweepstakes in *Nebraska* (2013).

Despite the down-at-the-heels characters he often plays, Dern was perfect casting in *The Great Gatsby* as Gatsby's rival, because "I *am* Tom Buchanan." Dern grew up in Illinois, a scion of two prestigious families: "My great-uncle Archibald MacLeish won Pulitzer Prizes as a poet and playwright." Dern's father was a very successful lawyer, "and legal partner of Adlai Stevenson." Bruce had no interest in law; his passion was running. "I was national high school champion at 800 meters. I went to Penn for two years, basically because my dad had gone there. My sophomore year, 1956, was an Olympic year. And I was very discouraged that I did not qualify for the Olympic team. So I quit college."

He'd never thought about acting before, but he started going to a lot of movies, "and they were touching me. I said, I'd like to be able to do that. So I looked for a dramatics school."

Bruce Dern tortures and terrorizes young Nicolas Beauvy in *The Cowboys*. *Courtesy Warner Bros.*

He was admitted to The Actor's Studio, and under the tutelage of Elia "Gadj" Kazan and Lee Strasberg, they finally deemed him ready for Hollywood. He was also, by this time, married to actress Diane Ladd, who has been nominated for three Oscars. Although the marriage didn't last, it produced Oscar-winning daughter Laura Dern. "In the limo on the way to the airport, Gadj said, 'When you get out there, nobody's going to know who the hell you are, so your roles are going to be the fifth cowboy from the right. Just make sure you're the most honest, unique fifth cowboy from the right, because you're an original.'"

After Dern guested in ten different series, in 1962 he sidekicked for Jack Lord in *Stoney Burke*. "I thought Jack Lord was the most egotistical individual I met in the business." Dern lasted the first seventeen episodes. He had greater success when he formed a secret alliance with fellow strugglers Jack Nicholson, Warren Oates, and Harry Dean Stanton. "If I read a *Gunsmoke* script and Jack would be perfect for it, my agent would call his agent, then Harry Dean's agent, saying these guys could play brothers in this episode." Of course, casting directors had to be convinced. After their disastrous meetings with legendary casting director Lynn Stalmaster, both Nicholson and Stanton were shown the door, and Stalmaster found Dern so arrogant he chased him out of his office with, "And take your two yokels with you," adding as a generous afterthought, "If you're ever in anything, let me know and I'll come look at it." Dern replied, "I'm in your office right now." Stalmaster laughed, and that broke the ice. He would soon become an ally to them all, and when the late Stalmaster received the Academy Governors Award in 2016, it was presented by Bruce and Laura Dern.

Dern appeared on all the major Western series, hoping to get killed. "If you were killed in an episode, you could come back the next year and play another character. If you were not killed, they couldn't have you back, because the residual had just come in, and they didn't want to pay you for showing that episode and continuing you for another year." About shooting one memorable *Gunsmoke* episode he said, "I look over and sitting there is Bette Davis, playing my mother." In those days, a star doing episodic TV meant their career was over. "Honestly, I cried. She sees the tears, and she said, 'Bruce, what's the matter with you?' I said, 'Bette, it's a *Gunsmoke*.' She said, 'Who's going to pay for my cigarettes? That's why I'm here.'"

"In one episode of *The Big Valley*, Barbara Stanwyck slapped me as hard as I've ever been slapped in my life. I knew it was coming, but I said a sixty-year-old woman is not going to clean my clock! She hit me, I went, 'Ow, that hurt!' The director called, 'Cut! That's not in the script!' Stanwyck said, 'Keep it—that's just what he'd say. I slapped the shit out of him!'"

Dern is famous for saying and doing things that are not in the script, lines or gestures that are startlingly real. Jack Nicholson calls them "Dernsies." For *Once Upon a Time in Hollywood*, Tarantino wrote the part of George Spahn for Dern, because he had known Spahn. "I shot at least five episodes out at the ranch," Dern said. In the pre-Manson days, he and Robert Conrad visited blind and largely deaf Spahn. When Brad Pitt's character comes to check on Spahn, after confronting the Manson "family," Spahn doesn't know who Pitt is, but he says, "But you did something very nice for me today. You touched me, because you came to see me." Not in the script. Nor is Spahn's response when Pitt wants to be sure Squeaky Frome is not abusing him, and Spahn says Squeaky loves him. "So suck on that!"

Over the years, Dern has worked with most of the important Western filmmakers of his time: *Hang 'Em High* with Clint Eastwood; *Support Your Local Sheriff* for Burt Kennedy; *Posse* for Kirk Douglas; unforgettably for Mark Rydell in *The Cowboys*, in which he kills John Wayne. "And he insisted on me. They'd cast Vince Edwards, and John Wayne said, 'No, I don't want a damned TV doctor to be the guy killing a legend.'"

There were disappointments. Dern didn't get to star in a series about Western painter Frederic Remington that Dick Powell produced a pilot for. The Michael Cimino film about the Donner Party never happened. But Dern remains optimistic, and busy. At last count he's been in twenty-one films and eight TV episodes since *Hollywood*, including a handful of Westerns. And he still runs. "I'm eighty-five. There were nine of us last Saturday, 800 meters, and I was second in that race for people over seventy-five."

MORGAN WOODWARD

Actor Morgan Woodward was known for many things, most of them unpleasant: he was so good at playing bad that "although it was an unwritten law that no actor could do more than one *Gunsmoke* a year, I did nineteen in ten years," he said. And Matt Dillon killed him in almost all of them. The man, whose appearance in *Cool Hand Luke* made mirrored shades a fashion necessity for lawmen, hadn't planned to act. "I traded Grand Opera for Horse Opera."

The actor, who was born in Arlington, Texas, in 1925, and died in 2019, explained, "I wanted to be an opera singer. Unfortunately, a chronic sinus condition prevented me from being in voice when I needed to be." Another early passion was flying. "I started when I was sixteen, and got my private pilot's license when I was seventeen, in preparation for World War II." He enlisted, but, he says, "they had so many pilots that they stopped the pilot training program. So I did not get Army Air Corps wings—a big disappointment to me." A civilian again, Woodward attended the University of Texas, majoring in business and minoring in music and drama, where classmates included Rip Torn, Jayne Mansfield, L. Q. Jones, and Fess Parker. He was getting serious about acting when he was recalled to active service for the Korean War.

When he returned, Woodward's entry into film came thanks to a fraternity brother. "Fess Parker had become *Davy Crockett*, and when Disney did his first live-action motion picture, *The Great Locomotive Chase*, Fess told Disney he knew this guy who would be just great as this wild-eyed Confederate master sergeant. I went to California to do a screen test and was signed to a three-picture contract."

With so many Westerns being made, it was perfect timing for Woodward to be in Hollywood. "I was six-foot three, and two hundred pounds, scarred and mean-looking, and had a cowboy accent already." Working on 1957's *Gunsight Ridge*, "Joel McCrea and I were in a fight, and I should have ducked. He did an uppercut and split my chin wide open. I'm still scarred, but on my face, it didn't make any difference."

He appeared in series like *Cheyenne*, *Sugarfoot*, and then with Hugh O'Brian in *Wyatt Earp*. "I did this episode in the *Earp* series, and I played Captain Langley of the Texas Rangers." When it was decided Wyatt needed a sidekick, "All they had to do was change the name Langley to Shotgun Gibbs. I was with Hugh for four years. That was the first series that I had a running role in, and that gave me a great deal of confidence." But after the 1962 season, O'Brian quit.

"I knew Hugh was unhappy. Chuck Connors was getting $15,000 a week [for *The Rifleman*], and Hugh was getting maybe $2,500."

"*Gunsmoke* was simply the best series on television. Everybody was top notch." But he noted ruefully, "I couldn't do *Gunsmoke* for the first ten years because the casting director and I'd had a run-in at Goldwyn Studios before, and he wouldn't cast me. And then he died—unfortunately for him, fortunately for me—and Pam Polifroni started casting *Gunsmoke*. The first thing she did was to bring me in." One of the unexpected dividends was his long friendship with star James Arness. "Jim knew that I was a pilot, and said he'd thought about taking flying lessons. I said, 'I've seen the shooting schedule, and we're going to be finished right after lunch, so let's get in my plane and see how you like it.' We just had a marvelous time. I had a surplus Army airplane that you could push the canopy back and let the breeze blow on you, and he just absolutely loved it. I bought him a private pilot's course, and said, 'Okay, pal, here you go: take off!' Jim went on to get a commercial license. Quite a pilot, he did very well."

By his screen retirement in 1997, Morgan Woodward had amassed nearly 130 credits, including 12 appearances on *Wagon Train* and 6 years as Punk Anderson on *Dallas*. His favorite film? "*Firecreek* (1967) was probably the most interesting because of Henry Fonda and Jimmy Stewart and all of the great character actors that were on the picture—Dean Jagger, Ed Begley, Jack Elam—it's loaded with them."

If Morgan Woodward is one of the most intimidating visages to ever grace the screen, part of his secret was a skill that children have competed at for years. "I can go forever without blinking. And a lot of times I'd get into a *mano a mano*, a showdown when I had an asshole for a leading man. I didn't blink, and I waited for him to lose. Then he'd want to retake. And then, I did blink." It doesn't matter, Morgan: you'd already won.

L. Q. JONES

L. Q. Jones, the sandy-haired giant with the high cheekbones, warm smile, and ice-cold blue eyes, celebrated his final birthday, his 94th, in August 2021. He'd been a constant, mostly menacing, screen presence for five decades. His last film was 2006's *Prairie Home Companion*. The veteran of hundreds of big- and small-screen performances had recently recalled, "We didn't know it while it was taking place, but when we did *The Wild Bunch*, it changed the way the pictures were accepted, changed them 180 degrees. And, oddly enough, I happened to be in another picture, *The Mask of Zorro*, that changed it back."

He explained that the former brought an unflinching look at brutal violence, and the latter marked a return to thrills with less realistic bloodletting. It's no surprise that his lengthy career had bridged many cinematic trends.

He got his boot in the door thanks to his former University of Texas in Austin roommate, Fess Parker, who also got a fraternity brother, the late Morgan Woodward, his first role. Woodward recalled, "Fess sneaked him in to see director Raoul Walsh, and L. Q. is so crazy, he convinced him that he ought to be in the picture." It didn't hurt that Fess, by then TV's *Davy Crockett*, also got writer and future director Burt Kennedy to rewrite L. Q.'s dull audition scene. L. Q. was so pleased with the role that he took his character's name for his own; until then he'd been Justus McQueen.

From 1955 on, he recalled, "Between war movies and Westerns, work was constant." He was sidekick to Clint Walker on *Cheyenne*, did three movies with Elvis Presley, including the excellent Western *Flaming Star*, and guest-villained on series like *Annie Oakley*, *Rin Tin Tin*, *The Rebel*, *The Rifleman*, *Have Gun—Will Travel*, and *Laramie*.

"I was regular on about seven Westerns." About *The Virginian*, on which he played ranch hand Beldon, he said, "We became a family. We were putting on a new *Virginian* every other week. You had two weeks to make an hour-and-a-half show, which is a full motion picture."

The seed of one of his biggest breaks was planted in 1955 but took a few years to flower. *Annapolis Story* director Don Siegel's dialogue coach, Sam, took a liking to L. Q. "At the end of it, he said, 'Listen, kid, I guarantee you we're going to be working together, because I'm going to be a director, and I will remember you.' And I said, 'Yeah, thanks a lot. Heard that before.' Later I was in my agent's office and they called and wanted me for *Ride the High Country*, and I realized it was Sam Peckinpah." Counting shows that didn't work out, "We ended up doing, I think, seventeen projects together."

"Sam, if he was good at two things, it was attention to detail and casting the right people. The man was a genius, but Sam had a strange way of operating, sort of like John Ford's." He purposely created hostility between members of the cast and crew. "He has you so overwrought that everybody detests everybody else. And then he starts to put you back together. And within a week, there's only one human being in our universe, and that's Sam Peckinpah. It worked for him until we got into *Pat Garrett and Billy the Kid*. He tore us down, and then Sam was so sick that he couldn't put us back together."

A man of many talents, Jones adapted and directed Harlan Ellison's sci-fi novel, *A Boy and His Dog*, which starred Jason Robards and helped make a star of Don Johnson. He produced *The Brotherhood of Satan*, giving his frequent co-star, Strother Martin, one of his best non-Western roles, "And in one scene, he's completely nude. Just for a few frames."

But above all, L. Q. Jones was an actor. "I know this sounds Pollyannish, but any show I do is my favorite for the moment." But for TV Westerns? "I did seven *Gunsmoke*s. Over the years, almost everything I'm in, they ask me to change it, to fit me. Not on *Gunsmoke*. You take what they give you, hit your mark, say your words, and pick up your check. Because they've done a hell of a job, the writers, the producers, the crew. They were so professional in what they did.

"I did the *Gunsmoke* where the entire cast, with the exception of the regulars, was black (1969's *The Good Samaritans*). And I played a terrible person. A racist, I kicked dogs, beat kids, chased women. The Monday after they showed it, I had about a forty-five-minute trip to the studio. I was driving my MG, top down, and I was booed and hissed for the entire thirty miles. They had all seen the show, and they were throwing things. You know you made an impression. The other shows I enjoyed as much, but that is my favorite because of what happened after the fact."

CHAPTER 6

THE FILMMAKERS

NORMAN LEAR

When, in 1959, one of America's most popular and respected actors, Henry Fonda, announced that he would be starring in a Western TV series, the almost universal reaction was, why?

From 1943's *The Ox-Bow Incident* to 1948's *Fort Apache*, Fonda was already a Western icon. But conventional wisdom said no one would pay to see movie stars once they could see them for free: TV was considered career suicide.

Fonda's explanation was disarmingly frank. "Gold convinced me," the fifty-four-year-old actor told *Newsweek.* "'Residuals' is a magic word. It means it rains gold. It is the only chance an actor has to save money these days."

A seemingly unlikely pair fashioned the story that got Fonda to sign on to the NBC series: Roland Kibbee, who'd written for Fred Allen and the Marx Brothers, and Norman Lear, who'd been crafting gags for Martha Raye and Martin & Lewis.

The pair had met on NBC's *The Tennessee Ernie Ford Show.* "The head writer was Roland Kibbee," Lear recalls. "I learned a lot from him. He was an important mentor."

Both writers were WWII veterans—Kibbee, an Army Air Corps pilot, Lear, a gunner on a Flying Fortress. And yet their war experiences hadn't jaded them. They both strongly believed that you could find humor in any aspect of life, and they wanted to make a Western together that would stand out through its sly comedy.

"You could not be an American kid without being a fan of Westerns," Lear remembers. "My favorite guy was Ken Maynard."

Kibbee was no stranger to the genre. He'd already written the excellent 1954 Western *Vera Cruz*, beginning a long association with Burt Lancaster.

To lure Fonda in, the writers offered the busy actor an irresistible accommodation. Fonda would not play the "deputy" of the title but US Marshal Simon Fry. He would appear in all thirty-nine episodes per season, often narrating and riding endlessly through the desert. But he would star in only a half dozen, leaving him free to work on stage plays and films. The rest of the episodes would feature young Broadway star Allen Case as Fry's reluctant deputy Clay McCord. Three years earlier Fonda had a huge hit with *The Tin Star*, teaching a wannabe sheriff, played by Anthony Perkins, the ropes. The difference here was humorous.

"Kibbee's idea for *The Deputy* came from the play *The Front Page*, by Ben Hecht and Charles MacArthur," Lear says. "The [newspaper] editor had this great investigative reporter who was quitting all the time. And the editor played one trick after another on him to get him to stay."

Similarly, Fry cheerfully misleads and manipulates McCord into situations where he has to help the marshal.

A shop owner with a lightning draw and perfect accuracy, McCord wasn't merely reluctant to pin on the badge. "A guy came in with a handgun that was shooting a little high and to the left. And the deputy said, 'I don't do handguns, just rifles,'" Lear remembers.

Because a handgun is just for killing men: after McCord's father was murdered, he became a pacifist. More than a character quirk, it proved a seminal choice in outspoken liberal Lear's career, he admits. "What's the earliest evidence of my having that kind of sensibility? *The Deputy*."

Of course, Westerns being what they are, Deputy McCord had to become Sergeant York—the Tennessee pacifist-turned-war-hero who earned Gary Cooper an Oscar—and strap on a gun nearly every week.

The range of plots and subject matter was unusual for the time: racism, rape, the taboo of backshooting, the presumption of innocence, the evils of lynching.

Still, *The Deputy* kept faith with the classics. Wallace Ford was cast as aging Marshal Lamson, in part because he was a member of John Ford's stock company. Episodes featured plum roles for Western stalwarts, who included Bob Steele and *Red Ryder*'s original Little Beaver, Tommy Cook. They also featured fledgling stars, including Clu Gulager and James Coburn.

Kibbee and Lear always balanced the dark drama with humor, some of it pretty broad. In one episode, Fry and Lamson "torture" a side of beef to get an outlaw in the next cell to talk, a scene that could have been created for Martin & Lewis.

The series' downfall was built into its premise: audiences wanted to *watch* Fonda, not *glimpse* him. Case's talent was not enough to eclipse the reason they tuned into the show.

The Deputy began to be viewed as a bait and switch. Fonda began disappearing as soon as he arrived, starting with episode two. James Arness got away with flipping most *Gunsmoke* episodes to the supporting cast because he didn't start doing that until eight or nine seasons in.

After two seasons, Fonda voluntarily pulled the plug. He later turned his image on its head in 1968's *Once Upon a Time in the West*. He died at the age of seventy-seven in 1982.

The last major Western Kibbee wrote was 1971's *Valdez Is Coming* before he died at the age of seventy in 1984. Case's biggest success after *The Deputy* was playing Frank James to Christopher Jones's Jesse in 1965's ABC series *The Legend of Jesse James*, before he died of a heart attack at the young age of fifty-one.

Lear went on to ever-greater success with revolutionary comedies that include *All in the Family*. Ironically for a Western fan, his CBS series *Maude* is what finally killed off NBC's longest-running Western, *Bonanza*. Passing the century mark in 2022, Lear continued to develop new series and had branched out to documentaries as well. Lear died in 2023. Largely forgotten today, *The Deputy* was an innovative and original Western series when many were interchangeable.

SAM PECKINPAH

Back in 2017, Hollywood's famous Chinese Theatre celebrated L. Q. Jones's 90th birthday with a screening of the controversial masterpiece that saddled Sam Peckinpah with the moniker "Bloody Sam," 1969's *The Wild Bunch*.

Jones roared with laughter when I told him the theme of my article. "Peckinpah's kinder, gentler side? Did he have one?" Then he quickly clarified, "It was a privilege to work with him. In spite of the stories I tell, I adored the man."

Peckinpah had written nearly fifty Western TV episodes and directed more than a dozen when MGM greenlit 1962's *Ride the High Country*. The story of two aging, threadbare lawmen-gunfighters transporting gold from a mining camp, and inadvertently transporting a naive would-be bride, would be the career capper for two great Western stars, Joel McCrea and Randolph Scott.

Jones had first met Peckinpah as Don Siegel's dialogue coach on 1955's *An Annapolis Story*. "Sam said, 'Listen, kid, we're going to be working together, because I'm going to be a director, and I'll remember you.' True to his word, once he got a little foothold, here came the calls, and we ended up doing, I think, seventeen projects together," Jones said.

For the role of runaway bride Elsa Knudsen, Peckinpah cast stage actress Mariette Hartley. "The very first thing I did was that wonderful movie," she recalls fondly. Hartley wore a blue checkered dress to the audition, "And walking up those MGM steps, I felt like I was Alice in Wonderland. There he was, behind the desk, with his cowboy hat on and his feet on the desk with his cowboy boots on. They don't do that in Connecticut. Sam read with me, that beautiful scene with Heck [Ron Starr] when I'm doing the dishes. He looked at me, and he said, 'I think I'm in love with you.' And Alice said to the Cheshire cat, 'Thank you, I think.'"

For her screen test, Hartley says, "I wore a dress that was stuffed with a lot of stuff for breasts, and Deborah Kerr's wig from *Quo Vadis*. My hair was very short because I'd just finished doing *Joan of Arc* in Chicago. Two days after that [producer] Phil Feldman called and told me I got the movie, and I about died."

James Drury, who would soon gain fame as TV's *The Virginian*, was wanna-be groom Billy Hammond, whose brothers figured Elsa would be bride to all of them. "Originally, Sam wanted Robert Culp for my part, and Culp's agent said, 'No, we don't want Robert playing a bad guy,' so he got me. I was able to play the part with great gusto, and I surely did enjoy that," Drury remembered.

"We had John Davis Chandler, Warren Oates, and L. Q. Jones all playing my brothers," Drury added. "My God, you put that bunch of actors together—we were electric! It was truly a worthy group of bad guys to oppose Joel McCrea and Randolph Scott." As L. Q. Jones said, "One of the things Sam was good at was casting. He found the right people to do the right parts. (John) Ford could do that."

Hartley agrees with the comparison. "Sam hired people the way John Ford hired people. He saw me as that girl—I was not a typical Hollywood beauty. I think he knew that I could be her, not play her."

There were problems in production. When an unexpected snowstorm hit their Mammoth locations, the producers unceremoniously ordered Peckinpah and his crew back to L.A. Hartley remembers, "Sam felt the earth had been pulled out from under him. He was going to have to do the Hammond Brothers' den as Bronson Canyon (in Griffith Park), covered with soapy foam, that looked like dirty snow." Even when it was finished, the studio didn't realize what it had. *Newsweek* called MGM out for releasing *Ride* as the bottom half of a double bill with *The Tartars*, adding, "everything about this picture has the ring of truth, from the unglamorized settings to the flavorful dialogue and the natural acting. *Ride the High Country* is pure gold." A more appropriate release was quickly arranged.

Eight years later, Peckinpah, who was finishing *The Wild Bunch*, called Jones about a script called *The Ballad of Cable Hogue*. "Sam was absolutely in love with it, but he had no money," Jones says. "So he borrowed $17,000—all my money! Sam bought the project, sold it to Warner Bros. for a fortune, and never paid me back."

For that 1970 Western, Jason Robards starred as Cable Hogue, a desert rat left to die by rivals who take his water. But instead of dying, he miraculously "found water where it wasn't," as he says in the movie, then builds a stagecoach stop and woos Hildy (Stella Stevens), the gorgeous, soiled dove who must choose between love and wealth in San Francisco, California. Hogue's spiritual advisor is a libidinous preacher played by David Warner.

"Hate that son-of-a-bitch!" says Jones, with a laugh. "I was supposed to be the preacher. But Sam was right; he did such a better job than I could have ever done."

A newcomer in Peckinpah's cast was Western novelist Max Evans. They had become friends after Peckinpah lost out on filming Evans' novel *The Rounders*. For years, they tried to find a mutual project. In the film that finally joined them together, the stagecoach is prominent in the story, and Evans rode shotgun beside his close friend, driver Slim Pickens.

The Ballad of Cable Hogue was plagued with weather problems. The night before filming began, a terrible storm engulfed the Nevada desert, washing out seven bridges. L. Q. recalled, "The first day, we (go to) location. It's where we're trying to kill Jason by not letting him have water. Sam is looking, and as far as the eye can see, is water. It may have only been an inch deep, but there it was."

Evans concurred. "It rained fifteen days, and we were jammed up in that hotel. Then it turned hotter than Hell. It was 107 to 110 degrees where we were shooting. For Sam to hold that together and make that beautiful picture is one of the marvels of directing of all time."

A quirky mix of slapstick and sentiment, the Western was viewed by Peckinpah as a comedy, but Stevens insists it is a love story. It's also her best work, and maybe Robards' as well.

At the time the film was made, "Jason Robards was down; he was a drunk. Had a bad reputation," Evans recalled. "Sam took him, got him to quit drinking, and made a great actor out of him. Jason went on to win two Oscars and an Emmy after Sam got him straightened out."

Neither of these Peckinpah films were nominated for any major awards, but their reputations grow with each passing year.

JOHN WILDER

"My parents loved Westerns. My mother's family were pioneers; they were the first four wagons into Seattle, Washington. When I was five, in a little house on American Lake in Washington, we'd listen to the radio, to the *Adventures of Red Ryder*. Two years later I'm at the microphone doing the voice of the little Indian boy."

John Wilder's journey from kid to kid actor, to TV writer, to writer-producer seemed almost predestined to prepare him for the crowning achievement of his career: writing and producing the monumental twenty-six-hour miniseries, James H. Michener's *Centennial*. It also nearly did him in. "I had basically a nervous breakdown working on that," he recalls. "My marriage blew up, my world fell apart because of the stress. I'll never do anything as hard again; never anything I loved as much, because I loved the characters."

"I had bad allergies as a little guy. The doctor told my parents to go east of the mountains, or south to, like, Pasadena." Pasadena won. He was directed by Maria Riva, Marlene Dietrich's daughter, in a production of Lillian Hellman's *Watch on the Rhine*. "She took my mom aside and said, 'Johnny can read way above his years, and in radio they look for children that can read.' So [Mom] took me over to CBS for a general audition, and the next day [we] started getting calls. Within a month, I was doing *Lux Radio Theater*. In the five years I worked radio a lot, I had thirteen running roles on different series."

Among Wilder's other radio appearances, starting in the late 1940s, were *The Jack Benny Show*, *The Roy Rogers Show*, *The Gene Autry Show* and he starred in the radio version of *The Adventures of Champion*. His first movie would be a 1946 P.R.C. Western, *Tumbleweed Trail*, where he played Freckles Ryan opposite Eddie Dean. "He was a good singer, and I got to sing a duet with him."

The world of early television opened up opportunities for adventure, not all of them pleasant. "People think it's all make-believe. But I almost rolled a stagecoach [on *Rin Tin Tin*], almost got mauled by a lion [on *Circus Boy*], and on *Broken Arrow*, the wad from a blank set my face on fire." But there were many more positive experiences: working with Lloyd Bridges on *Zane Grey Theatre* and making friends with Steve McQueen on *Wanted: Dead or Alive*.

He graduated from Van Nuys High and started at USC on a baseball scholarship. He had leading-man good looks, but, he says, "I wasn't going to be a star. I really wasn't a character actor. So, I thought I should direct. And I started writing."

Film work both paid for, and interrupted, his education—*The Benny Goodman Story, Summer Love, Five Guns to Tombstone*. But his most important role was in the World War II movie *Hold Back the Night*. On location, he bonded with roommate Chuck Connors over baseball. "And that changed my life because Chuck knew I wanted to get behind the camera. He got cast as *The Rifleman*, called me and said, 'You're going to write an episode.'" Frustratingly, that sale didn't lead to more work. "Friends who could've thrown me a bone, didn't. I couldn't get arrested." Just as he was starting Loyola Law School, he "got a call from Chuck. 'I just got a series, *Branded*. You're going to write all my dialogue,' what he called John Wayne dialogue: good and tight and lean. I went onto *Branded* as a story editor. It was terrific."

From there Wilder moved to the hottest show on TV, *Peyton Place*, writing 119 episodes, then to Universal, then to Quinn Martin, writing and producing *Streets of San Francisco*. "I loved it," but as he told Quinn when he left, "I really want to be doing what you're doing." Wilder was set to run drama development at a little Grant Tinker start-up called M.T.M. Until lunch with Universal President Frank Price changed everything. Price asked, "'What can I do to get John Wilder to come back to Universal?' I said, you have one property, *Centennial*. And he said, 'That's yours.'" This was the time of the grand miniseries. *Roots*, in 1977, was ten hours long. "I've got a commitment for thirteen hours," Price told Wilder, "and an option for thirteen more." Wilder bailed on M.T.M.

In his vast and wonderful novel, Centennial was the name Michener bestowed on a fictional town that was a microcosm of the history of Colorado, as well as a cautionary tale. "Michener's ultimate message," says Wilder, "[is] that we have an obligation to take care of the planet, and we're not doing a very good job of it. It's the ultimate ecological editorial, to see how the Indians lived with the land and thought only the rocks live forever. Who are the villains of *Centennial*? The real estate brokers.

"*Centennial* spoke to me because there are moments in [my] family history that were replicated in Jim's book. Like the part that Dick Crenna played. We called him Skimmerhorn, but it was really Chivington, and it was the

Sand Creek Massacre." Although he wasn't contractually obligated, Wilder sent every script to Michener for his approval. Michener loved appearing in the opening. They were close friends for the rest of Michener's life.

"My philosophy of producing television was, get the material as good as you can in the time you're allotted, hire a director who's a shooter, and hire bulletproof actors." With 128 characters in a nine-hundred-page story that reaches from the 1740s to 1974, casting was an immense job. Wilder would jot the names of actors in the margins as he read. Actor Jesse Vint recalls Wilder introducing himself at a gas station. "He said he knew a part I was right for. Go ahead and read the book, then give him a call. It was one of the most amazing historical books that I've ever read. I came across a character named Amos Calendar. I called him, he said, 'That's the one!' He's one of the few creative geniuses that I've ever known."

For the first important character, Lame Beaver, he wanted Michael Ansara, who'd played Cochise with him on the *Broken Arrow* series. "Michael, please tell me you have Native American heritage. And he said, 'No, but I'm blood brothers through the ceremony with five nations.' I said, that'll do." For his daughter, Clay Basket, he wanted Barbara Carrera. "Any Native American heritage? 'Well, I'm Nicaraguan. And that's Indian.' That'll do."

The core character for the first several episodes was a feisty, heroic French-Canadian trapper named Pasquinel, the first white man in the region. Richard Chamberlin would be McKeag, his Scottish partner. Carrera would be his wife, and Sally Kellerman would be Lise Bockweiss, his other, German, wife, "and she learned German, as did [her father] Raymond Burr." But who could play Pasquinel? Robert Conrad had been vigorously campaigning for the role, but was he a strong enough actor? A moving episode of *Baa Baa Black Sheep* suggested he was. They met. Wilder had three provisos he insisted upon, that Conrad wouldn't like. This was no Maurice Chevalier role: he'd have to learn an authentic French-Canadian accent. Pasquinel's wife is described as larger than her husband, and Kellerman was four to six inches taller than Conrad. And he'd have to say to her, "Maybe I'm a coward," words that the genuinely tough actor would despise uttering. Finally, "Richard Chamberlain is playing McKeag. We both know that he's gay. The line of dialogue I won't let you change is 'Maybe you're a better man than I am.' I'm trying to do an authentic movie. If you can't do those things, it's not going to work. And Bob said, 'Hey man, I'm an actor,' and we shook hands."

A few days into shooting, the tiny amount of footage coming in indicated that the wrong director had been chosen. Wilder remembered a director he'd used on *Streets of San Francisco*. "Virgil Vogel is an artist. He's not the most articulate man, he doesn't talk to actors at all, but boy, does he know where to put the camera. I sent him the script, he came into my office in the morning, and he cried. He said, 'I've been shooting shit all my life. And you send me something this beautiful, and I don't have time to prepare.'" Wilder offered to shut down the set to give Vogel three weeks to prepare, but Vogel flew up that night, "And, by God, he gave me more film that afternoon than the other director had given me with weeks to prepare." Vogel, Conrad, and many in the cast and crew considered *Centennial* the best work of their careers.

Since *Centennial*, Wilder has produced and written many shows, notably creating the contemporary Western series *The Yellow Rose*, and developing *Spenser: For Hire*. In 1993, Jeff Sagansky, who had been an executive's assistant on *Centennial*, had become the president of CBS, and asked Wilder to write and produce a sequel to the miniseries *Lonesome Dove*. "It's a great novel, a Pulitzer Prize winner. What could I do with that story? It ended. What's left? And I thought, father and son. Newt is Call's son, but Newt doesn't know it, and Call won't admit it. So I sat down and wrote the last scene of *Return to Lonesome Dove*, where they say goodbye, and Call, in effect, gives him his name without saying, you're my son. And it made me cry at the typewriter. I thought, okay, that's powerful. I called Jeff and said, I'm in. My agent said, 'Don't; sequels are never any good.' And I said, 'Nobody's making Westerns. I love Westerns. And I think I can do a good job, and that's good enough for me.'

"Why do we keep coming back to Western stories? The best of them are about right and wrong, meeting challenges, of maintaining integrity and honor, at least the Westerns that you and I love."

TAYLOR SHERIDAN

When I spoke with writer, producer, and director Taylor Sheridan in August 2021, he was less than a week from beginning to shoot the *Yellowstone* prequel, *1883*, which would begin streaming on Paramount+ just four months later. His fans expected it to be good. Few expected that it would be the best miniseries or limited series since *Lonesome Dove* or that it would be one of the finest Westerns of any format ever made for television.

It would be the Texan's first historical Western, but he'd previously written two excellent contemporary Westerns, *Wind River* and *Hell or High Water*, the story of two brothers who pay off their late mother's ranch by robbing branches of the bank that holds the note.

"I wrote that at a time when all my friends I grew up with—cowboys, ranchers—were losing their jobs and their land. It was the worst drought we'd ever seen in West Texas. There was nowhere to graze. Everybody's calling in the credit lines. It was a death knell for a lot of families that had ranched for a hundred or more years, and no one knew about it, so I decided to make a movie about it; a love poem to Texas."

It wasn't easy. "I had a lot of trouble convincing anyone to let me make anything Western, until *Yellowstone* proved that there was a real appetite for the genre. Then I devised a mechanism to make a legitimate period Western about something that no one's really successfully done, a 'wagons west' story that's really been impactful.

"If you study the pioneer movement west, you understand that there were plenty of other villains along the way, but the journey itself was a villain. The vast majority of people who went west [were] from eastern urban areas, Europe, Asia, Scotland, Ireland—from places where they were desperate, and this seemed like the best option to change the course of their lives. So many did not speak the language, had never ridden a horse, had never seen a rattlesnake, didn't know how to swim. And now they're gonna find themselves crossing between twenty-five and fifty rivers and creeks. They put themselves in situations that are almost impossible for someone who's prepared for it. That's the thing I've never seen in other films, the misery of the journey. Oh, and by the way, there's bandits everywhere because there's no law."

Sheridan was thinking about the world of *1883* long before *Yellowstone* premiered. "As a storyteller building a world, I need to know the origins: how it started, and how it ends, or I don't know what I'm writing toward. So, when I came up with the idea for *Yellowstone*, I plotted out from when the family came to the United States. When did they come to Bozeman? How did they become what they are?"

The fictional family who created Yellowstone, the largest private ranch in America, are James and Margaret Dutton, great-great-grandparents of Kevin Costner's character, John Dutton. As to their origins, Sheridan says cagily, "You're gonna have to watch it. But I will say this: they arrive in Texas and follow the Chisholm Trail north until they go west. And then they go north again. Or do they?" They're portrayed by husband-and-wife Tim McGraw and Faith Hill. Though the real-life duo is best known as country music superstars, they both have acting experience. "Tim's performance in *Friday Night Lights* was spectacular. I think musicians make this transition easily: they understand applying emotion to dialogue, because they do it for a living; they just do it to a rhythm."

Adding cowboy gravitas to the proceedings, the Duttons are guided by Shea Brennan, played by Sam Elliott. Sheridan is a big fan, he said, "going back to *Conagher*, *Tombstone*, *The Sacketts*. But my favorite Sam Elliot movie is *Roadhouse*," not a Western, but the story of bar bouncer Patrick Swayze. "When I bring it up, Sam shakes his head and goes, 'Oh, God, Taylor,' because I quote [his character] all the time."

Much of *1883* would be filmed at Sheridan's thousand-acre Bosque Ranch Complex in Weatherford, Texas. "Bosque is Spanish for river-bottom forest. I was raised in Bosque County, Texas, so that's where the name comes from, even though Bosque Ranch is on the Brazos River in Parker County." Much more than a filming location, it boasts a main arena, multiple barns, a practice pen, restaurant, bar, and offices, with plans to include not only regular cutting events, but large rodeos and concerts. Sheridan's goal with Bosque Ranch is to revitalize and revolutionize the performance horse industry. Pointing to the success of NASCAR and professional bull riders, Sheridan says confidently, "The prize money will be immense. The music will be loud. The excitement will be unmatched. In short, a niche industry will become a spectator sport. And I will show the world how to do it."

Westerns have long been a part of Sheridan's life. "As an eight-, nine-, ten-year-old boy, I watched all the early John Wayne and Clint Eastwood movies. Then [around 1990] you have sort of a triple whammy: *Dances with Wolves* had a tremendous impact on cinema when it came out. *Silverado*, *Tombstone* . . . *Lonesome Dove*'s a miniseries, but I put it in the same category. I think *Unforgiven* is the best Western ever made. It did something that I try to do, which is turn a genre on its ear, and play with our expectations of what that genre is. I thought it was masterful."

Unlike *Yellowstone*, which Sheridan co-created with John Linson, *1883* is his alone. "I've already written the whole thing." He would also direct an episode. When I asked how many seasons were we likely to see, he replied, "Well, *1883* only goes one season—that's it. Then we may jump ahead to 1922, to 1935. I haven't figured that out yet." In fact, he jumped ahead to *1923*, where an interim generation of Duttons, led by Harrison Ford and Helen Mirren, deal with the Roaring Twenties and the Great Depression.

While Sheridan's astonishing output covers many genres and eras, it's no surprise that he plans to continue returning to the Western. "It's all I've ever wanted to do."

CHAPTER 7
THE WRITERS

MAX EVANS

"Ol' Tony Hillerman told me one time, 'Max, you know, if you option a novel, you've got to hope they don't make the movie. Because then you can't option it again.' He was giving me advice long after the horses had entered the corral." The late, legendary Texas-born cowboy, artist, and author Max Evans—who was ninety-three and still writing when we spoke—recalled, "I lived off options for a long time."

His first novel, *The Rounders*, was published in 1960 and became a hit movie in 1965. His second novel, *The Hi-Lo Country*, was published in 1962, and despite being optioned repeatedly, didn't reach the screen for thirty-seven years—it was a contemporary story when he wrote it, but a period picture when they filmed it. Celebrating the 20th anniversary of the release of the film version of *The Hi-Lo Country*, Evans talked with *True West* about his Hollywood adventures.

"I'd read everything from Shakespeare and Balzac to dozens of shoot-'em-up Westerns. Enjoyed 'em all. But I wanted to write about what I really knew. I was a cowboy before I was twelve. By the time I was fourteen I was drawing a grown man's wages. When those cowboys'd haul me off to town, I'd observe them playing, having fun. When I started writing I realized that I had some really original material. I decided to write post–World War II. When I left for that war, ranchers were working cattle mostly from horseback. After I got back, the West was changed forever by pickup trucks replacing the horse."

The Rounders, the comical adventures of two down-at-the-boot-heels cowboys, reinvigorated the careers of stars Henry Fonda and Glenn Ford, and established Burt Kennedy as a top Western writer-director. But Fess Parker, fresh from his success starring for Disney as Davy Crockett, was the first to option *The Rounders*. He'd even convinced an Oscar-winning writer-director to pen a script. Evans recalls, "William Wellman came out of retirement because of *The Rounders*. We all had a meeting, and Wellman is talking about who Fess was going to play. And he looked at me and said, 'Well, Max is just right for the other part.' Ol' Fess just threw a damn fit. He made a real mistake: Ol' Wellman just dropped the project. Fess killed the whole thing."

Kennedy optioned the book three times before he got it set up at MGM. "Sam (Peckinpah) lost *The Rounders* to Burt Kennedy, and it really pissed him off. I had just published *The Hi-Lo Country*, and my agent sent it out to him. Sam optioned that at least five times. He was obsessed with that thing, and he never did get to make it." They became close friends to the end. Although there could be friction.

"We'd been in some joint in Malibu with Lee Marvin, drinking. On the way out, there was a swimming pool. Sam knew I couldn't swim and the 'sonuvabitch' pushed me in! I went to the bottom, (came up), caught the edge of the pool, and Sam started kicking my fingers! Ol' Lee jerked him back to save my life! (Back at Peckinpah's house) I had an impulse, picked him up and whammed him on the floor. He said, 'Oh, you s.o.b., you've broken my leg!' I just patted him on top of the head. 'I'm sorry Sam. I meant to break your goddamn neck.' That's how we got to be real deep friends."

Although Peckinpah would never film an Evans story, he would direct him, as the stagecoach shotgun rider, in *The Ballad of Cable Hogue*.

The Rounders became a TV series, with Chill Wills returning as rancher Jim Ed Love, Patrick Wayne in the Fonda role, and Ron Hayes in the Ford role. But it didn't last a full season. Max remembers meeting Wills, who was holding court in a Beverly Hills bar. "He punched me in the chest, and says to everybody at the bar, 'I cost this boy $2 million, I ruined his TV show. I took it over and ruined it.' Damn good actor, but that's exactly what he did."

Then Gene Kelly, planning to direct, optioned Evans' sequel to *The Rounders*, *The Great Wedding*, which would star Henry Fonda again. But the option ran out, and a couple of years later Kelly and Fonda were joined by James Stewart in the rather similar *The Cheyenne Social Club*. "Well, they did sort of plagiarize it," Evans notes but had no hard feelings. "They had wanted to make *The Great Wedding*, and this was a substitute for it. They were good guys."

Indirectly, Peckinpah's interest in *The Hi-Lo Country* helped get it made. Evans explains, "Martin Scorsese read it simply because of Peckinpah's interest. He produced it, but he hired ol' Steven Frears to direct it." As dark as *The Rounders* is carefree, *The Hi-Lo Country* was inspired by the murder of one of Evans' closest friends. The Western *noir* stars Woody Harrelson and Billy

Crudup as cowboy friends drawn to the same dangerous woman, played by Patricia Arquette, and features Sam Elliot as the same character Chill Wills played in *Rounders*. "Frears did his research and made a legitimate post–World War II Western. There's very few of them made, you know."

JIM BYRNES

With 635 television episodes, 480 radio shows, and 5 movies, no other series in any genre has equaled the longevity of *Gunsmoke*. And to fans who read the credits, Jim Byrnes is a familiar name, having penned 34 of the very best episodes, and 1 of the movies.

The Iowa-born writer always knew what his specialty would be. "I loved *Rawhide, Wanted: Dead or Alive*, and of course I loved *Gunsmoke*, never dreaming I'd ever write for *Gunsmoke*. I was in high school when I sold my first script." His older brother Joseph was taking a writing course at Los Angeles Valley College from prolific Western telewriter Richard Carr. "My brother said, 'They want us to write something, and you watch all the Westerns. Any ideas?' We wrote a story called *Desert Flight*. Carr read it and said, 'You guys should submit it: this is pretty good.'" It became an episode of *Zane Grey Theater*, "and James Coburn and Dick Powell starred. Then I didn't sell anything for six years."

Byrnes wrote scripts on speculation, and drove taxis and trucks until his script, *Gaucho*, landed him an agent. *Gunsmoke* producer John Mantley read *Gaucho*, and called Byrnes in. "They said, we want you to write a *Gunsmoke*. Come up with a story." The problem was, they'd already been on for thirteen years. "I started pitching stories. 'We did that ten years ago.' I think, this is my great chance; I can't blow this. I finally found this story about a wolf." The episode became "Lobo," and the late Morgan Woodward, who was *Gunsmoke*'s most frequent guest star, named it his favorite. He recalled with a laugh, "Watching it, I got so involved, I forgot I'm watching *me*!"

Before Byrnes had finished writing "Lobo," Mantley offered him a six-week job as story consultant. "I said yes. Then they said, 'We want you to stay,' so six weeks turned into two years."

The late 1960s was a tough transitional time for TV, especially Westerns. The back-to-back assassinations of Martin Luther King Jr. and Bobby Kennedy led to demands for less violence on-screen. "They had to change the opening of the show: Matt in a shoot-out [became] Matt riding a horse. We were warned constantly about violence—the network called me Mr. Blood-and-Guts because I kill a lot of people."

While Dillon was making mostly cameo appearances, Arness preferring to spend his time surfing, Byrnes's skills often earned him plum assignments with Dillon in the center. "The Badge" is one of the few shows to deal with the Matt Dillon/Miss Kitty romance. Byrnes also tackled history that was uglier than TV generally dealt with, as in one of his several two-parters. "'The Valley of Tears' was a real place. Indians would raid ranches and farms, kidnap the women, then meet in the Valley of Tears with the Comancheros, who'd trade for them, to sell them into prostitution in Mexico. I got really pissed off when they changed the title to 'Women for Sale.'"

Another element common in Byrnes's stories, but rare in the black hat/ white hat world of Westerns, is moral ambiguity. By the end of "Women for Sale," our sympathies have turned against a girl victim, in favor of her young kidnapper! Similarly, in "Shadler," a killer about to hang (Earl Holliman) gets a chance at freedom because he gets so annoyed at a priest trying to comfort him that he cold-cocks the priest and escapes in his robes. Byrnes laughs and adds, "I grew up in a very Catholic family, so I threw little anti-religious things in there." Byrnes's episode "Thirty a Month and Found" won Best Episodic Drama from The Writers Guild, and the Spur from the Western Writers of America.

In 1976, MGM came calling, asking him "to do a series based on the movie *How the West Was Won*." They screened the original movie, "but it was too episodic, and I wanted a family. I did what they call a [series] bible, almost a hundred pages, with storylines for the first season." Initially, James Arness wasn't considered for the lead, but when *Gunsmoke* was abruptly cancelled, its star was a natural for Zeb Macahan.

The Sacketts miniseries made a star of Tom Selleck in 1979. "[It was] based on two Louis L'Amour books, and Ben Johnson's character wasn't in both books. I had to do a lot of shuffling to get it to work. I met Louis L'Amour several times, and what a gentleman. That was a great experience because of Tom, Sam Elliott, Ben Johnson, Glenn Ford—it was a dream, all those guys!"

In 1982, Louis L'Amour's *The Shadow Riders* was a follow-up to *The Sacketts* with the same cast of leads, only the Sacketts became the Travens. "They pitched the same bunch but didn't have the rights to *The Sacketts*. So, Louis and I got together; he gave me the first scene. He says, 'You do the first scene my way, then you just take it where you want to go and I'll go where I want to go.' His novel and my screenplay are entirely different."

In 1980, Byrnes turned Kenny Rogers' hit song "The Gambler" into a Western. "We hit it off very well. Kenny was very humble; he'd never acted before. I said, 'I think we could be friends for a long time.'" They did *The Coward of the County*, then Rogers did a Western with another outfit. One of Byrnes's frequently used actors told him that when the cast arrived on-set, "they all got notes saying, do not speak to Kenny Rogers unless he speaks to you. Including Ben Johnson, who'd won an Academy Award." Byrnes wrote the second *Gambler* movie but left the final three to others.

Over the years, Byrnes has written numerous Western TV movies, and pilots about gunfighters, Buffalo Soldiers, and a rodeo story that starred Slim Pickens and Bo Hopkins. Looking back on nearly sixty years of screenwriting, Byrnes recalls, "The movie that really got me into Westerns was *Red River*. I saw that, I said, I gotta do this. I've got to do Westerns."

JEB ROSEBROOK

The literary successes of author Jeb Rosebrook, who passed away in August 2018, included plays and novels, and although he worked in many genres, he was best known as a screenwriter of Westerns. His masterwork was *Junior Bonner*. Many consider the film to be the best work of both director Sam Peckinpah and star Steve McQueen. It was McQueen's personal favorite among his films. Both a rodeo film and a family drama, it tells the story of aging rodeo star Junior Bonner (McQueen) returning home for the Prescott Rodeo to find that his brother Curly (Joe Don Baker) has bought the family ranch from their profligate ex-rodeo-star dad Ace (Robert Preston), put their mom (Ida Lupino) to work selling antiques, and is turning the family land into a mobile home development. Shortly before his passing, Rosebrook had published the book *Junior Bonner: The Making of a Classic with McQueen and Peckinpah in the Summer of 1971*, which he wrote with his son, Stuart Rosebrook, senior editor of *True West*. I was very fortunate to have the opportunity to interview Rosebrook about the film.

Henry C. Parke: How close was the finished film to your original script and what inspired you to write *Junior Bonner*?
Jeb Rosebrook: *Junior Bonner* is very, very close to my expectations. The creativity and collaboration with Sam brought it full circle. Junior and Ace, Ace and Mom, Curly selling senior living mobile homes, Mom and the antiques, the changing of Yavapai County from ranching to housing subdivisions, this is the result of my time spent with Sam right from the start. He went through every line of dialogue, beginning to end with me. The past is the past, but my love of the land never left me. I grew up on the Orme Ranch with the Orme

family in Yavapai County from the age of nine. The ranch was a major influence on me. The changes on the landscape from ranching to housing developments was dramatic to see after so many years away from the Prescott area.

Parke: How does a writer go directly from a single TV credit to writing a movie for the highest paid, and coolest, star in film, Steve McQueen?

Rosebrook: The path involved a few projects that never got filmed. Actually, I had a shared teleplay credit on *The Virginian* ("The Bugler"). From there I wrote for the Mirisch Brothers at United Artists my story "Keeper," about an American Indian from Appalachia in Chicago. It did not work out. Then I was inspired to adapt and update a story from my novel, *Saturday*, to a contemporary Western, *Ward Craft*, which was my first original screenplay. My agent at CMA gave it to James Coburn, who optioned it. The picture was not made but it put me inside the creative walls of CMA, eventually leading to *Junior Bonner*.

Right from the beginning, producer Joe Wizan wanted it for Steve. I began with meeting Steve at his home, with Wizan, and ended up buying him a beer in Jerome, Arizona, at the end of the film. We were not alone, but in a way we were. There's no denying Peckinpah's brilliance as a filmmaker, but he enjoyed giving manhood tests, and had no qualms about firing people who displeased him. Sam had a habit of what we called putting people "in the barrel." During the fight sequence he called me over in front of the entire cast and crew accusing me of not giving script changes to script supervisor Johnny Franco. Over and over, he repeated the accusations and just as often I denied it. He knew damn well I turned in the changes. We soon went back to work. I was not put on the bus as an example of his firing. And we moved on. Was he jealous of my relationship with the cast and crew? Was I at times his dilemma? Could be. But like the wild cow milking [in which Peckinpah unexpectedly put Rosebrook on camera, taking part in a rodeo event he hadn't done since he was a boy], I could prove to him and the cast and crew who I was.

Parke: Who else made important contributions to the film?

Rosebrook: Cinematographer Lucien Ballard was Sam's eyes, and the respect Sam had for him could not have been overstated. Lucien was all class. As was composer Jerry Fielding. Sam could not have created the creative works he did without his genius. It was a treat for me to have worked with them both.

Parke: Why have you always maintained that *Junior* changed your life, but not necessarily the way we might guess?

Rosebrook: When *Junior* was a financial flop I was consigned to television. Because of my background in New York, I landed with director Fielder Cook on *Miracle on 34th Street* (1974). Later there were Writers Guild of America nominations for *Prince of Central Park* (1977), and for *The Waltons* episode "The Conflict."

Parke: Looking back on a career of over three decades, both as writer and producer, which were your favorite collaborations and collaborators?

Rosebrook: Producers Stan Margulies and David Wolper, for *I Will Fight No More Forever* (Rosebrook shared an Emmy nomination for the screenplay of the 1975 Chief Joseph biography). Polishing screenplays for Larry McMurtry and Pat Conroy on 1990's *Montana*, with no credit. And I had a chance to meet and collaborate, without ego, with director Dick Lowry and Kenny Rogers on two Gambler movies, Jane Alexander on *Miracle on 34th Street* and Ruth Gordon on *Prince of Central Park*. And a great creative collaboration with my partner, producer-writer Joe Byrne and our characters in *A Hobo's Christmas* (1987).

With credits as varied as *Junior Bonner*, numerous *The Waltons* episodes, the Wright Brothers' biography, *The Winds of Kitty Hawk*, and science fiction favorites like Disney's *The Black Hole*, Rosebrook's cinematic legacy will entertain and enlighten for generations to come.

JOHN FUSCO

An 1880 tintype of Henry McCarty, alias William Bonney, alias Billy the Kid, planted the seed in writer John Fusco's imagination that would blossom as 1988's *Young Guns* and its sequel. "Looking at these old photos, being fascinated by the myth, but then trying to see this real person behind it. There had been forty-one movies made about Billy the Kid; Audie Murphy and Johnny Mack Brown and Paul Newman. It had always been this 'loner' story. And he *wasn't* a loner. I became fascinated by The Regulators, and their allegiance to John Tunstall; this was disenfranchised youth in the wild west. I felt it would be really interesting to do a flip on *Oliver Twist*'s Fagan and his den of thieves."

Similarly, the selfie-like snapshots that Clyde Barrow and Bonnie Parker took of each other would trigger a thirty-year obsession that what would lead to the 2019 Netflix movie *The Highwaymen*, starring Kevin Costner and Woody Harrelson as the retired Texas Rangers who ran down Bonnie and Clyde. In both cases, writer John Fusco was motivated by a desire to get a mistold story right. "Those old photos of Barrow and Parker, leaning on their stolen 1932 Ford V8 Sedan, downright haunted me." His investigation revealed that the real Bonnie and Clyde were the antithesis of romantic Faye Dunaway and Warren Beatty, and the real hero of the story was the Ranger who ran them down. "As I researched, I became fascinated by Frank Hamer, one of the greatest lawmen of the 20th century, and I was really disturbed [by] his portrayal in this classic movie."

Hamer, portrayed by Denver Pyle, is the lawman the outlaw duo capture, photograph, and humiliate in the press, motivating him to hunt down and kill them. It never happened: Hamer and the Barrow gang never "met" until the brief moment when Hamer tried to get them to surrender before opening fire. "[He'd] been shot seventeen times over the course of his career, had killed more than fifty men. He'd patrolled the border on a horse, with a Winchester. He was an old-time Ranger, in an era that had passed him by." That is until Texas governor "Ma" Ferguson (played in *Highwaymen* by Oscar-winner Kathy Bates) reluctantly asked Hamer to come out of retirement to get the Barrows.

The story simmered on the back burner until 2004, during the shooting of Fusco's *Hidalgo* in the Mojave Desert. "Producer Casey Silver asked me what my passion projects were, and I told him about Frank Hamer. Coincidentally, we were staying at Whiskey Pete's Casino Hotel, where the actual Bonnie and Clyde death car was on display." Silver was quickly onboard.

Fusco wanted the cooperation of the family, but the Hamers, who'd won a settlement from Warner Bros. for defamation, weren't talking. "Frank Jr. like his father had been a Texas Ranger, one of the last of the flying game wardens, hunting down poachers from a Cessna plane. I happened to have a few game warden contacts; I did ride-alongs in three states." They interceded for Fusco, and a meeting was set. At a lunch of mostly bourbon, Fusco convinced eighty-six-year-old Frank Jr. of his righteous intentions. "We walked out into the sun. He said, 'I only ask one thing: to do right by my daddy.' He had his friend take a [picture] as we shook hands, and he said, 'Here's our contract right here.'"

Fusco's initial dream-cast to play Hamer and partner Maney Gault were Robert Redford and Paul Newman. Redford got the script first. "He said, 'Don't send the script to Paul. I'm going to bring it to him and I'm going to make sure that we do this. After *Butch and Sundance* and *The Sting*, [this] will be a perfect last one for us to do together.'" Newman signed on, and the new pairing was the talk of Hollywood. Sadly, Newman was soon too ill to work, and the deal fell apart.

Fast-forward a dozen years, to Netflix, where Fusco was writing and producing the *Marco Polo* series, and Casey Silver was making the Western mini-series *Godless*. Director John Lee Hancock had long been a supporter. "We knew there had been interest from Kevin (Costner), and Woody (Harrelson) had been circling it for quite a while. Casey called me and said, 'You've got a relationship with Netflix; I do now. What about taking *Highwaymen* to them?' And bingo: they were on board and we were off to the races."

Fusco grew up on his father's farm in rural Connecticut, dropped out of high school to ride the rails, then got a G.E.D., and went to NYU Film School. Screenwriting teacher and Oscar-winner Waldo Salt took Fusco under his wing. "He had hoboe'd with Woody Guthrie. We were kind of kindred spirits. He got behind my work and I just idolized him." His bachelor's thesis script became the 1986 movie *Crossroads*. Then Fusco defied all his agent's entreaties to do something commercial, and wrote a Western, although "A Western had not made money since *Butch Cassidy*." *Young Guns* was a hit, as was *Young Guns II*, beginning the genre revival that led to *Dances with Wolves*, *Tombstone*, and *Deadwood*.

"Working with the 'Young Guns' was great," Fusco recalls, "but working with the 'Old Guns,' that was the career highlight. We were casting Lawrence Murphy. I said I wrote it as Jack Palance and everybody looked at me like, he's still alive? And so they reached out. He's retired, he's happy, he's not reading anything. I said, don't give up. Tell him this Western's being made with all these young guys, and we want the old guard, the icons of the American Western to take on the 'brat pack on horseback.' He read the script and came out of retirement. From there he'd go on to win an Academy Award [for *City Slickers*]. I think of being down on the Mexican border during *Young Guns II*, drinking tequila with Kiefer Sutherland, Emilio Estevez, Lou Diamond Phillips, James Coburn, and Christian Slater. James said, 'You know, that Emilio, that's the best fucking Billy the Kid there's ever been.' He said, 'I played opposite Kristofferson. Kris is a good actor. But he was a pacifist. He never aims his gun directly at anybody. But Emilio, he just breathes life into the character. That's what made me want to do this.'"

"There are projects that get offered to me, and I'll say to my wife, I just can't find my way into this. She always says the same thing to me: think of it as a Western. As soon as I do that, I've got it. The Western's in my blood and it always will be. After this thirty-year dream of telling the story of Frank

Hamer, I'm making good on my word, and helping to keep the interest in the West and the Western going."

DUSTY RICHARDS

With all the pseudonyms he used, it's hard to say how many Westerns novels Dusty Richards wrote, but he was pleased and proud that his 150th novel, *The Mustanger and the Lady*, was made into the movie *Painted Woman*, and glad that it had been published under his own name. "Our girl is a hell of an actress," he crowed about Stef Dawson. "She's gonna be a star."

The former Tyson Foods executive retired at age sixty-five, traveled the American West in an RV with his wife, Pat, and found a second life as a novelist. Dusty, who was age eighty at the time of this, his final interview, recalled the 2016 writer's convention in Branson, Missouri, where this movie journey began.

"This lady had made a film [2015's *Hush*] about a little cafe in a little town up here by me, and I vaguely remembered her. She was talking about how to write a film-script there. She looked over the books on the table, and she asked, 'Have you ever had one made into a movie?' I said, 'I had a couple of 'em sleep in Hollywood.' I'm thinking she's got some contacts somewhere. I picked up four books. I said, 'Take them home. Read them. You want one; we'll work out a deal.'"

Dusty met writer/producer Amber Lindley on Saturday. The next Wednesday, she offered a movie deal. Dusty wasn't surprised that *The Mustanger and the Lady* was her choice.

"If I was making a movie, that's the movie I'd make. There ain't no big Indian wars, fights, battles, cattle drives. That's going to be the bargain movie to make. I think to get that girl bucked off the horse was going to be like $3,500 or $4,000. And she just flies off the horse!"

They struck a deal. "I didn't have any doubt about her. She had enough experience on that small movie she made, and contacts and stuff. But, you know, I had a good friend who sold a damn book to that actor, Ted Danson.

"Ted Danson paid her—not an agent—paid her $125,000 for her book. It was a cute story. It would have fit him, and they never made the movie. . . . It was the only book she ever wrote and ever sold. . . . Hell, she got the money, [but] she'd a lot rather have had the movie.

"But I just had in my mind that [Lindley] had it set on this deal. And by golly, they have to pay you when they start filming, when they turn the camera on. So I had my small chunk of money, and I'd tell people that it wasn't

Metro-Goldwyn-Mayer, but it was about the price a good book would bring you if you sold some [publisher] a book. I appreciated that, I damn sure did."

Toward the end of filming *Painted Woman*, Lindley invited Dusty to the set in Oklahoma. "Oh, it was wonderful! There's a part where [Dawson] is escaping [with her horse], and they had two cameras. One of them is on railroad tracks, so it could run up and down, back and forth. And the other one is a telephoto. They made three shots with both cameras at the same time. So whoever edited had six pictures to choose from. . . . It took three-and-a-half hours to make that three-minute deal. When he said cut, the kids—just young people out there—they screamed and hollered and laughed, applauded like they'd just won a ballgame.

"I was sitting there beside the director, and I said, 'You know, I could have wrote that thing in four paragraphs.' He turned to me, and he said, 'I bet you could.'"

Painted Woman wasn't Dusty's first time on a movie set. He did some acting while attending Arizona State University in Phoenix, but "no one discovered me." But he enjoyed his work, especially the day they blew up the barn for the climactic scene in 1959's *Rio Bravo*. No one had noticed what was being stored in the building. "I mean, it was an explosion of explosions. So here comes the pink snow: somebody had stored some damned pink paper in that thing. It ruined the whole scene. I learned some new swear words—that director [Howard Hawks] was having a fit. They had to build another barn and blow it up, I guess."

Dusty also worked as an extra on the series *26 Men* that former Hopalong Cassidy sidekick Russell Hayden produced, about the Arizona Rangers. "It was a really kind of slapstick deal. One time, we wrecked a wagon. I was riding in a posse, chasing, the wheel went off, and two of us went off into the cactus. And [Hayden] said, 'Save it! Save it—we'll use it next week!' He didn't have to pay a stuntman.

"I met Steve McQueen; I was on the set a couple of times with him. And boy, he had a catered luncheon and everything else. Have a beer bust on the end, and someone to pick up the bill for it.

"You did one of those *26 Men*, you brought your canteen water with you. Somebody told me, he made those things for $10,000, and they made a quarter of a million dollars a week."

Dusty got an early taste of filmmaking in Arizona by ditching school for a bit part with a goddess. "The guy said, 'What did you do with your life?' I said, 'You want to hear about the time Marilyn Monroe and I made *Bus Stop* together?' I sat two to the right and two above Marilyn Monroe. You have to have a big screen to see me. I was that thirteen-year-old cowboy."

Dusty grounded *The Mustanger and the Lady*'s plot in history, and *Painted Woman* co-writer and director James Cotten was particularly curious about the character Vince Wagner, the Mexican-Apache horse trainer (played by David Thomas Jenkins), a person lost between two worlds.

"Vince came from the American South, and all that trouble. [Vince was] not the first guy to take a body and turn it in to the US marshals [for the reward]. I've read some actual accounts for that happening. Didn't have fingerprints, they had some kind of a description. They had some stuff that belonged to him, like letters. They didn't have things like we have today: he's blond headed, six foot tall or whatever he was. 'Oh, I see him, and I'll swear to it. I've known him all his life.' [Laughs.] Get $100 reward. But you got [not actual cash, but] scrip that the government would agree to pay, when Congress would vote some money to pay that. And that's when you got your money. Otherwise, you took a discount on it. In Fort Smith, [Arkansas], barbers, everybody, made money off that, because people would need their money, and they'd take 20 percent off, 25 percent off, and if they had $100 scrip, they'd pay them maybe $75. But Hell, you had your money and gone. Might be eighteen months before the government got around to paying."

In adapting the novel to a screenplay, changes are always made to story. "What they did was, they took a dance hall girl who knew about a murder, [but] that girl didn't know about a murder in the book. Took that and shortened it up for the movie, because, in the other deal, [the Papagos Indians] were running all over the country."

Dusty was pleased overall, but disappointed at losing the subplot about the Papagos, who were enemies of the Apaches. "I wrote that book to show when the tables turn for the Apaches, it wasn't no damn wonder they had a problem. They had them down there at San Carlos. When you come over that mountain to San Carlos from Tucson or Tombstone, there isn't even a saguaro that grows on the San Carlos side of the mountain. They stuck [the Apaches] in a hellhole."

In 1985, with two Western short stories published, Dusty joined the Western Writers of America and attended his first conference, in San Antonio, Texas, where he met everyone of note except for Louis L'Amour, who'd stopped attending.

"I would like to have met him—and cussed him. Because, when I began to write books, I would get these people who would write and say, 'Louis never done it like that.' I must've got 150 letters, saying, 'Louis never done it like that.' Louis is not the only damn guy who ever wrote a Western book, you know? I think *Sacketts* is probably one of the greatest bunch of books that was ever written. But he's got a bunch of other crap that I don't like. I'm sure there are some books of mine that somebody'd say, 'I don't like the one about the dog-tailed horse' or whatever. That's their privilege. But I never would have wrote anybody to say, 'Louis L'Amour told me how that was done.'

"I really think that he leaves women out. Women were part of the West. And people like this dance hall girl in this book, were sold by parents to somebody who said they were gonna get her a job; that went on all over. And Hell, there was one woman to eleven or twelve men, or maybe even a greater number, in a lot of places on the frontier."

When he was just starting out, Dusty paid book editor Frank Reuter $250 to critique one of Dusty's novels. "Oh my God! He wrote on the front. He wrote on the back. He wrote in between. That had enough red ink in it, it would have saved a bloodmobile." Impatient for a critique on the third novel he'd sent, Dusty drove the forty miles to Reuter's house to hear the verdict. "I asked, 'Frank, how'd you get along with this book?' 'Well, I probably didn't critique it as good as I did those others. I was goddamn busy reading it.' It went off in my head that I would sell that book. I mean, here's a guy that did bestsellers and everything else, and he's so interested in my old cowboy story. I've got a shot at selling that book. Absolutely."

LEE MARTIN

When Western novelist and screenwriter Lee Martin visited the set of *Shadow on the Mesa*, the first film based on one of her books, the cast and crew were astonished to meet the author. "When my sweetheart and I went to the location, they all thought *he* was Lee Martin. One of those crusty old guys almost swallowed his cigarette. But [leading man] Kevin Sorbo didn't bat an eye when he saw that I was female; he was very gracious. I've always wanted him to be in my Westerns; he's attached to *Hang Town* right now, when we get the funds."

For the author of twenty-eight Western novels, with three Western movies made, the romance and mystery of the West was a perfect fit. "My father came to California on horseback. He was part Cherokee and French and German. He worked on different cattle ranches. And he had a cattle ranch at the end. We lost him when we were young, so my brothers became my heroes, and they are probably in some of my novels. My sister and I followed them around the rodeos."

Martin hasn't been influenced by any particular Western authors. "Actually, I was influenced by movies, all the Westerns, and John Wayne especially. In third grade I started writing stories in spiral notebooks. I didn't *decide* to be a writer: I never had a choice. I just began writing stories because they were in me and had to come out. When I write, even now, it's spontaneous, without planning; and sometimes the hero demands it."

She skipped fifth grade at her one-room schoolhouse. "Best education you can ever get is in a one-room school. You have to tow the mark." She graduated from high school at age sixteen. "I had the highest grade in the county in the English/Subject A exam given by the University of California at Berkeley, and could have gone, but had no money. We were struggling on the ranch, so I went to work as a waitress in a truck stop." She kept writing. At age twenty, she was married to, then divorced from, a bull rider. She moved back to the ranch. "My first short story sold when I was in my late twenties."

One of the last of the pulps, *Ranch Romances*, started publishing her short stories in 1959, and would publish about twenty of her forty-three short stories. "Jim Hendryx was the editor, and he gave me a second pen name of M. Lemartine so he could use two in an issue." Other Western stories appeared in *Zane Grey Magazine*, *Great Western Short Stories*, and various men's magazines. "The last seven were in *Woman's World*, after the Western market ended," around 1970.

In her early forties, "[w]hile I was working full-time and trying to write, I met my sweetheart, Jim. We both went to night law school. In California, if you've only been to high school, you can pass a two-year college equivalency exam. I sold my first novel to Avalon about eight years later, and then sixteen more. I did practice law for about thirteen years. I didn't like it, so I just retired and went into writing full-time."

While she continued to write Western novels, she knew the screen was her real calling. "What really sent me was the Saturday afternoon matinees with Red Ryder, *The Lone Ranger*: that's what I wanted to do. To me, a screenplay is like the short stories I used to write, which were small movies in print with a beginning, middle, and climax."

Her break came when Martin found InkTip, a website where writers pay to have their screenplays made available to producers. "I sold all three Westerns off of InkTip."

Michael Feifer has directed two films based on Martin's novels, 2021's *Last Shoot Out*, featuring Bruce Dern, and 2022's *The Desperate Riders*, featuring Trace Adkins and Tom Berenger. He's also signed on to direct *Hang Town*. "I have never met him and only spoke with him on the phone once or twice," Martin says, "but I dearly love him. He has shown so much respect for my writing and made very few changes."

"Actors will stick to the script if they like the dialogue," Feifer explains, "if they feel it's strong. I think actors like Lee's dialogue because it's rich and of the period. It feels right to them. And that's a compliment to Lee's writing that actors don't change it too much." What makes Martin's scripts stand out? "An attention to detail, a care for story, and an interest in women in the Old West, too. A lot of times I receive scripts, or I write scripts myself, and it's just like, men killing men, and you don't really get the backstory. You don't really see the romance."

"I'm big on happy endings," Martin agrees. "The guy's gotta get the girl in the end. You know, my big, tough rodeo brothers, they wanted to see the guy get the girl too."

PAULETTE JILES

While Texas novelist Paulette Jiles liked the idea of *News of the World* becoming a movie, this wasn't her first rodeo. "Larry McMurtry did a script for *Color of Lightning*, but he couldn't sell it to Hollywood. Twentieth Century Fox bought *Enemy Women*, but they shelved it. So I'd gotten used to disappointment." When her agent said she'd sold *News of the World* to Universal, "and Tom Hanks is playing the captain, I said, 'Has he signed?' He had, and I was just on top of the world. Oh, he does a superlative job with the captain."

Eleven-year-old German actress Helena Zengel is new to the United States, but she won the German equivalent of the Best Actress Oscar for 2019's *System Crasher*. She plays Johanna, a child of German immigrants taken captive by the Kiowa band who slaughtered her family. After six years, five since the end of the Civil War, she is rescued. When the black soldier entrusted with returning her to relatives is murdered, the obligation falls to ex-Confederate captain Kyle Kidd, who scrapes out a living traveling the hostile Army-occupied countryside, giving public readings from the world's newspapers. It's the first Western since *True Grit*, a decade ago, that would interest a child and be appropriate for them to see. "Helena does a really good job," opines Jiles. "She worked very hard at learning Kiowa to play that part. And Kiowa is difficult because it's a tonal language; it's not easy to do."

Although perhaps never portrayed in fiction before, Captain Kidd's profession, news presenter, is not Jiles' invention. The character was created for her earlier novel, *The Color of Lightning*, "Which is partially about Britt Johnson, the African American frontiersman that *The Searchers'* story was based on, [although] they changed it to a white guy—John Wayne. His wife and two children are taken by a joint raiding force of the Kiowa and Comanche people, and Johnson went alone into Indian Territory and got them back. It was the most amazing thing.

"Because he's a freed slave, it had to be conveyed to the reader that the 13th, 14th, and 15th Amendments had been passed. Some good friends who live here in town, their great grandfather was a traveling newsreader named Cornelius Kidd. I said, 'That is fascinating.' I put him in a brief scene where he does a reading, talking about the new amendments. Then I thought, this character is too good to let go. So I gave him his own novel.

"What suggested the story to me was my research into captives, and what happened to them after they returned. So many, when taken young, did not want to come back. There were some successful returns, but only of children who were much older when they were taken, and remembered more of their former life. But [most], they just didn't readjust."

The screenplay was co-written by Oscar-nominated English director Paul Greengrass, famous for three *Bourne* thrillers, and directing Tom Hanks in *Captain Phillips*; and Australian Luke Davies, an Oscar nominee for his *Lion* script. Usually filmmakers of very contemporary stories, they successfully tackled the 19th-century plot. "They did a good job," Jiles believes. "They changed many things, and the captain is not the same man that is in the book, [but] they stayed with the basic story."

There were also many subtle changes from screenplay to movie. Dialogue is almost always shortened, as good acting eliminates the need for many speeches, and Kidd's news readings are trimmed. In the movie, Kidd is more dignified when speaking on stage, and less stilted offstage, than in the script. The most striking revelation in the screenplay comes on page ninety-four, when Johanna has led Kidd off the main trail, suddenly sure of where she's going. "Close on the shack as they approach. Everything about this—the wide-open space, the sky—reminds us of something. Something deeply rooted in our imagination. The opening of *The Searchers*." The family homestead, bloodied, death-scarred, abandoned.

They were lucky to get the movie in the can when they did, Jiles reveals. "They were pretty close on to the COVID, coming right up to the edge.

Lockdowns were on the horizon." And for a film that's so highly regarded, it was not the Hollywood premiere that Jiles dreamt about. "Texas is pretty open. Our theaters are open, but they're holding down the capacity. My friends got together and rented one in The Rim, a big shopping area North of San Antonio, and thirty of us went. It was very different [from] a big premiere, but there was lots of cheering, and booing the villain, and it was fun. It is a beautifully told story, beautifully photographed. The sets are terrific. The girl is wonderful, and they just made a gorgeous film out of it. You'll love it."

So will you.

EILEEN POLLACK

The primary job of the biographical Western *Woman Walks Ahead*, starring Jessica Chastain, Michael Greyeyes, and Sam Rockwell, is to entertain. It succeeds admirably: the largely unknown story of Caroline Weldon (frequently misidentified as Catherine), the Brooklyn widow who became Sitting Bull's friend and advisor, is beautifully told.

But how close is the movie to the truth, and does that matter? People nowadays seem to learn history more from fictional depictions than from nonfiction, and schoolkids learn less history than any previous generation. Accepting what's presented as unvarnished truth is far too easy for folks today. After all, Wyatt Earp may have been a hero or a villain, but he's popularly considered a hero because his history is based on a book he helped shape.

Was Weldon truly the heroine the film portrays? As newspaper reports in her time make clear, she was then roundly despised, at least by whites: a recent *New York Post* article short-handed her as "The *Hanoi Jane* [Fonda] of the Victorian era." One of the few existing letters of Weldon's, addressed to Chief Red Cloud, was preserved only for amusement, passed from one official to another with the addendum, "a letter from a female crank." No word on whether Chief Red Cloud ever got to read it.

"She was crazy as hell at Standing Rock," the late historian Robert Utley said. The author of twenty-two volumes, including his *Sitting Bull* biography, added, "She was certainly not helpful in his relations with white officialdom. Whether she was harmful in the attitudes of his own people toward his liaison with a white woman is unknown. I suspect they didn't like the idea."

"This white woman had given up everything to trek from Brooklyn to the Dakotas to be an ally for people she felt had no allies and deserved them. I thought the movie captured much of that," Pollack says.

Not that Pollack isn't dismayed at some points the film got historically wrong. "They have her going there very naively, to paint Sitting Bull's portrait, and then becoming politically aware and active. Weldon went there primed to help Sitting Bull fight the Dawes Act [of 1887]," which divided tribal lands into individual farms and sold the "excess" to whites.

"She'd already been sending him lists of prices for land and translating for him," Pollack says, "being his lobbyist in Washington, DC, working with the NIDA [National Indian Defence Association]."

Weldon, age fifty-two, traveled to Standing Rock reservation in June 1889 and May 1890. She did paint four portraits of Sitting Bull, but the point of her visits was to act as the Hunkpapa Lakota chief's advocate and translator.

Casting made Weldon and Sitting Bull much younger than they were, probably to create a potential romance more appealing to audiences. The movie does not include Weldon's fourteen-year-old son, Christie. "She brought him out; they intended to live on Sitting Bull's homestead," Pollack says.

"What they leave out [when we see Weldon moving in] is that [Sitting Bull's] wives and kids were there. You see them running around, but you don't really get who they are."

Tragically, Christie stepped on a rusty nail, contracted lockjaw, and died. "He was very close to Sitting Bull," who had taught the boy to ride, Pollack says. "If I'd written the movie, it would have been forty hours long and twenty times sadder. As it was, it was so sad that you could barely stand it."

Yet the movie gets much of the history right. "The part that I thought was most effective was showing how much the whites hated Weldon for talking with the Indians, for going to live with them," Pollack says. "The scene in which she gets beaten so badly, even though not literally true, was so emotionally true and historically true. That was a very effective [way] to portray something that I needed lots of pages to get across."

The movie shows the extremes of white views about Indians at that time, and how far beyond the extremes Weldon stood. "The conservative position was: kill them all. The liberal position was: help them assimilate, divide up the reservations," Pollack explains. "Weldon was one of a handful of people who had the belief that the Indians should just be allowed to be Indians."

Indian Agent James McLaughlin (Ciaran Hinds) is one of the more controversial real people in the story. "McLaughlin was probably the best agent in the service, his influence enhanced by marriage to an Indian woman,"

Utley said. "But best agent means best at advancing civilization and best at controlling his charges."

"I was impressed with how they portrayed McLaughlin, because he wasn't really a villain," Pollack says. "I've spoken to his grandson, who considers himself Lakota. [McLaughlin] really thought that he knew what was best for the Indians. He saw Sitting Bull as an old fuddy-duddy who was clinging to the old ways and keeping the more progressive members of the tribe from becoming assimilated."

The best part of the story that isn't in the movie is what Pollack learned after the book's 2002 publication. Daniel Guggisberg, inspired by Pollack's book, conducted research that is shared in the e-book edition of *Woman Walking Ahead*: "Weldon wasn't a widow. She'd had a terrible marriage to a doctor, ran off with some guy. [Her husband] divorced her very publicly and shamefully; she was prohibited from remarrying. She was a divorcee with an illegitimate son," Pollack says, adding that was the reason she changed her name from Susanna Karolina Faesch Schlatter to Caroline Weldon.

"So, she was just remarkable in about every way, shape, and form."

CHAPTER 8

THE WOMEN OF THE WESTERNS— ON BOTH SIDES OF THE CAMERA

WOMEN WHO DIRECT WESTERNS

While Western films tend to be stereotyped as "boy stuff" just as Romcoms are tagged as "girl stuff," the truth is, Westerns have always had a sizable female following. But while we've long had female on-screen icons like Maureen O'Hara, Barbara Stanwyck, and Dale Evans, scarcely half a dozen have sat in the director's chair. Unexpectedly, half of them have done their directing in the 21st century, and of the entire group, only one was born in the United States.

In the "silent" days of 1913, Canadian Nell Shipman began writing and starring in Westerns. By 1920, she was co-directing her own features. In films like 1920's *Something New*, 1921's *The Girl from God's Country*, and 1923's *The Grub Stake*, rather than playing the typical waif in need of rescue, the outdoorswoman was more likely to rescue the male lead.

Shipman retired in 1924, and it would be thirty-five years before another woman would take on the mantle. Sixteen-year-old British beauty Ida Lupino was already a star when, in 1934, she came to Hollywood. While continuing to act, in 1949 she began to write and direct tough *films noir*. Ten years later she directed her first Western, an episode of *Hotel de Paree*. Series star Earl Holliman recalls, "She was a movie star, and I had watched her for years. Directors who've acted can be very helpful. She was sharp, knew exactly what she wanted, where she wanted the cameras." Still, on her first Western, communication wasn't always easy. "She was English, and she talked about when the heavies go up to the bar, 'to have a couple of hookers,' which in England means a tall whiskey. And the assistant director asks the producers, 'Where will we get these hookers?' Ida was talking about drinks; they were talking about whores." Lupino would go on to direct episodes of *Have Gun—Will Travel*, *The Rifleman*, *The Virginian*, and others.

Nine years later, Lina Wertmuller, the first woman ever nominated for a Best Director Oscar, became the first and probably only woman to direct a Spaghetti Western. *The Belle Starr Story* was shooting in Yugoslavia when star Elsa Martinelli insisted the director be replaced, with Wertmuller. "I thought it was a great move," recalls male lead Robert Woods. "I love her films; she's a true artist." Wertmuller worked for hours on scenes with Martinelli and wrote her a poignant speech about Woods' character being the only man she ever loved. "Then halfway through the picture, they had the Indian girl kill me! But I still got my sixty grand."

Now in the 21st century, three women have picked up the megaphone and riding crop. Beijing-born Chloé Zhao has directed two contemporary films, neither truly a Western but both with Westernish aspects and elements. In 2017 she directed the remarkable true story *The Rider*, about the second act in the life of a rodeo cowboy recovering from a near-fatal head injury. She followed it in 2020 with *Nomadland*, starring Frances McDormand, who sees herself as a modern-day pioneer. *Nomadland* won Oscars for Best Picture, Best Director, and Best Actress.

In 2021, New Zealand–born Jane Campion wrote and directed *The Power of the Dog*, adapted from Thomas Savage's novel. It's set in Montana in 1925, but was magnificently shot in New Zealand by Australian cinematographer Ari Wegner, also a woman. It's about the struggles between the ranching Burbank brothers, Benedict Cumberbatch and Jesse Plemons, and the woman and her son—Kirsten Dunst and Kodi Smit-McPhee—who come between them.

Campion won the Best Director Oscar, and the film received an additional eleven nominations.

Kelly Reichardt, the only American in the group, has directed two fine, critically acclaimed Westerns. *Meek's Cutoff* (2010) is the story of a tiny wagon train whose Oregon Trail journey is waylaid when wagon master Meek takes them on a "shortcut." Her next Western, 2019's *The First Cow*, is the seriocomic story of the first cow introduced into an Oregon frontier and the entrepreneurs who build a business on filched milk. The director did not set out to make Westerns. Reichardt recalls, "The only Western image that really impressed me as a kid growing up in Miami was the Marlboro Man." In *Meek's Cutoff*, "[there's] a bossy man on a horse, a wandering Indian, wagons, oxen, and cooking over an open fire. So, the Western was hanging over me while making that film. The visual language of the genre is strong. With *First Cow* I didn't feel I was walking in the footprint of the genre. I could do whatever I wanted, maybe because many of my influences came from Asian films and French painters."

What challenges does she face making period pictures? "Harsh landscapes, extreme weather, rattlesnakes, oxen, and a volatile actor. *Meek's* pushed people to their limits and brought out the best and worst in us all. The rewards, to name a few: times of a perfect synchronicity with crew, actors, and nature; the lovely animals; shared research." That shared research, which included the lead actors, produced films of startling accuracy. About *Meek's*, she said, "The art department research brought [production designer] David Doernberg and me in contact with a lot of strange and interesting people. Michelle Williams was reading the diaries from the pioneer women, and Zoe Kazan had been researching the frontier since she was a little girl obsessed with *Little House on the Prairie*."

First Cow is not as grim as *Meek's*, and one can imagine Laurel and Hardy doing what her characters do, but Reichardt doesn't call it a comedy. "I really don't put it in any certain category. I think it has weight and humor and a searching quality. But it was fun cutting the film and it often made me laugh."

Considering the striking but nontraditional beauty of the films, it's no surprise that Reichardt and cinematographer Christopher Blauvelt have many influences. "Winslow Homer for certain, and Robert Adams' photography, pioneer wildlife photographer William L. Finely, the paintings of Michael Brophy, who also took me on scouts out in the high desert of Oregon. The Westerns of Anthony Mann and Budd Boetticher."

Would more women assuming the Top Hand role make a significant change in Westerns? "The genre already is what it is. That language is already in stone. Now that more women are getting the chance to direct, they can comment on the genre, but creating a whole new language for it is probably impossible."

MARIETTE HARTLEY

"I knew that it was something special; Sam (Peckinpah) was terrific, everybody was terrific, especially Randolph Scott and Joel McCrea—who I'd never heard of." Before Mariette Hartley made her film debut as the female lead in Peckinpah's 1962 masterpiece, *Ride the High Country*, she had no expectation of becoming "Queen of the West." "We only had one movie house in Westport, [Connecticut]" she said. "The first movie I ever saw was *The Red Shoes*, as a young ballet dancer. Then Olivier's *Hamlet* and *Henry V*. I didn't know anything about Westerns. My next-door neighbor had horses, and I would ride bareback."

One day, "a wonderful, crazy directress, Claire Olsen, from Chicago rounded up the kids from Westport, and made us actors and actresses." Four years with her led to two "with Eva Le Gallienne, who taught me Ibsen and Chekov." At age fifteen, "she handed me off to John Houseman of the Shakespeare Festival. So, I was passed on from one really great theatre person to another."

Surprisingly, what led Hartley to Hollywood was not the film business, "but a bad marriage. He wanted more than anything to go to California; and I hated California." The father of an actress friend steered her toward the William Morris Agency. In four days, she was meeting at MGM with Peckinpah. Three days later, the studio set up a screen test, she recalls, "and I said, what's that? I tested with Wayne Rogers, Ben Cooper, Richard Jaeckel, and Ron Starr" in the scene where Elsa washes dishes with her romantic interest, Heck Longtree. Starr would win the role.

Elsa runs away from her father, played by R. G. Armstrong, to marry James Drury, and learns to her horror that she will in effect also be marrying his three brothers—Warren Oates, L. Q. Jones, John Davis Chandler—and father, John Anderson. "The time I got really scared was the dancing during the wedding. Sam wasn't soft on that: he wanted it to look the way it looks. Those guys pulled me into it, and I was terrified." She liked them, and would work with them all again. "But Johnny Chandler terrified me! I mean, he *was* that guy."

Hartley frequently catches Scott's and McCrea's films on TCM. "I asked Joel, is there anything that you do to prepare? He said, 'Because we never do things in sequence, and have to know where we are emotionally, I read the scene *before* the scene I'm doing right now, get prepared for that. Then I suck in my gut and go on.' He was a dream to work with; both of them were."

And there was a special reward for being "introduced" in *Ride the High Country*. "The joy of that was that my father was alive when it came out in 1962. We shot it in 1961. My mother, father, and I saw it together, and when 'introducing Mariette Hartley' came up in gold letters, I was so grateful that he saw that. I felt very blessed."

Ride the High Country was an international hit, and Hartley was in demand in all genres. Although she did a great deal of Western television, she did only two more Western features, both co-starring Lee Van Cleef. In 1970's *Barquero*, Warren Oates and his gang are fleeing the Army after a robbery, and Van Cleef's barge is their only means of escape. As the townspeople panic, the voluptuous bad girl and the "virtuous" married Hartley make plays for Van Cleef. "I called me and Maria Gomez, not the long and the short of it, but the concave and the convex of his life. Lee covered himself with Coppertone. He looked really greasy and sexy, he thought. One time, he takes me in his arms and I slipped out and landed on the ground. Not one of my best experiences."

Still, it was better than *The Magnificent Seven Ride!* "You mean *The Magnificent Seven Ride* for twenty-four pages? Until I got raped and killed. That was a juicy role."

Her TV work was much more satisfying. "I did two *Virginian*s, and four *Bonanza*s. I just adored *Gunsmoke*. 'Cotter's Girl' was my very first television show, written by the great Kathleen Hite." A man forces Matt Dillon to kill him, so Matt will be responsible for the daughter he's kept hidden on his farm. "It was *Pygmalion*! I just loved it. I loved Jimmy [Arness]—he made me laugh harder than anybody except maybe Hoss [*Bonanza*'s Dan Blocker]. And Michael Landon.

"The nice thing about *Bonanza* was, you could stretch yourself a bit. I mean, from playing an Indian to playing a famous actress. I went through the whole Cartwright family, one brother at a time. And then I dated Ben." After which, one irate fan wrote to complain about Ben's foolishness, "Didn't [you] recognize her as the Indian a year and a half ago?!"

She enjoyed working with Dennis Weaver in *Gunsmoke*, "But he was odd when he did *McCloud*: he'd discovered his best side, and they could not use his left." She liked working with Warren Oates and Bruce Dern on *Stoney Burke*, "but (not) Jack Lord. I'd gotten the script the night before, had no time to study, and he did nothing but put me down. 'This isn't what happens when you do Shakespeare, is it?'" Kurt Russell was just twelve when he starred in *The Travels of Jamie McPheeters*, "I sang *Greensleeves* to him. It was a sweet show." Also guesting was Charles Bronson. "I went up to him in my innocent, virginal way, shook his hand and said, 'Hi. I'm Mariette Hartley.' And he said, 'Who gives a shit?'"

There were rewards even working on the lower-budget shows, like *Death Valley Days*, "where I had to bring my own red shawl, and the name of the episode was "The Red Shawl." But I worked with Robert Taylor, for crying out loud!" In other series, "I acted with Dan O'Herlihy, Raymond Massey, Mary Astor, Henry Hull, Lee J. Cobb. Really wonderful actors."

"I'd like to keep working. I'd love to do comedy again." Or a Western? "Sure, if it's a good script, and as long as I don't have to ride *too* much—you know, my bones are getting a little bit brittle."

KATY HABER

Film is the most collaborative of arts: no one makes a movie alone. So, how important might an assistant be to an auteur like Sam Peckinpah? A woman who was constantly by his side for eight movies in seven years? According to Mark Kermode, film critic for the BBC, "It wouldn't be completely fanciful to say she was the co-director. She was allowing the director to direct."

Sam made *Straw Dogs, Junior Bonner, The Getaway, Pat Garrett and Billy the Kid, Bring Me the Head of Alfredo Garcia, The Killer Elite, Cross of Iron*, and began *Convoy* with Katherine "Katy" Haber, MBE (Member of the British Empire), by his side, and as his "demons"—alcohol and drugs and paranoia—became more pronounced, her job of holding things together became ever more demanding.

It was certainly an unexpected life for the daughter of Czechoslovakian Jews who had fled to England when Hitler's troops marched into Prague in 1939. It was always planned that Katy would follow her dermatologist father into medicine. But when his depression led him to suicide, she says, "I decided that I would not have my mother pay an inordinate amount of money to get me through university. I decided to go into the film business."

In the late 1960s she'd worked as assistant producer to Ronald J. Kahn on theater and film productions, including *Prudence and the Pill* and *Girly*. Peckinpah was in England in 1971 to make *Straw Dogs*. Producer Sir James Swann called her. "'Sam's been through three or four different assistants, and all of them wanted to have lunch breaks and have their hair done. They couldn't take his odd curriculum.' So I went to see him, and he said, 'Can you type?' I said, yes. He threw me the script, and I started typing." Of course, it was the rape scene. "Nothing prepared me for working with Sam Peckinpah—nothing."

She began on *Straw Dogs* as a secretary, and by the end of the shoot, she was dialogue director, and so much more. That wasn't the only way their relationship changed. "There was no romanticism about it; it wasn't idyllic. But if romance means intimately involved, yes." And then, the film was in the can, and it was over. "He said, 'Thank you so much for everything that you did. Next time I come to England, we will work together.'" Then he was rushing off to Prescott, Arizona, to direct leading man Steve McQueen in the rodeo film *Junior Bonner*. They had to shoot key scenes during the actual World's

Katy Haber, on the right, self-described "Girl Friday, Saturday, Sunday . . ." to Sam Peckinpah, on the left, was at his side constantly, here on the set of *Junior Bonner*, and on the seven other films they made together. *Courtesy ABC Pictures*

Oldest Rodeo and Frontier Days Parade in June and July 1971. "Two days after he left, I got a call, saying, 'Get your fucking ass over here! We've got another movie to make! I can't do it without you.'"

"Wherever Sam went, I was next to him, earphones on, script in front of me. Sam wasn't concentrating on the actual prose of the film. I was able to tell him when they missed a line. He was not one for ad-libbing."

She would run interference to protect the crew. "Sam would work all day, work all night, and then sleep at funny times. And if he had a thought, he would say, 'Call the crew!' And I would say, 'I can't find them,' so that they could get a good night's sleep."

Toward the end of the shooting of *The Getaway* (1972) in El Paso, Texas, Sam crossed the border into Juarez and married his girlfriend Joie, so Katy was summarily fired and she returned home. She was immediately hired to work with Sam Fuller. When that project collapsed, as did Peckinpah's marriage, he called Katy back, this time to Durango, Mexico, where he was two weeks into production on *Pat Garrett and Billy the Kid*. During other gaps in her Peckinpah career, Katy would work with Michael Cimino on two movies, *The Deer Hunter* and *The Sicilian*.

Often, she was protecting Sam from his producers. While he was editing *Pat Garrett and Billy the Kid* (1973), "[producer] Jim Aubrey was cutting it in another editing room, taking out all the lyrical, prophetic, and emotional sides to it. He just wanted it to be a bam-bam-thank-you-ma'am action film. When Sam finished editing, I would hide the film in the fridge." Decades later, when they decided to release the director's cut, Katy was able to provide it.

Sadly, when Peckinpah made the transition from liquor to cocaine, his paranoia increased to an intolerable degree. "He was very, very emphatic about knowing where I was at every second of the day, down to even bugging my room on *Convoy*." That was the end: she quit. They never spoke again.

Katy went on to a long career in cinema in Hollywood, including as a producer of the sci-fi classic *Blade Runner*, using her Peckinpah-honed skills to unite a hostile American crew and dictatorial British director Ridley Scott. She has gone on to produce several documentaries.

Her dedication and service to underprivileged and underserved communities in Los Angeles, including the creation of the Compton Cricket team in 1995, was recognized by H.M. Queen Elizabeth II, who awarded Katy the MBE in 2012. She also helped start and served on the British Academy of Film and Television Arts, Los Angeles, for twenty-three years.

And she still has a couple of film projects in the works. She's planning a miniseries about her family and the Holocaust. And there's a novel she wants to film. "It's called *My Pardner*. It's Max Evans' coming-of-age story about a kid who goes cross-country with a cattle rustler. I made a promise that I would get that movie made. Hopefully I can fulfill that promise."

Sam Peckinpah died more than thirty-five years ago. "He loved me, but loved to hate me, and hated to love me. I loved him and hated it. It was one of the most compatible-incompatible relationships, but it lasted seven years and eight films. So, something must have worked."

DIANE LANE

Let Him Go (2020) may be the most remarkable female-driven Western since Joan Crawford and Mercedes McCambridge came to blows in 1954's *Johnny Guitar*, but even its star is a little tentative on the genre. "What *is* the criteria for a Western?" Diane Lane asks. "Is there a horse in it? Is it the zip code? Is it the time frame? This film, *I* think, qualifies; we have several boxes checked."

In *Let Him Go* she plays Margaret Blackledge, who is married to retired lawman husband Kevin Costner and is thrilled—and a little overbearing—to be a grandparent. The couple's son is killed in a farm accident, and after their daughter-in-law (Kayli Carter) remarries, the Blackledges have little contact with their grandson—then *no* contact when overnight the three move away to live in the boondocks with the husband's criminal family, dominated by nightmarish matriarch Blanche Weboy (Lesley Manville). The Blackledges must fight tooth and nail—on the ground, not in the courts—to save the boy.

"I hoped (writer/director) Thomas Bezucha could picture me in this character because she was a grandmother, and I understood this internal struggle of trying to get through something emotionally that you're not ready to do. The fact that that issue is the propellant for the plot is pretty unusual." With a laugh, she added, "Also, any excuse to get on a horse is good for me. It's wonderful. The only time I really got to [ride] was in *Cattle Annie and Little Britches*, when I was a kid. And once again in *The Virginian* with Bill Pullman for TNT. I think of horses as more than animals, probably because they interact with us so much. There's a special sensibility and sensitivity; I suppose they have to, because they're defenseless: all they can do is run."

Lane made her screen debut in 1979 at age thirteen, co-starring with Laurence Olivier in *A Little Romance*. In *Cattle Annie* a year later, playing Little Britches to Amanda Plummer's Annie, she was excited because "She was based on a true young woman, Jennie Stevenson, who really did run off with her friend, and they really did cohort and assist the Doolin–Dalton gang."

She had another great, older leading man on Universal's *Cattle Annie*. "To work with Burt Lancaster was just epic. Sometimes [director Lamont Johnson] and Burt would really get into it. There was one time everybody had to go to their trailers—we had to call a fifteen-minute cool-off period between the star and the director. We were down in Durango, Mexico, on John Wayne's ranch, which is vast, like a county. It was Amanda Plummer's first film. What a debut! She was just the personification of a pistol. We had so many wonderful actors: John Savage, Scott Glenn."

Eight years later Lane played her defining role in the Western genre as Lorena Wood to Robert Duvall's Gus McCrae, in the miniseries *Lonesome Dove*, widely considered the best made-for-television Western of all time; some say the best Western, period. "That's right, Lori Darlin'. Something magical happened there between the page and the screenplay and the performance and the audience that was . . . in bowling, it's a strike. Larry McMurtry won the Pulitzer Prize, rightfully so. It was brave writing, tough writing. The fact that [teleplay writer] Bill Whitliff didn't win the Emmy for bringing it to the screen blew my mind."

Tommy Lee Jones delivers his most dour performance, and Duvall his most delightful. "Robert was in character the whole time, but I didn't know it. When it came time to promote the piece, I hadn't seen him for quite some time, and looked at him and I thought, who is that? And what have you done with Gus? Because he was the actor, not the character. I had so much fun with Gus, but that lives forever on film."

It wasn't an easy shoot. "I had a scorpion in my petticoat at one point—I did a little jig that day. Riding side-saddle is not something that any person should do willingly. I contracted ringworm because I was in that water with Blue Duck (Frederic Forrest); that wasn't pleasant." Playing the captive of Blue Duck was a bigger challenge. "It was harrowing to go to the bottom of the barrel, the truth of what was going on emotionally and physically for this woman. Just the bestial way that things can go wrong for women in a lawless land."

In her next miniseries, *The Oldest Living Confederate Widow Tells All*, Lane played the child-bride of fifty-year-old Donald Sutherland, who was a soldier at age thirteen in the Civil War. Lane plays her for the first half century, and Anne Bancroft plays her preparing to turn age one hundred. "Getting to work with Donald Sutherland was amazing, and Bancroft was fascinating. The only sad part was that [Bancroft and I] never had any scenes together. I had just had my daughter like three weeks before I was in front of the camera. I was trying to breastfeed and be in a corset. I thought the challenge was so exciting, and I'm glad I did it, but it was kind of a blur."

In 1995's *Wild Bill*, Walter Hill, who had previously directed Lane in 1984's *Streets of Fire*, cast her in the brief but central role of the woman who ruins the life of Jeff Bridges' Hickok. She's only seen in dreams. "Walter was experimenting with different film stocks and lenses, trying to give the sense of what is a flashback, a premonition, an opium-addled memory. I don't always mention it, because I don't think people know I'm in it."

Having completed *Let Him Go*, would Lane be interested in doing another Western? "Oh, I would love to. I just want to find material that allows me to be who I am and where I'm at in my life right now. They say we [actresses] have one season: we get spring. That's not so true anymore, but it's always good to keep reminding people that there's a lot more to mine out of somebody besides what God gave them when they were under twenty-five, you know?"

CHAPTER 9

THE CLASSIC TELEVISION WESTERNS—OLD AND NEW

THE LONE RANGER—1949

Of all the people the Masked Man and Tonto saved,
the most crucial was Clayton Moore.

In September 2019, *The Lone Ranger*, TV's first Western series, turned seventy. At that time, incredibly, every weekday an average of 16 of the 221 episodes were aired on various channels.

When actor Clayton Moore was asked to audition, he was already well-aware of the radio show, which had begun in 1933. Clayton's daughter, Dawn Moore, explains, "He listened to it with his own father. The Lone Ranger was already a beloved character in their house."

Producer George Trendle and writer Fran Striker had co-created *The Lone Ranger* (although Trendle alone owned the copyright) and engineered the transfer from radio to TV. According to Moore, in his autobiography, *I Was That Masked Man*, Tonto was cast first. "No one but Jay Silverheels was considered to play Tonto." Both men were physically up for their athletic roles that rarely employed stuntmen. Silverheels, a Canada-born Mohawk, had been a professional lacrosse player and Golden Gloves champion, and Moore had been a trapeze artist and acrobat. Both men's acting careers began with bits in Poverty Row Bs. Silverheels had graduated to small roles in big films like *Captain from Castile* with Tyrone Power and *Key Largo* with Humphrey Bogart. Moore had become "King of the Serials" at Republic. When, after a long interview, rather than an audition, Trendle asked the actor if he wanted the role, Moore replied, "Mr. Trendle, I *am* The Lone Ranger."

The Lone Ranger was John Reid, a Texas Ranger who was ambushed with five other Rangers, including his idolized older brother. Butch Cavendish's gang thought they had killed all six, but Tonto found Reid and nursed him back to health. Tonto inadvertently gave him a new identity when he commented, "Now you lone Ranger."

Moore, who always wanted to be a policeman or a cowboy, fulfilled both goals in one role. "I fell in love with the character, and never wanted to play another role." While that was doubtless true, there was more to it, and the part could not have come at a better time in his life, his daughter reveals. "Dad was thirty-four; his father had died of a heart attack. His eldest brother had committed suicide. His middle brother was in an asylum. Then he's handed a script for a character who's devoted to finding justice for his brother's death. Who spends his entire life saving people. How much could that have resonated with him, to do something, on a much larger scale, that he couldn't do for his own family?"

The shows hold up well, thanks to strong casts and crews. The writing was surprisingly unrepetitive, as nearly all episodes were based on radio plays, with nearly three thousand to choose from. Jay Silverheels as Tonto was not only the first American Indian playing an American Indian on a TV series, he was also not a sidekick, as he was never used for comedy relief—any comedy was handled by Moore as his "Old Prospector" character. Tonto, although with a limited English vocabulary—"Me go." "Get 'em up, Scout!"—was an equal partner to The Lone Ranger.

Everything was great, until Moore was fired. "Trendle was famously shrewd and tightfisted," says Dawn. "Someone told Trendle that Dad was selling silver bullets at some personal appearance." Sure that the mask made the actor instantly replaceable, Trendle hired John Hart, who was not a bad actor but was no Clayton Moore; the audience knew the difference, and the ratings dropped. Hart was happy to leave. "They made every [episode] in two days," he told James Van Hise, "and we didn't get paid worth a damn. I made fifty-two episodes in 1952."

Moore was hired back the following year. Trendle was selling *The Lone Ranger* to Texas oilman Jack Wrather, a deal dependent on Moore being back in Silver's saddle. Trendle would receive $3,000,000; writer Striker's cut would be a $4,000 bonus.

While Silverheels would go on to appear in more than thirty movies and TV series, Moore would never portray another character; he spent two decades making Lone Ranger personal appearances, barnstorming cross-country, appearing at rodeos, store openings, and carnival midways.

Although the Wrather Corporation would later claim that they "allowed" him to make those appearances, Moore's daughter clarifies, "When Dad was on the road, (he) had to pay Wrather $1,000 a week . . . Once, Dad had to sell his own car so he could get back home."

Always concerned with living up to the ethics of his character, "The Lone Ranger Creed became his Bible," she adds. He and Silverheels did well with a number of commercials, famously the Geno's Pizza Rolls ad that spoofed Lark cigarette ads. The problem on-set was "Dad won't eat the product, because The Lone Ranger doesn't eat junk food." The sponsors were insulted, but the day was saved when someone suggested, what about if Tonto eats them instead? "Dad puts his hand up to refuse, Tonto takes a bite, and starts shoveling them in his pockets." They missed out on Coors' Silver Bullet Beer, because Moore wouldn't drink the product on camera. Moore worked for Wrather once again in 1970, promoting a short-lived Lone Ranger Family Restaurant chain that hoped to compete with the Roy Rogers Restaurants.

Then, in 1975, Wrather's lawyers told Moore, age sixty, he was too old to make appearances as The Lone Ranger, or even as the actor who played The Lone Ranger. Never mind that for twenty years he'd paid dearly for the privilege of keeping Wrather's character alive and followed Trendle's edict to never appear in public without the mask. They were making a new Lone Ranger movie, and Moore was finished.

Only he wasn't. "Dad didn't have a legal leg to stand on, (but) took Wrather to court—then lost, then carried on anyway. This textbook example of moral courage is when he started to shift from a long-ago faded TV star to an American folk-hero."

Unable to wear the mask, he switched to sunglasses; Corning hired him as spokesmodel for their shades. The controversy brought new interest, and soon Moore was earning more than he had in years. In 1996 I shook Clayton Moore's hand at a book-signing two blocks from Republic Studios. Hundreds of fans waited in the store and down the block: soldiers, CHP officers, police—people who came to tell Clayton Moore that his example inspired them to choose a career of service.

L.A. deejay Rick Dees campaigned and got Clayton Moore, like Jay Silverheels before him, a star on the Hollywood Walk of Fame. Of the then 2,686 stars, only one names an actor and the role he's beloved for: "Clayton Moore—The Lone Ranger." Rick made sure they could never take it away again. Hi-yo Silver! Away!

THE RIFLEMAN—1958

September 2018 marked six decades since a Western series premiered, starring a ballplayer-turned-actor and a one-season Mouseketeer as father-and-son ranchers in New Mexico. Despite being a black-and-white drama, *The Rifleman* continues running on cable, on streaming platforms, and on DVD. Why does it endure?

The answer begins with the creators, Jules Levy, Arthur Gardner, and Arnold Laven, who'd met in the Army Air Force's Motion Picture Unit during WWII. They were given the chance to create a Western story for *Zane Grey Theatre*, produced and hosted by song-and-dance-man turned leading man turned TV impresario Dick Powell.

"Powell used *Zane Grey Theatre* as a proving ground for pilots," Gardner recalled. *Johnny Ringo*, *The Westerner*, *Black Saddle*, *Trackdown*, *The Rebel*, and *Wanted: Dead or Alive* had all begun on *Zane Grey Theatre*. The problem was, the trio didn't have a story, only a title.

Enter an ex-Marine screenwriter who'd learned his craft by adapting nearly a dozen episodes of the CBS radio series *Gunsmoke* for TV. Sam Peckinpah gave them a script: a skilled marksman enters a shooting contest, but the town powers have bet on someone else. They let him know that if he wins, he'll die. He throws the match: the end.

The trio hated it—this guy was a coward, at least by Western standards.

Then Laven asked, what if he has a son, and the son will be killed if he doesn't lose the match?

That premise, the studio loved. Lucas McCain became an unusually realistic hero for the genre: powerful, wise, independent. But even he couldn't always triumph when the cards were stacked against him, although, in the long run, good won out over evil.

Peckinpah, who grew up on his family's ranch in Fresno, California, based the father-son relationship between Lucas and Mark McCain on his relationship with his own father.

Casting was crucial. Chuck Connors, six-foot-five and lantern-jawed, was a Brooklyn-born natural athlete. After the US Army, he played basketball for the Boston Celtics, then switched to baseball, playing for the Brooklyn Dodgers, then for a Chicago Cubs farm team in Los Angeles. There, he was given a small role in 1952's Spencer Tracy and Katharine Hepburn comedy *Pat and Mike*.

"They paid me $500 for my week's work in that movie," he recalled. "Baseball, I told myself, just lost a first baseman."

Johnny Crawford, a busy actor from age four, had appeared in more than thirty movies and TV shows by the time he auditioned for *The Rifleman*.

Obsessed with silent Westerns, "I was a fan most of William S. Hart," the late actor recalled in 2018. "I remember my audition vividly. I'd gotten several Western episodes, and I hadn't been so convincing as a cowboy. My mother, who was an actress, gave me lessons in cowboy talk."

Johnny auditioned for the partners, then for Connors. "I didn't see him right away, because he was only twelve feet tall," he recalls with a laugh.

That tall cowboy, Connors, remembered: "We must have interviewed twenty or thirty, then Johnny came in and before we even talked to him I said, 'That's him. That's the rifleman's son.'"

They shot 40 half-hour episodes that first year, 168 over five seasons, with three days of shooting each, and a starting budget of $38,500 per episode. In that first season, unprecedentedly, thirteen-year-old Johnny was nominated for a Best Supporting Actor Emmy. He lost to *Gunsmoke*'s Dennis Weaver. The series lost Best Western Series to *Maverick* and never earned another Emmy nomination, but that may have been their own fault: the producers walked out on the banquet because they were seated so far back, and Connors, though seated in front, went with them.

The plots were a blend of stark violence and family values. "I killed on average two-and-a-half people per show," Connors recalled. "We had the benefit of the father-son relationship, so I could have a scene at the end where I would explain to Mark, essentially, that sometimes violence is necessary, but it isn't good."

Peckinpah wrote six episodes and directed four, before quitting. He wanted an evolving storyline, with Mark growing to manhood; the producers wanted to keep Mark a kid. Peckinpah had a point: while the series never jumped the shark, seen over a period of years, the viewer wondered why Mark never learned a distrust of strangers who would inevitably kidnap him or try to kill his father. Peckinpah's extraordinary originality and storytelling ability would create a very high bar, which the series would strive to meet, and often succeed, for five seasons.

Connors had four sons. Johnny's brother, *Laramie* star Bob Crawford, guested on *The Rifleman* and remembers, "They had great relationships with their fathers and sons, and John and Chuck had this extra father-son relationship."

Because Johnny was a minor, his grandmother was on-set every day. "Chuck could be rowdy now and again, but when Grandma was around, Chuck was a pussycat—a Bengal tiger pussy cat," Bob says.

When *The Rifleman* found itself opposite the new *Lucy Show*, it was time to ride into the sunset.

Chuck Connors recalled, "When Johnny came on the set in 1958, he was a little twelve-year-old boy. He called everyone in the cast or crew 'Sir' or 'Ma'am.' During the course of the five years of our run, he had two hit records, and he was nominated for an Emmy. And yet, when the show was finished after five seasons, Johnny went around and thanked everyone in the cast and crew, and he still called them 'Sir' or 'Ma'am.'"

Levy-Gardner-Laven would go on to produce many movies, as well as the series *The Big Valley*.

Connors would have a long acting career in features and TV series, perhaps remembered best as the soldier falsely accused of cowardice in the series *Branded*. He and Johnny would remain close friends until Connors' death in 1992.

Johnny, who became a genuine cowboy during the making of *The Rifleman*, would have a rodeo career, an acting career, and a stretch in the US Army. He had the starring role in the Oscar-winning short film *Resurrection of Broncho Billy*, and a singing career, notably as orchestra leader and singer for the Johnny Crawford Dance Orchestra. In his final movie, *Bill Tilghman and the Outlaws*, Johnny starred as his idol, William S. Hart.

Why does *The Rifleman* series endure? Gardner, who passed away in 2014 at age 104, summed it up: "It has an eternal theme; father and son. It was a good show. We had five years of good directors and writers and actors. It makes me feel very proud."

THE HIGH CHAPARRAL—1967

A half century ago, a new Western arrived on NBC, and four seasons later, it was gone, leaving a legacy of just fewer than one hundred episodes—less than a fourth of the *Bonanza*s or a sixth of the *Gunsmoke*s. Yet this show's popularity grows, here and abroad, with daily airings on several channels. Director-writer Quentin Tarantino credits it as an inspiration for 2015's *The Hateful Eight*. When, in September 2017, the remaining cast and crew—and 150 fans—of *The High Chaparral* gathered at a hotel in Burbank, California, to celebrate the 50th anniversary of the rugged and romantic Western series, most of them knew it would be for the last time. Series creator David Dortort had died seven years before, and stars Leif Erickson and Cameron Mitchell had been gone for decades. In the years since that last roundup, we have lost star Linda Cristal, who could not attend; Henry Darrow, who played Manolito; Don Collier, who played foreman Sam Butler; and Kent McCray, the series production manager. McCray and his wife, Susan, who helped cast the series, were the hosts of the opulent affair.

David Dortort was the already incredibly successful creator of *Bonanza* when he branched off from the almost too-perfect Cartwrights to create what he'd later call a "dysfunctional Western family."

Kent, who also managed the production of *Bonanza*, enjoyed the older show but preferred the newer one, recalling, "In *Bonanza*, they had money, so people came to them; the stories were in and around the Ponderosa. *The High Chaparral* was a location [Old Tucson in Arizona] and had a lot of action."

Not only action, but also a palpable sense of danger and that rarity—unpredictability. It started with the pilot, when John Cannon (Leif Erickson) brings his lovely wife Annalee (Joan Caulfield), rebellious son Billy Blue (Mark Slade), and disreputable brother Buck (Cameron Mitchell) to the Arizona ranchland he's bought. Incredibly, Annalee is immediately killed by Apaches and, almost as quickly, John Cannon acquires a new Mexican wife!

"We had the Mexican family of high esteem south of the border, and then we had the Tucson family, the (socially lower) Cannons," recalled Henry Darrow, the ladies' favorite as lovable wastrel Manolito, of the elegant Montoya clan. "And the man who played my father, Frank Silvera, negotiated a romance between his daughter [Victoria, played by Linda Cristal] and the old man, John Cannon."

The quick marriage doesn't sit well with Billy Blue, who has just lost his mother and was attracted to Victoria himself. And that's just the pilot!

One revolutionary element for the series that aired from 1967 to 1971 was the number of Hispanic actors who appeared in it. "The people in Latin America, people all over the world, love it. They all can relate to it," Susan says.

Darrow agreed. "Dortort had such an affinity for Latin actors, and he used us. He hired almost every Latin who I had ever known of, about a hundred-odd people a year."

The High Chaparral surely came along at the right time for actor Cameron Mitchell, who was represented at the reunion by his children, fellow actors Chip and Camille Mitchell, who said, "I think it saved his life."

Cameron had acted with the best in the business—John Wayne, Clark Gable, Marilyn Monroe—but the Hollywood studio system had collapsed.

He was busy making European Westerns and horror films, but Camille remembers, "He was almost fifty, and in those days, fifty was old for an actor."

While flying to Rome to act in a movie, Cameron found himself sitting next to Dortort. Chip remembers, "They'd done *The Ox-Bow Incident* on TV together [for *The 20th Century-Fox Hour*], which got David an Emmy nomination."

Dortort gave Cameron a copy of *The High Chaparral* script: "'I thought you might want [to play] John Cannon.' But Dad read the script and he immediately fell in love with the role of Buck," Chip says.

"Cameron Mitchell was a character. He'd eat [while] wearing gloves. Show up blond without warning," Kent remembered.

His costumes were made of black velour. "After a take, he'd jump in a water trough to cool off. With the velour, it didn't show. But I thought he was the best actor on the show," Kent said.

Deep-voiced Don Collier had already performed in three films with John Wayne. His favorite episode on *The High Chaparral* was "Follow Your Heart," where Sam Butler finally gets a romance. "Though they killed my wife off," Collier added. "My favorite writer wrote that show, Denne Petitclerc."

Petitclerc, who also wrote the pilot episode, was a protégé of author Ernest Hemingway.

With stories so dependent on action, a strong stunt crew was indispensable. The stunts were overseen by Henry Wills, who had spent two decades performing stunts on Republic serials and B-Westerns before becoming stunt coordinator on 1960's *The Magnificent Seven*.

Stuntman Steve DeFrance, who calls Wills "my best mentor," remembers the job as a fifty-two-episode blur of action: "It was like working in a real ranch; every day was a day of work. In one [episode], we were Chaparral guys, running from the Comancheros, shooting back at them. Then we traded hats, rode back shooting this way *as* Comancheros. But in the afternoon, we changed into cavalry uniforms and came to our rescue."

What killed the series? Assassinations.

Kent believed the "death of Robert Kennedy changed the attitude of television. They didn't want to see people get killed, and that hurt us terribly."

For what had been a life-and-death action series, adopting a "no-kill" policy became a credibility nightmare. Jackie Fuller, Cristal's stunt double, recalls, "You'd have an Indian attack. A stuntman could act like he was shot, fall off the horse, but then you had to show him getting up and running off-screen."

Soon, viewers were running away as well. The final episode, "A Man to Match the Land," aired on March 12, 1971.

The *High Chaparral* family has gotten a good deal smaller since that 50th anniversary get-together. Linda Cristal, Kent McCray, Henry Darrow, and Don Collier have all passed away. Kent had just written his autobiography, and Susan said they were looking for a way to revive the series. That suited Collier fine: "It was fun to do. Sure wish we had time to do it again."

DEADWOOD—2004

"It's Doc Cochran's office—I'm sure of it! And there's the Bella Union!" More than a decade after HBO's *Deadwood* had left the air, fans attending the Santa Clarita Cowboy Festival at Melody Ranch were making their pilgrimage from holy site to holy site. They *loved* that show.

The gritty, greatly fact-based *and* greatly fictionalized story of the founding of Deadwood, South Dakota, was and is as controversial among Western fans as *High Noon*. But beyond question, *Deadwood* is the most popular, important, and influential Western thus far in the 21st century. It also introduced the word cocksucker to the Western lexicon. And then there was the ending that was intended only as a cliffhanger: George Hearst, father of future publishing giant William Randolph Hearst, and played with stylishly deadly charm by Gerald McRaney, is the victor. With the show's abrupt cancellation after three successful seasons, fans were devastated. As Robin Weigert, whose performance as Calamity Jane has redefined that character, puts it, "I thought, it's the anti-Western: the bad guy rides off into the sunset!"

Deadwood is the brainchild of David Milch, who both studied and taught literature at Yale before going to Hollywood. A man of great talent and passions, he's won four Emmys for writing, three for *NYPD Blue* and one for *Hill Street Blues*; he's had two nominations for *Deadwood*. He's also struggled with heroin and gambled away more than $100 million. For thirteen years, while working on many short-lived HBO projects, Milch and other members of the *Deadwood* team have made countless attempts to finish the story of the building of the town, and finally they've succeeded: a new *Deadwood* movie premiered on HBO on May 31, 2019, featuring Timothy Olyphant, Ian McShane, Molly Parker, Gerald McRaney—virtually the entire surviving cast and crew.

From the start, *Deadwood* was a show that everybody wanted to be a part of. "I was always fascinated with Westerns, because of all of that untamed lawlessness and danger and larger-than-life characters," recalls the production designer, Maria Caso, whose work on the series earned her an Emmy. She'd been highly respected in her field for two decades when the original series was announced. "HBO and Paramount already had production designers lined up, but my young son said, 'Mom, you have to try to get the show because that's your dream, to work on a Western.' I spent three days researching the real Deadwood. I went and met with David Milch and [producer] Gregg Feinberg. I told them I would kill to work on a Western. I promised I would sleep in my office and make the show look amazing if they hired me. They both said, 'Great, you are hired.'"

From there, the research began in earnest. "We were trying to re-create the town the way it really was. I flew to Deadwood and the museum curator had a photograph [of the town] that nobody had ever seen before. I brought it back and said, 'This is what we want the street to be,' so we copied everything on the street." Gene Autry's old Melody Ranch studio went through a major transformation. "We put a gold mine in the middle of the street, we had the street undulating, we brought in eighty truckloads of dirt. The roads back then were steep, muddy pathways. We watered the streets down every day. There were so many buildings we had to remove thirteen when we first got there."

Brad Dourif was a screen legend long before he was cast as Doc Cochran in *Deadwood*. Oscar-nominated for *One Flew Over the Cuckoo's Nest*, he also has a cult following for playing the voice of Chucky, the homicidal doll in the *Child's Play* films. He has a strong presence in Westerns, from *Heaven's Gate* to *Grim Prairie Tales*. Right before *Deadwood*, he'd even starred in an Australia-lensed prequel series to *Bonanza*, titled *Ponderosa*. "David said, 'I just want to see what you're going to do. I have a real instinct about it.' And I did my little audition; then next was my audition in front of HBO. Before we went in, David said, 'I'm looking around. Do you notice you don't see any other actors who look anything like you do? That should tell you where you're at.' So, whatever I did, he really liked it."

Respect is clearly mutual. "You know, I worked with David Lynch. I've worked with John Huston. I've worked with Milos Foreman. I've worked with tons of really extraordinary directors. But [Pulitzer Prize–winning playwright] Lanford Wilson and David Milch were the smartest people I ever worked with. And the most instinctive—their instincts were impeccable. David would come in, polish almost every single thing that we shot. I was really impressed with him."

Calamity Jane (Robin Weigert) returns to Deadwood not greatly changed in her habits but changed a lot in her confidence. By now she's a famous historical figure and an entertainer.

On the other hand, Brandeis graduate Robin Weigert had no long string of credits when she first read for the Calamity Jane role in New York. "I had not been on TV beyond an episode of *Law and Order*, where I'd been a traumatized victim of a shooting. In pictures the real Calamity Jane looks scary, tough. So I did my toughest rendition of the character, and the feedback came, 'Loved the vulnerability. But could you please make yourself a little more . . .' and I got a list of all the things I had *tried* so hard to be." For the callback she rented a Western costume, "to cover up the parts of me that looked softer, delicate. I got a kerchief to make my neck look more sturdy, and a hat to hide my hair."

She wore it again when they flew her out to L.A.—her first time in the West—for one last audition, where she turned on the roomful of studio executives. "I was cussing them out: I treated them like they were too cowardly to go look for the girl [lost] on the Spearfish Road. I used everybody in the room to be the folks in the bar. My nerves were vanquished by moxie and absurdity."

Weigert knew her version of Jane would be "a substantial distance from Doris Day's portrayal. David Milch had warned me off—not reading, but trusting—the various books too much, because Jane herself was an embellisher." She got help from an actress not associated with the show. "Jane Alexander, who's such a brilliant actress, played her in a movie some time ago. I wanted to pick her brain a bit. She was actually able to interview a centenarian who had met Jane, who as a tiny boy mended fences for Calamity Jane. She was such a generous help."

Another help to Robin was the man who played the object of Jane's unrequited love, Wild Bill Hickok. She was not happy, nor was HBO, when just a few episodes in, he drew aces and eights. "I was heartbroken. Keith Carradine had been such a bedrock element. I didn't know how I could be Jane without him. But it was great stuff to use, because I don't think Jane knew how to be Jane without Hickok for a good while. And Carradine used to take care of me, because I didn't know how to hit a mark, I had so little experience before a camera. He'd kinda put a hand on the base of my spine to gently guide me to open to camera."

William Sanderson, who plays hotel proprietor E. B. Farnum, gained recognition as the genetic engineer in 1992's *Blade Runner* and popularity in eight seasons of *Newhart* as Larry, with two brothers named Daryl. He's immensely proud to have been in *Lonesome Dove* as Lippy, the saloon pianist who the town's only whore refuses to sleep with at any price. "But my favorite role, even though *Newhart* was the longest running, was for *Deadwood*. For David Milch."

There's been a consistency to his nearly 130 film and TV characters. "The word I keep hearing, the nice word, is quirky. You can say lowlifes or misfits or steal from Strother Martin and say prairie scum." He got the role of Farnum with help from a great Western director. "I did *The Last Man Standing* with Bruce Willis, Bruce Dern—I liked him immensely. Walter Hill directed it. So when *Deadwood* came around, I got to meet with Walter [who would win an Emmy for directing the pilot], and read some material, and the genius-type David Milch was in the room, and seemed to like me."

Sanderson was surprised to learn that he was playing a real man. "Well, I was shocked. He was the first real mayor and he might've been the justice of the peace. He dispensed justice in a thoroughfare and was a successful businessman." As the series progressed, "David kept stealing from my own gargoyles of insecurity. He started to draw on my self-doubts and make Farnum into a cockroach or something. But they're hard to kill, cockroaches."

When season three of *Deadwood* ended, everyone involved happily prepared for the start of season four. Sanderson remembers, "Kim [Dickens, who plays Joanie Stubbs] had bought a house in L.A. And I had bought this one in Pennsylvania." Dourif recalls the call. "I could tell from David's voice I was not going to be in it anymore. So, I said, you're gonna fire me, right? And he was aghast for half a second and said, 'No. What I am saying is that they've canceled the series.'"

There's always been an aura of mystery as to why the popular series suddenly ended. Milch explained the cancellation in a 2012 interview with the Television Academy Foundation. "The budget was astronomical, easily higher than the *NYPD Blue* budget, and it was only half as many shows." But at that time, HBO seemed unconcerned about cost. Milch says, "I never got a note about cutting down the expenses." But no honeymoon lasts forever, and eventually the then-HBO president told Milch they were far over budget. "They said, if we agree to let you do four seasons, will you agree to cancel the show? And I said, no, I don't want to talk that way. So they said, okay, well then we're going to pull up at the end of the three seasons."

Fast-forward to late 2018, and a story that has jumped ahead a decade, to 1889, and a gathering of all the usual suspects to celebrate South Dakota's recently won statehood. The script is by Milch. The direction is by Daniel

Minahan, who directed four episodes of the original series, as well as many of *House of Cards* and *Game of Thrones*, and in 2018 shared the Outstanding Limited Series Emmy for *American Crime Story*.

Of course, in the intervening years, Melody Ranch had been busy as a location for many productions, including *Django Unchained* and *Westworld*, so Caso anticipated a lot of changes. "But no, *Westworld* used our *Deadwood* Street pretty much as is, just added a few things here and there. And *Django* did the same thing. I thought it was a compliment, using our street the way we left it." Not that Caso left it alone. "We tried to keep a lot of the old *Deadwood* and introduced some of the growth of billboards. We introduced brick buildings and electricity. Deadwood has its first telephone. We leveled out the street a little bit."

"The version of Jane I bring to this movie is already performing with Buffalo Bill Cody," Weigert explains. "Wild Bill haunts her still. It's kind of wonderful to get to return to a character after a dozen years, a very rare experience. She's been gestating deep inside me the whole time. I remember when almost all of the women found ourselves in the hair and makeup trailer at one point, and we just clustered together, grabbing hold of the hand of another. There was a lot of laughter and a lot of tears, and just a sense of absolute connection."

Sanderson, whose memoir, *Yes, I'm that Guy. The Rough and Tumble Life of a Character Actor*, was published to coincide with *Deadwood*'s release, was happy to be back at Melody Ranch. "Dan Minahan had directed me in *True Blood* and the *Deadwood* series, so that gave me a little confidence." Was it hard getting back into his role? Sanderson laughed. "You know, Farnum is me by another name. I had to accept that." He did miss two actors who passed away in the interim. "Both terrific actors. Powers Boothe won an Emmy for playing the biggest mass murderer in American history, Jim Jones." Then there was Ralph Richeson, who looked like a demented Gabby Hayes in his role as Richardson the Cook. "David [Milch] took an extra and turned him into, I thought, one of the most interesting characters."

Did Dourif find it difficult to get back into the skin of Doc Cochran? "No. The answer is, it was shockingly easy." How did it feel to be back at Melody Ranch? "Sad." After a very long pause, he explained, "'Don't it always seem to go that you don't know what you've got til it's gone?' It was such a shock when it ended; no one was expecting it. But in this business, your life is about getting a door slammed in your face. There are those people, and there is that level of commitment, and there's that love of what you're doing. And you realize you haven't gone anywhere near it since, and you've barely ever touched it before that."

Maria Caso feels no such sadness. "Working on *Deadwood* has been the most rewarding experience of my career. Re-creating a Western town with such rich characters and such a talented crew and a beloved writer like David Milch is truly a once-in-a-lifetime experience. And lucky me! I got to do it twice!"

HELL ON WHEELS—2011

If television is in the midst of a new Golden Age, *Hell on Wheels*, created by Tony and Joe Gayton, with its feast of characters and unsurpassed writing and direction, was one of the surest proofs.

For five seasons, from 2011 to 2016, *Hell on Wheels* told the story of constructing the Transcontinental Railroad through the jaundiced eyes of foreman and former Confederate slave owner Cullen Bohannan (Anson Mount). When we spoke, the show's days, and episodes, were numbered. The final season of fourteen shows was divided in half: seven in the summer of 2015 and seven in 2016.

Westerns, big screen and small, were undergoing an unmistakable resurgence. But when *Hell on Wheels* began in 2011, Westerns couldn't get arrested. How much credit does this railroad drama deserve for the reboot?

"That's impossible to say," admitted Mount, who was two-thirds of the way through filming when we spoke. "There was some hesitancy to get into the genre on the part of television because people chase each other's tails, and it hadn't been done for a while. Maybe it did spark a reemergence in the genre; who knows? But it's never gonna fully die: it's our martial arts film."

He was philosophical about the series ending. "It's time. I think we found a really good through-line to finish the story."

He noted that the final season, number five, has a theme. Season one's was "revenge," while season two's was "ambition." "I hate this word, because it is often misused or misinterpreted, but 'redemption,'" Mount said. "And I don't think the theme of 'hubris' has ever not been a part of the show."

Although the endpoint was always known, the route to get there, though blasted through rock, was not etched in stone. "Nobody really knows at the start of the season what's going to play out," Mount said. "You have some ideas up on the board; you may even have an ending in mind. If we'd started season three telling the network Cullen was going to end up married to a

Mormon girl in a Mormon fort, they'd have flipped out, and so would we. But that's where the season took us."

The series, like the railroad, has a high death toll. "You build relationships, and a storyline can end that very quickly," Mount said, about the fourth season. "Common [who played former slave Elam Ferguson] is one of my favorite people I have ever worked with. He had interests in other areas, and we found the best way to write him out. He did a heck of a job. And Kasha Kropinski [who played Ruth, the minister's daughter] was great to work with; she gave a heck of a performance in that final episode."

His favorite character to act with? The most wicked of villains. "It's been so much fun to plot that out with Chris Heyerdahl [the Swede]," Mount said. "He's a phenomenal scene partner. Things seem to crackle and spark when we get into a scene together."

After four seasons of filming the Union Pacific's race to Utah's Promontory Summit, where the Union Pacific and Central Pacific joined rails on May 10, 1869, the show's focus switched to the rival Central Pacific. "You can't really tell the story without showing both sides," Mount says. "[Showrunner] John Wirth wanted to show the Chinese experience in building the railroad. We've been as exacting as we can, to the extent that we're solidly all Cantonese, and not Mandarin."

What did Mount plan to do when he stopped working on the railroad? "I wouldn't do Cullen again," he said. "I'd totally do another Western; there's not a better genre. I like that it allows me to work outside."

Famous Westerns director John Ford would agree. He didn't call his films Westerns, but "outdoor pictures." Mount saw a transition in Ford's art when he made that switch: "Ford's best pictures weren't until he started moving outside. Look at Stagecoach: I honestly don't think it holds a candle to My Darling Clementine, and for an obvious reason; he was stuck in a studio."

But like Ford did many times, Mount had to move on to his next picture. "I'm really going to miss this crew," Mount said. "They're the best; they know the Western genre better than any crew knows any genre. I'll also miss riding the horses—best part of the job. What I won't miss are the elements."

The previous year, production was delayed when storms washed away the sets. "You know, it's hard not to get the crap beat out of you working on this show," the actor said. "I won't miss the bumps and bruises, but it's hard to come up with something bad about this job. It's really been wonderful."

LONGMIRE—2012

When the final episode of A&E's *Longmire*, season three, came to a close, audiences were left with some tantalizing questions: Now that Walt Longmire (played by Australian actor Robert Taylor) knows who killed his wife, how does he go on with his life?

Would Henry Standing Bear (Lou Diamond Phillips) ever get out from under the thumb of American Indian gangster Malachi Strand (Graham Greene)? Did Branch Connally (Bailey Chase) shoot his father, Barlow (Gerald McRaney), or vice versa? What fans did not wonder was whether *Longmire* would return to answer those questions. After all, it was the most successful drama series A&E had ever produced.

That's why jaws dropped internationally when the series was abruptly cancelled in late August 2014. The explanation was concise and insulting to the viewers: they were too old.

Zahn McClarnon, who played Longmire's frequent nemesis, Indian Officer Mathias, was told, "They wanted to advertise to a younger audience. So there was a problem with the demographics, because *Longmire*'s audiences tend to be thirty-five and above."

No one was more surprised than Walt Longmire's creator, novelist Craig Johnson. After all, "*Longmire* was pulling in close to six million viewers a week and had tripled A&E's expectations in ratings."

What was the real reason for the cancellation?

"A&E had a surprise hit on their hands and wanted to own the show," Johnson says. "You see, Warner Bros. produces the show and then the network pays a licensing fee to broadcast it. A&E figured that they could make more money off of the show if they outright owned it, but Warner was aware it was a hit and also had *Longmire* licensed to about one hundred other countries where it was also a hit, so they weren't about to sell it. Well, A&E told them that if they didn't sell it to them they would cancel it, and they did, cutting off their own hit to spite its ratings."

Longmire's producers went shopping for a new venue, and rumors swirled about where it might end up. TNT? USA? Perhaps FX, to replace the exiting *Justified*?

Instead, *Longmire* found a welcome at the last place you would expect a "geezer" show to roost, Netflix, then the home of *House of Cards* and *Orange Is the New Black*. It's a pretty edgy locale for a character who doesn't own a cell phone or a TV. Johnson concedes, "I think Walt would head over to the Red Pony Bar & Grill and watch *Longmire*, as only Henry would have Netflix."

Unlike A&E, which relies on advertising to determine which shows stay in the lineup, Netflix is a company that values what its viewers want. Netflix is delighted for the opportunity to lure some of those 5.6 million *Longmire* fans away from A&E and hopefully cultivate many more viewers along the way. As long as its 65 million subscribers are happy, Netflix is happy.

McClarnon has been pleased with the transition to Netflix. He has mostly worked with Taylor—"I like his process; I think he's a phenomenal actor"—and he says now he gets to work with more cast members. "I have a couple of scenes with Graham Greene, and he always brings surprises and lightens up the scene. And Adam [Bartley]—we say a couple of words to each other."

"My relationship really hasn't changed with the flip to Netflix," Johnson says. "I'm a writer, and the thing I can help with is the writing. The producers send me the scripts, and I go through them and send back my suggestions. Sometimes we agree, sometimes we don't, but that's the kind of collaborative relationship you have to have in a project this size."

One change is that, as with other Netflix series, the streaming media company does not offer a traditional "one-a-week" release. "They're going to drop all ten episodes this fall at once, which should really test the viewing fortitude of the fan base," Johnson says.

McClarnon approves. "Personally, I would rather sit down and watch the shows in my own time," he says.

One major positive change in the series is the definition of a TV hour. McClarnon recalls, "They screened the first episode in Santa Fe for the cast and crew, and it went an hour and six minutes."

"We used to be trapped in the basic-cable format of forty-two minutes with the burden of commercials," Johnson explains. "But now we're picking up at least twenty more minutes of content per episode, which is about a third of a season. That's a pretty dynamic change. It's going to give the writing and performances much more of a chance to breathe, which is one of the things that make the show different from everything else out there in the first place—that sense of silence."

THE SON—2017

On April 8, 2017, a new series, *The Son*, premiered on AMC. Starring Pierce Brosnan, the four-time James Bond who rode West in 2006's Western *Seraphim Falls*, *The Son* chronicled the rise and fall of a family and its cattle and oil empires.

Based on the critically acclaimed bestselling novel by Philipp Meyer, the series starts with a bang! We are taken to 1849, in lush, green Central Texas, where teenager Eli McCullough's turkey hunt has been spied by Comanches. They attack Eli's family cabin, rape and slaughter his family, and drag off Eli, to be killed or made a slave.

Suddenly, it's 1915, and the adult Eli (Brosnan), now the wealthy patriarch of a large family, is trying to shift the family fortune from steers to crude. Eli, his son Pete (Henry Garrett), and granddaughter Jeannie (Sydney Lucas) are trucking to town when they pass a tree with a lynched man hanging from a bough, the first fatal blow in a coming war between the Spanish gentry and the wealthy whites. Grandfather and granddaughter are each the most important person in the other's life—much to Pete's fury. Is Eli sheltering Jeannie or corrupting her? Is Eli involved in the lynching?

Eli McCullough's quest to assemble his wealth through ranching and oil triggers consequences that span generations.

Each of the two powerful storylines can stand alone, but juxtaposed, they are enthralling. "The Child is father of the Man," as Wordsworth wrote. How will one existence lead to the other? We go from the terror of younger Eli to the confident swagger of older Eli, entertaining guests with a sanitized version of his life's tale. Is he brave or horribly cynical? Is he a visionary or a swindler?

We know that beneath the charming Southern exterior beats the heart of a man taught survival by a Comanche war chief, lessons that have guided his life and will rule his descendants' lives.

Adapting *The Son* into a series had been a long commitment for Meyer, who sold his first bestseller, *American Rust*, outright to Universal. "But for the second book, I'd gotten a big enough paycheck that I thought, what if we adapt it ourselves and maintain creative control," Meyer says.

The book behind that five-year development process was a new type of novel for Meyer. Like Louis L'Amour before him, he traveled to all the settings for his story but took his adventure further, learning historical Comanche ways, skinning buffalo and drinking their blood.

The only cast member he had in mind was for the part of young Eli—Jacob Lofland, from 2012's *Mud*. "He's amazing. This guy dropped out of school in 7th grade; he's had no acting training, but he's a natural artist," Meyer says.

Meyer taught Lofland and others in the cast some of the skills he'd acquired. "I've never really shot with a longbow much," Lofland says. "Philipp

Meyer took me on two days of lessons. We practiced for a couple of hours each day, 'til we got to where we were both happy. He likes hunting and fishing. We get along really well. We're like the two rednecks on the set."

Playing Toshaway, young Eli's Comanche captor, was Zahn McClarnon, of 2015's *Bone Tomahawk* and Officer Mathias on Netflix's *Longmire*. "It starts off as a pragmatic relationship. He's captured for a reason—to work. Eli's a young, strong kid. And it grows into more of a father-son relationship, where Toshaway sees the potential in the kid and starts to care for him as his own son. Even more than old Eli, Toshaway is the patriarch of the series," McClarnon said.

Lofland recalls, "Getting dragged out of the house and across pretty much all of Texas, and getting beat in the back of the head with stuff; it was a little brutal." McClarnon agrees. "It was a difficult shoot, in the Austin heat, in June, July. People were passing out—it was that hot." McClarnon, who is Lakota, adds, "And Comanche is probably the hardest language I've had to learn. It's difficult to memorize a language that you do not speak fluently. Unfortunately, (many people) think we speak 'Indian.' There are thousands of different native languages!"

In the 1915 storyline, Madrid-born Carlos Bardem plays Pedro Garcia, the leader of an old and proud Tejano family, trying to keep a grip on his power as the more recently arrived whites, including Eli, try to squeeze him and his people out. It doesn't help, Bardem says, that Garcia has a willful daughter (played by Paola Nuñez), "who is the apple of his eye," and sons-in-law willing to rustle McCullough cattle for the revolution.

"It is a balancing act," he added, and with the utter contempt that Eli shows Garcia, "it is hard to keep his dignity."

Executive producer Henry Bronchtein, who won two Emmys for *The Sopranos*, saw a similarity between Eli McCullough and Tony Soprano. "They're alpha males," Bronchtein says. "One thing they have in common is that they get away with doing bad things, and people still love them. That's a charismatic thing that Pierce brings to the role, and yes, I think audiences will come to love Eli."

Brosnan charms everyone—even his horse has a crush on him, says line producer and writer Kevin Murphy, who explains: "Whenever Pierce goes somewhere, his horse wants to be with him, so you have to tie the horse up. They once neglected to tie the horse, and Pierce went into our ranch house to use the bathroom. We turned around, and the horse was walking up the steps of the porch, into the house, to follow Pierce to the bathroom."

It's a pity that *The Son* only ran for two seasons, because there was so much more story to tell. "As the 1849 storyline moves on over the seasons, we're going to be telling Civil War stories," Murphy said before the premiere. "And in the 1915 storyline, we're going to be telling stories about the Roaring Twenties, the Great Depression, and working our way up to WWII."

CHAPTER 10
THE AMERICAN INDIAN PERSPECTIVE

WES STUDI

When Wes Studi, fresh from the success of *Hostiles*, appeared on the 2018 Oscars to present a movie montage highlighting military service, the seventy-year-old mentioned that he'd volunteered for Vietnam, and asked if anyone else had.

He was met with silence.

"I wasn't surprised," he recalled with a chuckle. "I said it as a joke. I know the audience is not full of veterans, and their attitude toward veterans is not probably as complimentary as you'd find in other audiences."

He concluded his introduction with words in Cherokee, his native language. "It was to Cherokee veterans, as well as all military veterans, kind of a shout-out that it's a good day."

It was indeed a good day for veterans and American Indians. While that year, much was made of the racial diversity of nominees and the strides of women, most viewers were unaware that Studi was the first American Indian to be a presenter since fellow Cherokee Will Rogers hosted the Academy Awards in 1934.

Although lacking Oscar nominations, the critical and popular success of *Hostiles*, now available on Blu-ray and 4K, is no mystery to Studi.

"What sets *Hostiles* apart for me is simply the story. I think it speaks not only to the old Western of yesteryear, [but also] to the world we live in today.

"There's been a dearth of Westerns on the big screen for a number of years because nobody's been able to make a successful one since, say, *Unforgiven*. It's been a long time, and Western fans have been hungry for another one.

"Along comes *Hostiles*, and she'll go for another ride. I think we're probably going to see a few more in the next few years.

A wonderful portrait of Wes Studi as Toughest Pawnee in *Dances with Wolves*, taken by his wife, Maura Dhu Studi. *Courtesy Maura Dhu Studi*

"It was good to work with Christian [Bale] again. There was a threesome of us—Christian, Q'orianka [Kilcher], and me—who had worked on *The New World*. Rosamond Pike, I think she's a wonderful actor. [Writer/director] Scott [Cooper] was extremely open to ideas and had a good grasp of where he was going with the story."

Playing Studi's character's son was Adam Beach, who's shared the screen with Studi a dozen times.

"He's played my son to good effect and not so good effect at times," Studi says. "He killed me in *Comanche Moon*, and there was another one that he played my son and killed me. I think he gets a kick out of that."

In 1993, Studi starred as Apache leader Geronimo, in *Geronimo: An American Legend*, who surrenders to the Army in the end; in *Hostiles*, he plays Cheyenne war chief Yellow Hawk, who is freed from US Army custody and transported to his homeland to die.

"There's a continuity because the Cheyenne share an experience in dealing with the American military and the American government itself," says Studi, adding ironically, "They don't work hand in hand. The result being the kind of situations that our fictional character Yellow Hawk, and the real character Geronimo, ran into and had to deal with, and [we] continue to do so to this day."

Technically, Studi was born in Nofire Hollow, Oklahoma, on December 17, 1947. However, "The Cherokee Nation is where I was born, and my first language was Cherokee. That's what we spoke in the home. When I went to school, I learned English," he says.

"My parents did a lot of different things. The whole family raised crops and hunted, and survived in a way that people hardly do anymore. We bought salt and flour from the store. But we raised almost everything or hunted for it. Then my dad started working on ranches; that was pretty much his life and the whole family's life, living from one ranch to another in northeastern Oklahoma. We weren't living high off the hog."

In 1960, Studi's parents sent him to boarding school. "It was called Chilocco Agricultural School, and that's where my dad had learned most of his expertise in farming. I learned other things. We did half a day of academic work and half a day of vocational work, which was dry cleaning. It was a government Indian school."

Chilocco was originally one of the controversial institutions that tried to teach the Indian culture out of its students. "By the time I went there, things had changed. [We were] still discouraged from speaking our own languages, but it wasn't cracked down upon like it had been. The fact that a lot of Indians were involved in the administration of the school, and teaching, made a huge difference."

Studi enlisted in the National Guard in high school and entered the Army after graduation. "I volunteered to go to Vietnam. I was an infantry-man. We sought out the enemy, sometimes search and destroy, sometimes defend. For a while I was the RTO; I carried a radio for the platoon leader."

Despite the uniform, the physical differences between Indian soldiers like Studi and other soldiers were noticed by the Vietnamese. "They said they saw us as being very similar to the Vietnamese, you know? Because we kind of looked like them; our skin color was the same. And if they knew our history, they [knew] that we had been fighting the US Army just like they were at that point in time."

In the highly political Western films made during the Vietnam era, the treatment of Indians was used as a symbol of the US treatment of the Viet-namese. "Yeah, I think it was legitimate," Studi confirms. "I mean, we've all been the enemies of the US military. That may be hard for you to understand, but we've all been in that position."

The 1970s were an active time for Studi, who had returned from Vietnam in 1969. He attended Northeastern State University in Tahlequah, Oklahoma, on the G.I. Bill. Later, he would teach the Cherokee language there and within the community. He helped revive *The Cherokee Phoenix*, founded in 1828, the first newspaper established by Indians and published in Cherokee and English. He also became involved with A.I.M.—the American Indian Movement.

"The 'Trail of Broken Treaties' is when it started for me, in terms of activism," Studi recalls of the 1972 cross-country protests that culminated in Washington, DC, just before the presidential election.

Studi also went to Wounded Knee, where he was among those arrested in 1973. "The larger idea was to work toward a realistic approach to tribal sovereignty, and [we] continue to do so to this day.

"Russell Means was one of the leaders of the American Indian Movement, so I knew, and knew of, him back in the activist days of the seventies. And then we wound up on the film set of *Last of the Mohicans* in the nineties."

Studi's interest in acting began in the 1980s. "I decided to try at a community level and found that I liked it. That led to real theatre, led to educational television. I decided Los Angeles was the only recourse if I were to continue this line of work."

He made a powerful impression as the Toughest Pawnee in 1990's *Dances with Wolves*, which led to one of his most unforgettable characterizations, in *Last of the Mohicans*.

"Actually, when I slipped in to have an interview for Magua, I 'inadvertently' left a picture of myself from *Dances with Wolves* on somebody's desk," he recalls, with a laugh. "I don't know if it helped or not. After *Last of the Mohicans*, I continued to work."

That's putting it mildly. Studi has acted on-screen in more than ninety productions around the world. Recently, he co-starred in season three of Showtime's *Penny Dreadful*.

"Oh, that was a great job. Got to travel in Europe to Ireland and southern Spain. Where we worked was [Sergio] Leone-land, they call it. In fact, we worked in one of his old set towns. There are some subtle differences in the terrain in Spain, but only people from New Mexico or the Southwest can really figure out. I think it works pretty well."

He's worked on a number of films with his wife, documentary filmmaker Maura Dhu Studi, most recently *Defending the Fire*, an examination of the warrior in American Indian culture.

"I don't know if you'd call it a Western or not, but one of my favorite films that I've done is called *The Only Good Indian*." Set in 1900 Kansas, the 2009 film showcases Studi as an Indian bounty hunter, chasing down an Indian boy who's run away from a government school. "I'm pretty proud of having been a part of it."

Over the years, Studi has played many legendary chiefs, including Geronimo, Red Cloud, Crazy Horse, Buffalo Hump, even Cochise in *A Million Ways to Die in the West*.

"It carries a special responsibility. I'm going to have to play the character as he's written, and then also keep in mind that there are family memories and whether he was an icon.

"During *Geronimo*, we were playing with descendants of his. It's something that you have to be careful with, that's part of the whole process, putting together a character."

Since *Hostiles*, he has been in fourteen movies, TV episodes, and even voiced cartoon characters, and with at least ten others preparing to film, Studi shows no interest in slowing down.

"I continue to like it, and I will do it until the day I die."

As far as Westerns go, Studi remains confident of the genre's power over audiences, saying, "I think almost every director is going to try a Western, if they have any balls."

GRAHAM GREENE

One of the most recent of Graham Greene's 150-plus screen characterizations is in INSP's movie *Blue Ridge*, a contemporary Western about Appalachian backwoods clans, with a "Hatfields and McCoys" feel. The Canadian actor, a First Nations member of the Oneida tribe, explains that his character was "the patriarch of his family, and he ran everything with an iron fist. He hated the other family, blamed them for killing his daughter." Greene is happy to see the movie released. "I did a bunch of films that haven't been released yet because of COVID-19 that's going around."

For more than a decade, Greene was a busy actor on Canadian television, and in supporting roles in small features, until 1990's *Dances with Wolves* made him not just a familiar face but a star. He earned an Oscar nomination for playing Kicking Bird, a performance in an English-language film, but not in English. "It took three months to learn the dialogue. I had no idea what I was saying," Greene recalls, "and I had to learn it phonetically. I'd be running ten miles a day with my headphones on, listening to the translations, mumbling away in Lakota, and people were looking at me funny. But I got it down."

It was a tremendous undertaking for first-time director Kevin Costner. "He did fine," Greene says. "We stayed out of his way and let him make his decisions. I only questioned him once, [when Kicking Bird] was going nuts looking for a peace pipe. I said, 'He's a medicine person. He would never lose a

Kevin Costner as Lieutenant Dunbar and Graham Greene as Kicking Bird in *Dances with Wolves*, which earned twelve Oscar nominations and won five Academy Awards, including Best Picture and Best Director. *Courtesy Orion Pictures*

peace pipe. Why do you want me to do that?' He said, 'Because it looks good.' I said, 'Good enough.'"

Two years later Greene starred with Val Kilmer and Sam Shepherd in the groundbreaking *Thunderheart*, which defined the feel of contemporary 'Res' (reservation) Westerns like *Longmire*, *Yellowstone*, and the Tony Hillerman/ Joe Leaphorn films. It wasn't hard to convince Greene to do it. "I love The Badlands. My agent said, 'I got a film for you. It's in South Dakota. And you have to ride a motorcycle.' I said, 'I'm in.' 'Want to read it?' 'Don't have to.' Val was a strange fellow to work with. I just couldn't get into his head, what he was thinking, what he was doing. He was very to himself."

Greene's character, Walter Crowhorse, had one foot in the spirit world and one in the physical realm. "Crowhorse was fun because John Fusco wrote a great part. [Director] Michael [Apted] was great to work with. He just dropped the reins and let the actors go."

While he's done several period Westerns, Greene has done many more contemporary roles. "I like working in modern times. Doing period films is a lot of work. It's hard on the crew, the cast, everybody. I guess my favorite one was doing *Molly's Game*, playing the judge. Aaron [Sorkin], the director, was looking at me sitting behind the bench. I had a puzzled look on my face. He said, 'Are you alright?' I said, 'Yeah. I've just never seen the bench from this side before.'"

After a long career of playing good guys, he got to go to the dark side, playing the evil Malachi on *Longmire*. "Yeah, I had fun playing that. They wrote that because Lou Diamond [Phillips] kept bugging them. 'You've got to get Graham Greene on the show.' So they wrote the part of Malachi. I read it and went, 'Oh boy, that's perfect.' After the second season, they let me just go and do what I wanted because I knew the character so well. Like when I did *Goliath*, playing a nasty casino owner," opposite Billy Bob Thornton. "It was fun. It said I turned into a crow at night and watched people. I adapted these gestures; tilted my head looking at people, making a clucking noise. Playing villains is fun. Being nice all the time; it's boring."

Another of Greene's favorite roles was in the series *Defiance*, in which he and director Michael Nankin talked in a sort of shorthand, he says, "because we knew all these old films the kids had never seen. 'Do you want me to do a Bogart in this?' 'Yeah, that would be great.' And they go, 'What's a Bogart?' 'When you slowly turn around, look at somebody, and snarl at them.' One of the things that I really want to do, now that I am getting older and fading fast, is teach kids what to do in front of the camera. Because a lot of them don't know. They'll stare at the ground and mumble. I said, 'No, the camera's going to be over my left shoulder, look at my left eye; talk to me, not the ground.' I advise them to spend two or three years doing theater, because you've got to learn discipline, or you won't last very long. They ask, 'How did you last this long, Mr. Greene, forty-some years?' And I say, 'I've got a thick skin and a hard head.'"

INDIAN-CENTERED WESTERNS

The very first feature-length movie made in Hollywood, Cecil B. DeMille's 1914 film *The Squaw Man*, was an Indian-centered Western, and D. W. Griffith was making films like *The Red Man's View* five years earlier. Whether factual or fantasy, Indian Westerns have a long, if checkered, history. The points of view run the gamut: when Francis Ford directed and starred in 1912's *Custer's Last Fight*, the Indians were portrayed as savages. When younger brother John Ford directed 1948's *Fort Apache*, there was no doubt that Henry Fonda's Custer character was the savage.

While early films tended to show Indians as the enemy both of whites and of progress, there were always sympathetic portrayals of Indians— whether as noble savages, childlike innocents, or simply as human beings.

More evenhanded treatment became the norm by the 1970s, not coincidentally concurrent with the rise of Indian activism. The American Indian Movement's occupation of Alcatraz and Wounded Knee, and Marlon Brando's refusal of his *Godfather* Oscar over Indian treatment in films, were initially greeted by the public with amusement or annoyance, but these actions forced a spotlight on the unfair treatment of Indians by various government agencies. Three of the most visible participants and spokesmen for the movement would eventually become three of the most respected actors in the new wave of Westerns: Russell Means, Graham Greene, and Wes Studi, who in October 2020 became the first American Indian to be awarded a career Oscar.

Social justice warriors might dismiss older films simply because the Indians were portrayed by non-Indians, but that would be foolish. The suddenly widely accepted idea that people should portray only their own ethnic/racial/sexual identity is of very new vintage. Michael Horse, Yaqui and Apache, who played Tonto in 1981's *Legend of the Lone Ranger*, Deputy Hawk in *Twin Peaks*, and is in 2020's *Call of the Wild*, reminds us, "The process of acting is to portray something that you're not." He adds, "But if you're doing a cultural piece, and you don't bring somebody who comes with that culture, you're going to cheat yourself."

Michael Dante, an actor of Italian descent, played many a cowboy in Westerns but also played the son of Victorio, opposite Audie Murphy, in 1964's *Apache Rifles*; Crazy Horse in the *Custer* TV series; and most famously starred as *Winterhawk*. "The problem in those days, there weren't that many Native Americans that had a background in the theatre. They weren't professionals; they weren't given the opportunities."

In the early days of the silent movie, indigenous people often portrayed themselves. In 1908's *The Bank Robbery*, Quanah Parker, the last Comanche war chief, plays himself. In 1920's *The Daughter of Dawn*, Quanah's daughter Wanada, and son White, play lead roles. Shot in Oklahoma, the film tells the story of the struggles between Comanche and Kiowa, and tribe members make up the entire cast. Beginning her screen career in 1908, actress Red Wing was born on Nebraska's Winnebago Reservation and had appeared in more than sixty films when she starred in DeMille's *The Squaw Man*. Chief Buffalo Child Long Lance's swoon-worthy physique made a powerful impression in the Paramount early talkie *The Silent Enemy*, and stardom seemed a real possibility. Tragically, when word leaked out that he wasn't "pure" Indian but part black, his career collapsed, and he committed suicide.

With the coming of sound, DeMille filmed *The Squaw Man* yet a third time, with Mexican actress Lupe Valez as the Indian girl. In 1934, Valez would star in the remarkable *Laughing Boy*, based on Oliver La Farge's Pulitzer Prize–winning novel. The tale of a traditional Navajo lad (Ramon Novarro) who falls for "Americanized" city Navajo girl—and kept-woman Valez—was so daring and controversial that director W. S. Van Dyke kept his name off the credits.

End of The Trail, released in 1932, was a B-Western like no other. Tim McCoy, who'd lived on the Wind River Reservation and was adjutant general of Wyoming before becoming an actor, plays Cavalry captain Tim Travers, who has made enemies at the fort for being an "Injun lover." Framed for selling rifles to the Arapahos, he's discharged from the service but leaves only after giving a scathing speech denouncing the military and the government for not honoring any treaties made with Indians. Soon his son is killed by soldiers, and he's wrongly sentenced to death, and this is only partway through this unique fifty-nine-minute movie!

Throughout the 1930s and 1940s very few Westerns were built around Indian characters. Then came 1950, and *Broken Arrow*, director Delmer Daves' largely true story of the peace negotiated between former Indian fighter Tom Jeffords (James Stewart), and the Apache Chief Cochise (Oscar-nominated Jeff Chandler). The honor and wisdom of the protagonists is striking. The unspoken irony is that the peace would not be honored by the government. Jay Silverheels took a break from *The Lone Ranger* to give a powerful though brief performance as Geronimo.

In 1954, *Drum Beat*, Delmer Daves' story of the Modoc War of 1873, starred Charles Bronson as Kintpaush, the Modoc leader known as Captain Jack, opposite Alan Ladd as the frontiersman who's trying to prevent further bloodshed. In addition to being brave and daring, Kintpaush has a sense of humor and is more sophisticated than the ministers and generals he manipulates. Bronson's parents came from Lithuania. Eastern Shoshone actor and stuntman Cody Jones, who has worked on *The Son*, *Hostiles*, and the upcoming *Outlaw Johnny Black*, says, "At the end of the day, acting's acting. Charles Bronson, he was good." Michael Horse agrees. "Charles Bronson used to come pretty close."

Also in 1954, Burt Lancaster played Massai, a warrior who breaks away from Geronimo rather than live on the Florida reservation, in *Apache*. While his and his woman Jean Peters' pale blue eyes are distracting, it's a fine film full of original scenes, like Massai's first terrifying visit to a white man's town, and his meeting with a successful Cherokee farmer. Charles Bronson again excels as Hondo, a sellout to the Army.

Among the "White Man Who Is Made an Indian Because of His Bravery" films, the best is 1957's *Run of The Arrow*, from writer/director Sam Fuller. Rod Steiger plays an ex-Confederate who runs afoul of the Sioux, and when he survives their ritual "run of the arrow," he is made a member of the tribe by Chief Blue Buffalo (yes, Charles Bronson). A fine successor is Elliot Silverstein's 1970 film *A Man Called Horse*. From the pen of Dorothy M. Johnson, whose other filmed stories include *The Hanging Tree* and *The Man Who Shot Liberty Valance*, it stars Richard Harris as a British aristocrat whose hunting vacation ends when he's captured and enslaved by a Sioux raiding party. When he's allowed to join the tribe, and marry, the enemies they must contend with are not other whites but Seminoles, with jarring brutality on both sides. The rituals are historically documented, and unflinching, performed by Iron Eyes Cody. Cody himself is perhaps the best real-life example of tribe adoption. Beginning in silent Westerns in 1926, Cody became the screen's foremost Indian actor, with more than two hundred roles in his nearly sixty-year career. He's best remembered as the Crying Indian in the famous anti-littering Public Service Announcement. Most Indians were well aware that Cody was in fact the son of Italian immigrants, but because he always portrayed Indians in an honorable and historically accurate way, they kept his secret from the general public until after his death.

Horse's screenplay was by Jack DeWitt, whose Westerns were revisionist long before the term was coined. In *Sitting Bull* (1954), starring J. Carrol Naish, DeWitt pulls no punches in his contempt for Custer. And he daringly includes a historically accurate but rarely seen black Sioux (Joel Fluellen), a former slave adopted by the tribe. In DeWitt's *The Battles of Chief Pontiac* (1952), Pontiac (Lon Chaney Jr.) must deal with English allies and their homicidal Hessian mercenaries. "The industry has needed a good Indian for years," Chaney had said, "and I'd like to be it." He would be that in 1956's *Daniel Boone—Trailblazer*, and the following year in the Saturday morning series *Hawkeye and the Last of the Mohicans*, in which he played James Fenimore Cooper's Chingachook to John Hart's Hawkeye.

Although the often-glacial pace requires as much patience from the audience as the Congress expected from the Cheyenne, John Ford's *Cheyenne Autumn* (1964) is a pro-Cheyenne telling of the Army's attempt to force the Cheyenne from their homelands to a reservation. *Mad Magazine*'s parody, *Cheyenne Awful*, features a background Indian commenting, "Notice how the director gave the five leading Indian roles to three Spaniards, an American, and an Italian, while we *real* Indians play crummy extras!" To be fair to Ford, the three "Spaniards"—Dolores Del Rio, Ricardo Montalban, and Gilbert Roland—were all Mexican by birth and presumably of Indian as well as Spanish blood.

"Paul Newman nailed it," Michael Horse says of his performance in 1967's *Hombre*, Elmore Leonard's Western take on J. M. Barrie's *The Admirable Crichton*. Newman is the self-possessed white-raised-by-Apaches whose path crosses with a stagecoach full of "real" whites, including embezzling Indian Agent Fredric March and outlaw Richard Boone. Directed by Martin Ritt, the film makes social points that are organic yet startling.

Michael Horse recalls, "*Little Big Man* was the first time I saw one of those funny old elders that I grew up with, and Chief Dan George was just magic. 'Am I still in this world?' 'Yes, grandpa.' Dustin Hoffman tells him, 'I have a white wife.' 'Does she show enthusiasm when you mount her?'" *Little Big Man* (1970) is the story of the only white survivor of Custer's Last Stand. A jarring mix of broad humor and horrendous slaughter, the brutality in the depiction of the Army and Richard Mulligan's portrayal of Custer as a preening half-wit make it unforgettable.

In *Chato's Land* (1972), all Charles Bronson's half-breed Chato wants is to enjoy a drink at the saloon, but when a lawman gives him no other choice, Chato kills him. A posse pursues him into the desert, not realizing they've become Chato's quarry. With almost no dialogue, performing almost entirely alone, Bronson gives a calm dignity and perseverance to his character.

In David Wolper and Stan Margulis's 1975 Emmy-nominated production *I Will Fight No More Forever*, the unpunished murder of an Indian by a white begins an unwanted war. Famed one-armed Gen. Oliver O. Howard (James Whitmore) is ordered to force the Nez Perce onto a reservation. Chief Joseph (Ned Romero) befuddles the general with his superior tactics, keeping his tribe one step ahead of the Army for more than a hundred days, nearly reaching Canada before surrendering with the words that are the film's title. Written by Jeb Rosebrook and Theodore Strauss, the TV movie features a young Sam Elliott as Indian-sympathetic Capt. Charles E. S. Wood.

In 1975, independent rural filmmaker Charles B. Pierce wrote and directed *Winterhawk*. When a Blackfeet village is struck with smallpox, Winterhawk (Michael Dante) goes to a mountain man rendezvous to trade pelts for medicine but is instead bushwhacked and robbed by badman L. Q. Jones. Winterhawk captures a white sister (Dawn Wells) and brother to trade for medicine. Notable for its cast, the pursuers are Leif Erickson, Woody Strode, Denver Pyle, and Elisha Cook Jr. Dante notes, "When you're playing a Native American, you have to speak with your hands in the dirt psychologically, to relate to the moon, the wind and stars, the elements, the environment. They're very spiritual. He was not written as a spiritual man. I brought that." It was the last time Dante would play an Indian. "Now they won't hire a white man. They don't need to; they have a lot of wonderful actors. Graham Greene, Wes Studi, Zahn McClarnon, Adam Beach—he's an outstanding actor." Dante was delighted to learn that one of his favorite current actors made his first visit to a set on *Winterhawk*. "I grew up in Montana," says *Longmire*'s Zahn McClarnon. "They were looking for extra women. My mom is this gorgeous Lakota woman, and she went onto the set to be an extra. And I met Woody Strode. I was like six or seven, I wouldn't go ask for his autograph. But I finally got the nerve to."

What are some of McClarnon's favorite Indian films? "*One Flew Over the Cuckoo's Nest* and *Josey Wales*." Cody Jones concurs. "Clint Eastwood used Chief Dan George in *Outlaw Josey Wales*, that's one I enjoy a whole lot. Even today, the image of the native is the great warrior of the plains, the stoic. But reality is, American Indian culture has a lot of laughing. And Will Sampson: big guy, big presence. It was awesome to see Clint bring the natives into the forefront like he did." At least the first half of *Josey Wales*, one of Eastwood's best films, is about a farmer seeking revenge on the Union soldiers who slaughtered his family. But it's the humor and the humanity that stays with you.

In *Legend of Walks Far Woman* (1982), Raquel Welch's character, banished by her Blackfeet tribe, tries to make a life with her mother's Sioux people. This is a woman's story full of unusual situations, like dealing with her husband after a concussion suffered at the Little Bighorn makes him violent. The only whites seen are the dead cavalrymen whose pockets are emptied.

Dances with Wolves (1990) was the game changer. In addition to being an excellent film and an astounding first-time directing effort by Kevin Costner, no other film had ever given so many major roles to native actors: Graham Greene, Rodney A. Grant, Floyd "Red Crow" Westerman, Tantoo Cardinal, Wes Studi, and nearly a dozen others. *The Last of the Mohicans* (1992) continued the same trajectory. Michael Mann's film, the 9th version in America alone, starred Daniel-Day Lewis, Madeleine Stowe, and Wes Studi, and introduced many audiences to Russell Means and Eric Schweig. Both films combine romance and thrilling action, compelling characters, and seemingly doomed civilizations. They are both beautifully made films. *Mohicans* made a fortune, and *Wolves* is the most successful Western of all time.

Geronimo—An American Legend is the 1993 masterpiece of director Walter Hill, writer John Milius, and star Wes Studi. A lavish war movie as well as a Western, it follows Geronimo from his surrender to the Army, to his followers' and his own mistreatment, to his escape to Mexico, and beyond. The problems of the chain of command are highlighted, as Geronimo puts his faith in General Crook (Gene Hackman), and Lieutenant Gatewood (Jason Patric), whose actions are controlled from Washington.

Unlike Chief Joseph, Sitting Bull and his Lakota followers did manage to reach Canada, but not for long. *Bury My Heart at Wounded Knee*, the heartbreaking 2007 TV movie, is seen largely through the eyes of Charles Eastman (Adam Beach). As a Sioux child he's taken from his parents and sent to a school to be Americanized: his hair cut, his clothing replaced, forbidden to use his native language, he's even forced to take on a Christian name. But when the educators see how bright he is, he's sent to college and medical school, used as a PR tool by the government, and finally returns to Standing Rock, where he tries desperately to fit in and to save his people.

In the past several years, there have been three impressive Indian-centered Westerns. *Hostiles* stars Wes Studi as a long-imprisoned Cheyenne chief finally allowed to return to his ancestral home. Christian Bale is the Indian-hating Army captain who reluctantly agrees to escort him. It feels spiritually like a continuation of Studi's earlier *Geronimo*. *Woman Walks Ahead* stars Jessica Chastain as Catherine Weldon, a New York painter who journeyed out West to paint a portrait of Sitting Bull (Michael Greyeyes) and becomes involved in the Sioux battle to protect their land. *The Last Manhunt* is a tragedy based on the same historical events as *Tell Them Willie Boy Is Here*, in which Willie Boy (Martin Sensmeier) loves Carlotta (Mainei Kinimaka), but her father (Zahn McLarnon) forbids their marriage because they are cousins, and violence and a manhunt ensue.

EDWARD S. CURTIS AND THE HOLLYWOOD HEADHUNTERS

While Edward S. Curtis's photographs, and especially his twenty volumes of *The North American Indian*, are an archive of incalculable value, their sheer vastness predetermined that they would rarely reach the common man. And just like George Catlin, painter of Indian portraits before him, Curtis was on a mission: to preserve the history of a people the government was trying to—if not extinguish—homogenize out of existence. And what better way to

Edward S. Curtis's film crew worked closely with Kwakwaka'wakw artisans to build homes, totems, props, costumes, and war canoes for use in *In the Land of the Head Hunters. Courtesy Seattle Film Company and Milestone Film & Video*

reach the man-on-the-street than with the great entertainment form of the 20th century, the movie?

A dramatic story about Indian characters, set in the time before white men arrived in North America, would give Curtis the chance to show their way of life. Thus was born *In the Land of the Head Hunters*, a dozen years before the coming of sound films.

Focusing on the Kwakwaka'wakw people of Washington State and Canada, Curtis spent three years preparing and making the film. According to a 1914 issue of *The Clipper*, "Mr. Curtis had to live in a North Coast Village for a year before the Indians of that village and two others consented to enact for him the dramatic legends of their clans." He gained an ally in George Hunt, who despite his Anglicized name was a Kwakwaka'wakw member. The Potlatch, a centuries-old traditional gathering of people of the Pacific Northwest—involving dancing, ceremonies, giving of gifts, wonderful masks and costumes—had been banned by Canada under The Indian Act in 1884, as wasteful and anti-Christian. Any Indian who took part was "liable to imprisonment for a term of not more than six nor less than two months." The ban would not be repealed until 1951.

But moviemaking was not a crime; it was to be encouraged. And Curtis hired Hunt and many other tribe members to produce "movie props and costumes," which just happened to be identical to the banned artifacts, and filmed their rituals, whose performance would have been a crime, were it not "acting." On-set photos show that Hunt helped direct key sequences.

The story is of Motana, young son of a chief, embarking on a vision journey, fasting and performing brave deeds to increase his power. In a vision, he sees beautiful Naida, and when he meets her, learns that she has been promised in marriage to Kwagwanu, the evil sorcerer. This leads to war between their villages. Among the astonishing events filmed are Motana's attack on an island of sea lions, the hunting of an immense—and real—whale, sea battles between war canoes, costumed dances of the grizzly bear and thunderbird, all recorded gloriously by the eye of Curtis.

The reviews were spectacular: *Motion Picture Magazine* said, "As a drama, it is compelling in its charm, but as a gem of the instructive film, it has rarely been equaled." *Motion Picture News* noted, "Many of the scenes make one's hair stand on end, and there are not a few who are still wondering whether these headsmen really decapitated their victims during their various battles, so realistic and true to life are they enacted."

Motion Picture World was most impressed of all: "Mr. Curtis conceived this wonderful story in ethnology as an epic. . . . This production sets a new mark in artistic handling of films in which educational values mingle with dramatic interest."

Head Hunters was a disheartening financial flop. Why? Andrew Erish, film historian and author of *Vitagraph—America's First Great Motion Picture Studio*, says, "Curtis obviously hadn't gotten to the movies very much." The same year that Western blockbusters like *The Spoilers*, *The Virginian*, and DeMille's *The Squaw Man* were released, "Curtis's love triangle is entirely dependent on [reading] the inter-titles. It's almost impossible to identify anyone from shot to shot—there are no close-ups, no two-shots. There's no attempt at conveying romance. There's an utter lack of dynamics regarding individual characters or relationships."

Even in a spectacular moment, when Motana emerges from the mouth of the whale, instead of staying in character, he mugs shamelessly at the camera, like it was a home movie. As a contemporary, and very enthusiastic, review in *Motography* said, "While no . . . acting, in the theatrical sense of the word, is attempted by the Indians, every movement breathes the primitive life in which their people were raised." But acting is what audiences expected.

Despite a few high-profile bookings, Erish explains, "None of the big-time distributors picked it up. It ended up getting distributed by organizations that solely handled films for schools and churches." The general public never got a chance to see the film, although it was still being booked at churches and schools into the 1940s.

Curtis made two more films, both documentaries, in 1916: *The Alaskan Indians* and *Seeing America*, about the wildlife in Yellowstone Park.

This was about the end of Curtis's Hollywood sojourn. Although in 1923 he was named to co-head DeMille's Camera Department, which a Paramount press release described as "the most coveted job in motion picture photography," that job only entailed shooting stills for *Adam's Rib* and the silent version of *The Ten Commandments*.

More than a century after it failed to get a true theatrical release, a remarkable reconstruction of Edward Curtis's masterpiece, *In the Land of the Headhunters*, is now available from Milestone Film & Video. A 16mm print from Chicago's Field Museum, combined with recently discovered 35mm nitrate reels from UCLA and reference stills from the Library of Congress, created this version, which features original color-tinting and is accompanied by a newly recorded version of John J. Braham's original orchestra score. The two-disc set includes new and old documentaries, featuring memories of original cast members, their children and grandchildren, and visits to locations. There are audio recordings Curtis made in 1910 of Kwakwaka'wakw chants and songs, and a 1973 reconstruction, retitled *In the Land of the War Canoes*, which, though incomplete, adds convincing sound effects, dialogue, and authentic Kwakwaka'wakw music.

CHAPTER 11

THE NEW WESTERNS

FORSAKEN

"This was a film that I've been dreaming of making for thirty-some-odd years," Kiefer Sutherland told the audience when *Forsaken* premiered at the Autry Museum of the American West in Los Angeles, California. In *Forsaken*, he is directed by his cohort from Fox's *24*, Jon Cassar, who remembers, "We worked together for almost nine years. Between set-ups, we always talked about the kind of movie we'd love to work on together. And he always wanted to do a Western."

Considering their previous success with *24*, for which they both earned Emmys, you might expect a high-tech, edgy sci-fi Western from the pair. But you would be dead wrong. "I was taking a chance," Cassar admits, "looking backwards rather than forwards with the Western."

Kiefer plays John Henry Clayton, a Union soldier coming home from the Civil War. But he has taken a decade to return, years he spent as a gun-for-hire. He gives up the guns but arrives home to find his mother dead, his father, Rev. Clayton (played by Kiefer's real father, movie icon Donald Sutherland), unforgiving, and the love of his life, Mary-Alice Watson (Demi Moore), married and a mother. The hometown where he planned to settle down is under attack by land baron James McCurdy (*Deadwood*'s Brian Cox), whose gunmen are systematically driving out settlers who refuse to sell land so he can profit from the incoming railroad.

Cassar admits that Western movie lovers will find familiar themes in the story that has been developed over the years by Kiefer and scripted by Brad Mirman: "There are similarities to a million Westerns you've seen before. The land baron has been the villain of so many, but [the character so well] reflected the lengths these ambitious men would go to."

"It was interesting to get those characters we've seen before and give them some sense of reality. We did that with an incredible script and with incredible actors," Cassar says, from nervous townspeople to hired thugs, to an elegant, aging gunfighter exceptionally played by Michael Wincott.

Kiefer's Western roots run deep. He earned his spurs playing "Doc" Scurlock in 1988's *Young Guns* and in the 1990 sequel. He took a couple of years off from acting to become a rancher and rodeo cowboy, and not just for show: Kiefer and partner John English won the US Team Roping Championship in 1998.

This isn't Donald's first rodeo either. In 1974, he was the title character in *Dan Candy's Law*, a Mountie tracking a Cree fugitive. But *Forsaken* is the first time father and son have acted together in a film.

"My father is an actor who I've always wanted to emulate," Kiefer says. "I've had such a deep respect for his choices in storytelling, for his unbelievable breadth that allows him to move from character to character, just seamlessly and flawlessly."

"When you see two actors looking into each other's eyes, father and son playing father and son, there's something there that is magic," Cassar adds.

That magic is particularly true in a scene with them alone in church, son telling father about the war, and his life since. "Even Donald cried in that," Cassar says. "Donald said to me, 'I had no plan to cry whatsoever. But it was my son, and he was so hurt. Even though it was a fictional story, it was hurting him. So to tell that story that emotionally, it got to me too.'"

Filmed in Alberta, Canada, *Forsaken* is a tight, focused ninety minutes. "There was a sizable [secondary] story, a wannabe gunslinger and his love—a parallel love story to Kiefer and Demi's. Kiefer's character was trying to end his life as a gun-for-hire, and this young man was excited to start one. They did a wonderful job, but I wanted to keep the story focused on father and son. Having to tell them that they were cut out of the film was very difficult," Cassar says.

"We made this picture two years ago. We had financial problems; it was sitting on the shelf for a while. But it's coming out when there are a bunch of other Westerns, which is fantastic," Cassar says.

Cassar is proud of his non-CGI movie. "There are no phones, no computers. It strips down your story to such basic elements that all the other 'noise' goes away. There's a simplicity to Western storytelling that people are attracted to," he says. "It really gets down to who the characters are and how they interact. *Forsaken* is a pleasing movie to watch, without all that noise."

THE MAGNIFICENT SEVEN

Remaking a classic movie is daring, and director Antoine Fuqua made the challenge a double dare by remaking two at once: 1960's *The Magnificent Seven* and the Japanese classic that movie is based on, 1954's *Seven Samurai.* For the remake, Fuqua reunited with actors from 2001's *Training Day*, Denzel Washington and Ethan Hawke.

The remakers have attacked their challenge with gusto. Richard Wenk, one of two credited screenwriters for the 2016 film, told me, "Antoine is almost savant-ish in the way he approaches action. He's constantly trying to make sure it's real, and the action just kept getting better."

The action is, truly, magnificent. Stunt coordinator Jeffrey Dashnaw, of 2015's *The Hateful Eight*, with his crew of more than forty, does a breathtaking job, as does Oscar-winning cinematographer Mauro Fiore.

But when remaking a classic, one must not lose sight of the elements that made a work a classic in the first place.

In Akira Kurosawa's *Seven Samurai*, set in 16th-century Japan, a farming village hires unemployed samurai to defend against bandits who have been robbing the harvests, although the village can pay only in food. The brilliant story of character, action, humor, and hope made it appealing as a Western.

Producer Lou Morheim wangled the remake rights for $2,500. The only bona fide box office star going in, Yul Brynner, hoped to direct rather than star. Instead, producer Walter Mirisch, whose earlier fine Westerns were made at Monogram, starring Joel McCrea, hired John Sturges, who directed 1954's *Bad Day at Black Rock* and 1957's *Gunfight at the O.K. Corral.* Mirisch recalled watching the original film with Sturges: "The two of us sat alone in a projection room . . . and had the best time ever, translating all of the sequences of Mr. Kurosawa's movie into the Western motif."

Originally the '*seven*' were to be an older, world-weary group, led by Spencer Tracy. Anthony Quinn planned to produce and star, but his role, Toshiro Mifune's over-the-top comic character, was retooled to be the romantic interest, for young German actor Horst Bucholtz. Broadway star Eli Wallach likewise wanted the Mifune part but instead played bandit leader Calvera. They switched the locale to Mexico where, again, farmers were victimized by bandits. These farmers went north to buy guns but instead hired unemployed gunmen who were willing to risk their lives for about $20 apiece.

The 1960 Western is crisply paced; the 2016 remake, ambling. The 1960 Western is full of humor; the 2016 remake rarely provokes a smile. Fuqua's film shifts the locale from a Mexican village to a cliche frontier town under the thumb of the now-generic greedy land-cattle-oil-gold baron.

After a wincingly melodramatic opening, bounty hunter Sam Chisolm (played by Washington) rides into a different town, *Shane*-like, costume and whiskers in an homage to Fred Williamson's Westerns. A saloon arrest triggers a shoot-out, and Josh Faraday (Chris Pratt) comes to his aid. A woman who has fled the baron's town a widow (Haley Bennett) hires Chisolm to drive out the villains. He assembles his seven.

In the 1960 classic, you learn all you need to about the seven in succinct glimpses: Charles Bronson's character once made big money but is now reduced to chopping firewood for meals. Robert Vaughn's character is on the lam from an honor double murder.

In the remake, more time is spent introducing the characters, but you get less of a sense of them. While Chisolm's seven are more diverse, you learn nothing about these characters beyond "he's a Mexican; he's an Asian; he's an American Indian."

In all three versions, men who have been selfish in the past risk their lives to do good. The two classics are tales of redemption; the men face death without gain. In the remake, redemption is blurred because we never learn if the leather pouch that's being tossed around holds a little money or a lot.

This lack of crucial detail plagues the picture. Until the seven free the enslaved gold miners, you never have any inkling that enslaved miners are out there to be freed. When Chisolm has his showdown with the baron, revealing their personal history, with absolutely no foreshadowing, the moment comes too late to matter; it feels like the filmmakers' afterthought.

A hero can only be as heroic as his villain is formidable, and the baron villain, the talented but horribly miscast Peter Sarsgaard, comes off as the sort of twerp any one of the seven could have taken on with both arms tied behind their backs. The comparison of that villain to the bandit leader Calvera is ludicrous. Eli Wallach played Calvera so richly that it has become the portrayal by which all bandit characters are judged.

The 1960 Western was a career-making film for the actors, who had to be signed quickly, before a looming Screen Actors Guild strike. Bronson became the highest-priced actor in Hollywood. Vaughn grew into his world-famous role in the late 1960s' *The Man from U.N.C.L.E.* James Coburn parlayed his near-silent role into stardom and ended up with an Oscar in 1999. Steve McQueen, then starring on *Wanted: Dead or Alive*, wanted the part so bad that he caused a car wreck to get out of his series commitment;

the ultra-cool star earned an Oscar nomination seven years later. Brad Dexter would up his acting profile, then switch to producing. Mirisch would go on to produce three sequels and a TV series, and was an executive producer on the remake.

Washington, Hawke, Pratt, and Vincent D'Onofrio are already famous. This less-than-magnificent film in their otherwise stellar careers will, unfortunately for Westerns fans everywhere, disappoint more than reinforce their star power.

DEAD MEN

"The title *Dead Men* is in regards to our main protagonists, Jesse and Jake. The odds of their survival and subsequent overthrow of the main antagonist, Cole, were so impossible—improbable—that they might as well have been dead men," recalls director Royston Innes.

Walmart shoppers grabbing a DVD of the 2018 Vision Films Western *Dead Men*, directed by Royston Innes, starring Ric Maddox and co-written by the pair, might be surprised to learn that the three-hour drama first rolled camera more than six years earlier.

"The flashbacks work so well because Ric and the others look so much younger," Innes says. "It had literally been a couple of years, and the age shows."

"A couple of Hollywood years," adds Maddox, with a chuckle. "You know, a Hollywood year is like five years on a Texas ranch."

Which is where Maddox grew up. Innes left Australia when he was age nineteen, "and lived on several continents," before he arrived at Playhouse West in Los Angeles, California. Maddox, fresh from the Iraq War and from New York's Stella Adler Conservatory, met Innes doing a play. Each was impressed with the other's intensity and commitment.

To make their Western, they drew their inspiration from nearly the same source. "My favorite movie is *Lonesome Dove*; his favorite book is *Lonesome Dove*. I keep threatening to read the book," Maddox says.

But *Dead Men* didn't begin its life as a movie. "Our focus was to get a Western in the hands of a younger generation, eighteen to thirty-five, people who normally had little interest in the [genre]," Innes says. "We did it as a web series, to bring in the younger crowd."

Although their project first screened on the Internet, the format, in many ways, is an update of the Republic-style serial, telling brief chapters of a dramatic story, often with a cliffhanger ending.

"It was to be a celebration of a certain type of man," Innes explains. "The type of spirit that we wanted to bring back; that grit, that feeling of anything is possible. And we're living examples of this. Our grit, and the fact that anything is possible, is the only reason this thing got made."

Working with boundless enthusiasm and precious little money, the first season was posted in ten eight- to ten-minute chapters. Shot in Western movie towns and rugged locations all over Arizona, the story is about Jesse Struthers (Maddox), who barely escapes when his father is murdered by a hired gun (Craig Hensley) for his gold mine claim. When Jesse, his father's close friend (Brent Rock), and Jesse's ne'er-do-well brother Jake (Aaron Marciniak) try to go up against claim jumper and would-be politician Cole Roberts (Richard O. Ryan), blood spills. Jesse nearly dies, only to be rescued by an Apache warrior (Sam Bearpaw).

And that is just the first twenty minutes!

Although Innes and Maddox transformed their webisodes into a movie, their chapter format plays better as a two-part miniseries, which is how German TV aired the movie.

The cast may not be marquee names, but they are a fine ensemble with extensive credits on TV and in features. The longer-running format also gives secondary characters the chance to have their own intense stories.

"Roy's catchphrase, that I love, was 'Let's get salty, boys.' By that he meant, let's be intense, not namby-pamby. Roy was superb; he's an actor's director. I'm impressed as hell with what Ric and Roy pulled together," Hensley says.

Salty indeed, the film features powerful, memorable action scenes, including a knife fight between Brent Rock and Malcolm Madera, elegant bullwhip-work by Anthony De Longis, and a ferocious battle between Apaches and outlaws, all beautifully coordinated by the film's villain, Ryan.

Did Innes have any qualms about the amount of brutality in the film? "Well yeah—that it couldn't be more so. I have no problems with brutality if it's earned. The eighteen- to thirty-five-year-olds see a lot of Quentin Tarantino–esque violence," he says.

"But what I found within the first couple of months that we've been out, we've had a lot of success with the older generations as well, who're just looking for a good old-fashioned, honest Western. So that's been a win."

The role of Apaches grows as the story progresses, including a wife for Struthers, played by Marisa Quintanilla. "Hollywood tends to amalgamate tribes, and we wanted to stay true to who the Apaches [are]," Maddox says. "I think I'm the only white guy speaking Chiricahua Apache, but there's just something really powerful in that language, and I wanted to honor that."

Innes was grateful that the Indian actors stuck with them: "A lot of these guys came all the way down from White Mountain Apache reservation, six hours away. I'm so proud of the Apache attack at the end; all Apaches, and great riders, too."

The satisfying ending leaves an opening for a sequel. Innes says, "If this ends up being successful enough to be able to make the second chapter, we're ready to do it."

BIG KILL

Scott Martin has been cautiously optimistic about the future of Western films: "Until this resurgence, there hasn't been the appetite for them. But we're talking about doing them again—and I can't wait!"

At 2017's American Film Market, he shared his belief that filmmakers in that genre "have to either make them small, as best you can with the resources you have, or you have to go big; there's not a lot of middle ground."

Martin was nowhere to be found at the 2018 market; he was busy directing his first Western, *Big Kill*, from his own screenplay. At a budget of more than $1 million, this Western is small, but it's a big step up from his 2012 directorial debut, the WWII action film *Battle Force*, which he made for $35,000 in ten shooting days.

For *Big Kill*, released in September 2018, Martin attracted stars with strong Western credits, including Jason Patric, of 1993's *Geronimo* and 2004's *The Alamo*, Lou Diamond Phillips, Michael Paré, and Danny Trejo.

The attraction began with the writing. "Scott's script was a lot of fun," Phillips says. "From page one, I thought, wow, this is reminiscent of *Butch Cassidy and the Sundance Kid*."

Phillips, beloved as Henry Standing Bear on *Longmire*, but who will always be Chavez y Chavez to fans of 1988's *Young Guns*, adds, "It had this retro feel; it wasn't a cynical, gritty kind of Western. It was more of a real adventure, like *Silverado*."

"That's why I'm doing this, to have people be able to sit down and forget about the world problems, their own problems, and just be entertained for a couple of hours," Martin says.

Big Kill combines humor, a compelling story, a little attractive nudity and plenty of action, with several thrilling shoot-outs. Cinematographer Mark Atkins captures not only the action but also the stunningly beautiful New

Mexico vistas—sometimes the horses seem to walk slower than need be, just to hold onto the view a little longer. All of it is wrapped up in Kays Al-Atrakchi's rousing, classically Western score.

Big Kill is the story of two likable drifters who would put down roots if they weren't always being run out of places: handsome lady's man Travis Parker (played by Clint Hummel) and poor gambler but good shot Jake Logan (Martin—yes, he also acts). They're being run out of Mexico by General Morales (Danny Trejo) when they encounter tenderfoot Jim Andrews (*Last Man Standing*'s Cristoph Sanders), a Philadelphia accountant. Widower Andrews is responding to a two-year-old letter to join his brother in the silver boomtown of Big Kill. When Parker and Logan learn the brother owns a saloon, they agree to escort Jim.

When the trio arrives, the men discover the boomtown has gone bust, the brother is nowhere to be seen, and the Easy Lady Saloon and the town overall are in the clutches of a mysterious preacher (Patric), backed by his smiling gunslinger, Johnny Kane (Phillips).

With a career of playing good men and good bad men, Phillips relished playing a *bad* bad man in the Jack Palance mold. "I haven't played a bad guy like this. At this point in my career, it's getting harder and harder to find things that I haven't done. I'd actually grown that mustache as an homage to Charles Bronson."

The costume design, by former HBO *Deadwood* costumer Toby Bronson, is stylish, individual, and appropriate, but Phillips' burgundy ensemble is striking. "Scott asked me, do you want to go a little flamboyant with this? I said, absolutely man; my other Western characters had been on the subdued side."

Phillips felt at home filming at New Mexico's Bonanza Creek Ranch. "I had actually shot on that set for *Young Guns*. There were a number of buildings and locations in that town that I had been on before. Matter of fact, we stayed in the same hotel, and there were a number of people that were not only on that crew, but some *Longmire* people as well."

Every movie production has its challenges. "Shooting with animals just takes longer than you anticipate," Martin learned. "Great as the wranglers are, horses are still animals. If they're not wanting to stand where you want them to, you just have to go with it. The cold weather was a bit of a surprise. Shooting inside the saloon, you can see our breath."

Phillips laughs at that, saying, "Every time I do a Western, we do it in the dead of freaking winter. Even though the sun was shining, it hovered around thirty-five degrees; some nights it got down to seventeen. People were having to shed their massive arctic winter coats before a take."

Before he'd even rolled camera, Martin knew what was coming next. "I have a sequel that continues the adventures of Jake and Travis. It's called *Settle the Score with a .44.*"

HELL OR HIGH WATER

You know you're in Texas when a pair of ski-masked men rob a crowded bank, and nearly every customer pulls a gun and opens fire. The impromptu posse that takes off after the robbers would throw a scare into the James Gang!

Hell or High Water is the modern-day Western story of brothers who, like Jesse James and brother Frank, have problems with banks: in this case, the bank's imminent foreclosure on Ma's ranch. Ben Foster plays Tanner and is as frightening here, as a gregarious fellow, as he was playing Russell Crowe's humorless wingman in 2007's *3:10 to Yuma.* He's just out of prison, and brother Toby, played by Chris Pine (known for his role as Capt. James T. Kirk in the rebooted *Star Trek),* divorced and with sons to support, comes up with a wonderfully awful idea: raise the money for the mortgage by robbing branches of the bank that holds the paper.

Hell or High Water is also the story of the pair of Texas Rangers investigating the holdups: widowed, soon-to-be-retired Marcus (Jeff Bridges) and his esteemed, but much-badgered Comanche partner Alberto Parker (portrayed by a Comanche, Gil Birmingham, who first gained notice as Billy Black in the *Twilight* films).

Birmingham was happy to play Parker for many reasons. "It's rare that you see a character of that ethnic background portrayed in such a positive light," he says. "The natives are still here; we've been portrayed in the past as if we don't exist anymore. [This movie] had a special meaning for me because my father was a lawman for most of his career. He was a military policeman and also a Texan, so many of these aspects fell into place just automatically."

Hell or High Water is helmed by David Mackenzie, a director and writer who has elegantly tackled crime dramas that include 2003's *Young Adam,* sci-fi flicks that include 2011's *Perfect Sense,* and romantic comedies such as 2011's *Tonight You're Mine.*

"I did have qualms about making a Western," Mackenzie recalled. "Not necessarily as a Scot, because many of the protagonists of the story of the West were of Scots ancestry, but as someone with a strong admiration for the great films in that genre—it's hard to follow in those footsteps. I abandoned an attempt to write a Western a few years ago because I felt like I was at the bottom of a butte in Monument Valley looking up at a genre I couldn't possibly add to. When this script came along, it was like a gift that allowed me to connect to this lineage in a fresh and interesting way."

That script is by Taylor Sheridan who, though now legendary for creating *Yellowstone* and its decedents, was in 2016 best known as an actor. He'd starred in FX's *Sons of Anarchy* before turning writer, stunning audiences with 2015's clever and tough *Sicario*, about an FBI agent embroiled in the drug wars at the US-Mexico border.

"When I came across this script, I thought it was absolutely brilliant," Birmingham says. "I was curious to know how he had the sensibilities about the native character, and it turns out he lived on the Lakota reservation for six or seven years." Subsequent to *Hell or High Water*, Birmingham would star for Taylor Sheridan in the film *Wind River* and the series *Yellowstone*.

One major appeal of the film is Jeff Bridges' performance as a Texas Ranger, a fitting follow-up to his Rooster Cogburn portrayal in 2010's *True Grit* and a strong addition to a half century of Western roles that began on father Lloyd Bridges' series, 1965's *The Loner*. Like John Wayne, Bridges has matured into his later Western roles, bringing layered and nuanced qualities. Says Mackenzie, "I am an enormous fan of Jeff and his films. He was incredibly creative and a real gentleman—it's a fantastic performance with some real magic."

Birmingham says he and Bridges have a strong personal connection. "I was surprised at how similar we were—he's a very Zen kind of guy. We also connected in a major way, with music. Every time we went on the set, I can hear Jeff saying, 'Did you bring your guitar?' I said, 'We're working, Jeff. When are we going to have time?' 'Well, you never know. But if we do, we're going to jam!'"

The film's cat and mouse story, more rooted in character than elaborate plotting, features a gem of a scene early on in which an old man is showing a teller a shoebox full of coins when the robbers enter the bank. The old man is Buck Taylor, Newly from CBS's *Gunsmoke*, who has taken over for the late Harry Carey Jr. and Ben Johnson as the man you cast to prove you're making a real Western.

With two pairs of characters diametrically opposed, the question arises: Who do you root for? Birmingham's character has no pity for his quarry. "It's the Ranger creed: our job is to protect property and life. [The brothers'] motivations aren't pertinent to us," he says.

Director Mackenzie doesn't want the audience to see things quite so black and white. "It was always the intention of this film to have some sympathy for the outlaws," he says. "There's a long tradition of this sympathy in Scottish culture—the defiant outlaw-hero ballad—that was directly transplanted into American culture. I think we care about these guys because, in different circumstances, it could be us doing what they're doing."

THE LEGEND OF BEN HALL

Can a film be a Western if the story takes place on the other side of the globe?

Writer-director Matthew Holmes makes a convincing case. "In the 'Wild West' period, Australia and America had the same things happening at the same time—gold rushes, outlaws, lawmen, the frontier, conflicts with the indigenous people, rebellions—the list goes on and on," he says.

While the United States had its outlaws, Australia had its bushrangers, and Holmes has filmed the life of one of Australia's most famous, in *The Legend of Ben Hall*. "Ned Kelly is the most famous; Ben Hall is probably second—but he was far more prolific than Kelly when you compare criminal careers," Holmes says. "The Hall Gang roamed and robbed for over three years, and Hall committed over six hundred major crimes: highway robbery, mail coach robbery, store robbery, horse 'borrowing,' arson, assault, and gunfights."

Before Hall was born, his English father and Irish mother were convicted of minor thefts and sent to New South Wales, where they met as convicts, and married.

"Ben Hall distanced himself from his father. By age twenty-three, he was a successful landowner and cattleman, with a wife and son, well-regarded by all. However, the 1862 gold rush directly hit his area and brought the criminal element," Holmes says.

"Hall had no criminal record until his life fell apart—his wife ran away with his friend and took their young son with her," he adds. "He fell into depression and abandoned his work, becoming the friend of a highly successful career criminal called Frank Gardiner, who lured him in. His descent is fascinating, as he was somewhat a reluctant criminal."

Often described as an Australian Jesse James or Billy the Kid, the Kid comparison seems unfair. While the American outlaw claimed to have murdered twenty-one men, "Ben Hall himself never killed anyone, even though he was involved in numerous gunfights and scrapes. He had a very firm position against taking human life unless his own was threatened," Holmes says. "Unfortunately, his companions didn't share that code and they killed policemen, for which Hall was considered an accomplice."

The range of the "Gentleman Bushranger" was vast. "The state of New South Wales is larger than California and New Mexico combined; the Hall Gang roamed over twenty thousand square miles," Holmes says. "They were superb bushmen and riders, and since they were constantly stealing race-horses, catching them out in the wilderness was virtually impossible."

As with American outlaws, bushrangers were hard to catch in part because they enjoyed popular support. "Hall had a lot of allies who knew him before he was a criminal and respected him. The bushrangers became 'poster boys' for those who hated the harsh and corrupt British system. One coach service from Sydney to the goldfields had a timetable with the clause, 'Ben Hall permitting,' on it," Holmes says.

Desperate to catch Hall, the Australian government passed an astonishing law in 1865 aimed directly at him. "The dreaded 'Felons Apprehension Act' declared Ben Hall [and his accomplices] John Gilbert and John Dunn outlaws who could be killed by any person, at any time, without question. This act was only brought out again against bushranger Ned Kelly and gang thirteen years later," Holmes says.

The Legend of Ben Hall does not attempt to tell Hall's entire story. Holmes clarifies: "Our film focuses on the last nine months of Hall's life, when his criminal career was at its most critical and conflicted. It's jam-packed with action, adventure, tragedy, betrayal, and romance."

Most who have tried crowdfunding to finance their films have failed. But Holmes successfully raised money through a Kickstarter campaign to shoot a trailer of *The Legend of Ben Hall*, and he used the trailer to raise the money for the feature.

"If you can make the public love the project as you do—so much that they are willing to dig into their pockets now to ensure it gets made—then you have a chance," Holmes says. "When they make it a beg for people's charity, they inevitably fail.

"We've attempted to make an epic Western on a tiny budget. And because this is set 150 years ago, nothing from that time period exists any-more, so we've had to build all our own sets, props, and source costumes and weapons that are period accurate, which is never easy or cheap."

While the Western is not a documentary, "Authenticity has been my biggest goal," Holmes admits. "I've got Australia's leading authority on Ben Hall as my script consultant. It's risky sticking to history because it makes the story unpredictable and unconventional. But it makes the characters very three-dimensional. I think it's the reason people will embrace the movie, the fact that it is so close to history."

Holmes plans *The Legend of Ben Hall* to be part one of a trilogy. The other subjects would be bushranger John Vane and Hall's criminal mentor Frank Gardiner, who ended up in California, running a saloon in San Francisco's Barbary Coast.

CHAPTER 12

NOT YOUR ALL-AMERICAN, LILY-WHITE WESTERNS

BUFFALO SOLDIERS

The Buffalo Soldier and his crucial role in the post–Civil War West went unacknowledged for so long in history annals that his story was rarely told on film. Just shy of a century, from the 1866 formation of the black cavalry units, John Ford made the first and finest film on the subject, 1960's *Sergeant Rutledge*.

A courtroom drama as well as a Western, the movie was a complex and incendiary story—the court-martial of black Sgt. Braxton Rutledge (played by Woody Strode) for the brutal rape and murder of a child, and the murder of her father, all of which were portrayed with flashbacks of the 9th Cavalry's fight against the Apaches. Ford's film dealt bravely with subjects few movies of the time dared. When another soldier asked Rutledge why he ran if he was innocent, he replied, "Because I walked into something none of us can fight: white woman business."

The leading lady of the film, Constance Towers, remembers, "It was a project that John Ford wanted to make for a long time. He was a great champion of the men who became the most heroic unit in the United States Cavalry."

Legendary Gold Medal decathlon athlete Rafer Johnson made his film debut, between Olympics, as a corporal. He remembers, "It was an honor to work with John Ford in his very special part of the world, Monument Valley—one of the most picturesque parts of the United States."

In some unexpected ways, the 1860s and the 1960s were not all that different. Towers recalls that, while filming in Four Corners, where Utah, Colorado, Arizona, and New Mexico meet, "We had an unusual adventure. We were on the Utah side. But the black men, Rafer Johnson and the others, couldn't stay where we stayed. They had to stay in a neighboring town; they were taken in a private plane to a motel someplace that would accept black men. It's hard to believe that in 1960, it was still that difficult to blend the colors."

Nevertheless, Johnson's memories of making the film are positive. "It was a very pleasant experience. I was not very aware of the Buffalo Soldiers beforehand, but when we did the movie, I [learned] of the wonderful job they did," he says. "They were segregated, but they were Americans, and they continued to do their job, to protect the people."

A decade passed before the premiere of the next movie about the Buffalo Soldiers, and in 1970's *Soul Soldier*, Rafer Johnson was promoted to the lead, even though his rank was demoted to private. An earnest attempt to show the day-to-day life of the individual soldiers while fighting the Apaches, the movie featured a cast that included Cesar Romero, Barbara Hale, and Isabel Sanford, and it was shot at Fort Davis in Texas, the actual headquarters for all four regiments. While the film showcases effective moments and some good performances, it is an unfocused story with a threadbare production. Johnson explains, "*Soul Soldier* was a university film. They had to do a lot of fundraising to make it a feature."

Between those films, the Buffalo Soldier made an occasional appearance on television. In *The High Chaparral* 1968 episode "The Buffalo Soldiers," Sgt. Maj. Creason (Yaphet Kotto) leads the 10th Cavalry as they bring law to unruly Tucson, Arizona, and, with the help of the Cannons, contend with racism. On *The Big Valley* episode in 1967 called "The Buffalo Man," the Barkleys hire convict labor to pick their peach crop and discover that Damien (again Yaphet Kotto) was a member of an all-black platoon Jarrod Barkley (Richard Long) commanded during the war. Although identified as a Buffalo Soldier in the show, that designation did not come about until after the Civil War.

In 1979, a one-hour Western pilot *Buffalo Soldiers* featured troops protecting settlers from Apaches and Comanches. Written and directed respectively by prolific *Gunsmoke* collaborators Jim Byrnes and Vincent McEveety, the episode had a high quality, but it was never seen again.

The best film on the subject since *Sergeant Rutledge* appeared in 1997, a TNT movie called *Buffalo Soldiers*. Starring and produced by Danny Glover, whose credits include *Lonesome Dove*, it tells a substantially true story of the pursuit of Apache leader Victorio. Dynamically directed by Charles Haid, the movie shows an army trapped between two enemies: the Apaches and white officers who would welcome failure by the black troops, to confirm prejudices. Filmed in Cochise Stronghold in Arizona's Coronado National Forest, William Wages' stunning camera work earned the American Society of Cinematographers' Outstanding Achievement Award. Although the ending feels contrived, an otherwise powerful script and supporting performances make this an exciting and thought-provoking movie.

Finally, bookended by the dedication of the Buffalo Soldier Monument in Fort Leavenworth, Kansas, Bill Armstrong's modest, but informative, 1992 documentary *The Buffalo Soldiers* succinctly tells the soldiers' story in forty-seven minutes. It closes with a moving speech by Chairman of the Joint Chiefs of Staff Colin Powell.

Nothing yet on these legendary soldiers, though, has come close to topping *Sergeant Rutledge*. Ford certainly made movie magic, by whatever means necessary. Towers recalls one rather deplorable trick the director played: "He had [Strode's wife] Luana tell him that their marriage was over; she was going back to Hawaii. And poor Woody was beside himself; he stayed up all night, and Pappy got him to drink a little more than Woody would have normally consumed. So, by the next morning, when he went in to do his breakdown scene in the courtroom, which was fantastic, he was well prepared to break down. But that was a typical John Ford trick, which I thought was terrible, but he did get a great performance out of him."

THE FILMS OF PANCHO VILLA

Pancho Villa was admired by some of the finest writers of the 20th century, and a surprising number wrote screenplays about him: Ben Hecht who, with Charles MacArthur, redefined our opinion of the press with 1931's *The Front Page*; Robert Towne, whose *Chinatown* screenplay is arguably the most important work of literature of the 1970s; Sam Peckinpah who, from *The Rifleman* series to 1973's *Pat Garrett and Billy the Kid*, brought a combination of reality and poetry to the West in particular and to manhood in general. Their views of the Mexican Revolution general offered cinemagoers wildly differing results.

Certain elements in Villa's life so appealed to filmmakers that they are found in virtually all Villa films. The writers relished his illiteracy. They ate up the fact that he married women at the drop of a sombrero—unofficially, more than two dozen. They appreciated that the seemingly 1870s-style story was really 20th century, replete with cars and planes.

They especially delighted in his American supporters. In 1934's *Viva Villa!* Villa's American ally is a reporter played by Stuart Erwin. In 1968's

American reporter Stuart Erwin, left, had better show more respect to Wallace Beery as Pancho Villa, right, or he'll have to answer to Leo Carrillo, center, in *Viva Villa! Courtesy Metro-Goldwyn-Mayer*

Villa Rides, he's Robert Mitchum's gun-smuggling pilot. In 1972's *Pancho Villa*, he's Clint Walker's gunrunner.

Most of all, they loved that Villa had an instinct for using the press . . . and Hollywood. The heart of 2003's *And Starring Pancho Villa as Himself* is Villa's involvement with the film industry. But even back in 1972, Telly Savalas's Villa took time out from a battle to watch a newsreel of his own exploits.

Although the other films have considerable merit, the only undeniable classic is 1934's *Viva Villa!* Wallace Beery gives one of the finest performances of his career, reprising a role he played in 1917—when Villa was still alive and powerful—in the lost New Jersey–filmed Pathé serial *Patria*.

Hecht's script—written in two weeks—is brilliant, taking Villa from his childhood to his death, painting him convincingly as both brutal thug and patriotic idealist, undone by his own innocence. James Wong Howe's breathtaking black-and-white cinematography of Mexico makes one wonder why anyone would make a movie in color.

The supporting cast is exceptional. Leo Carrillo is hilarious and chilling as Villa's friend, whose impatient, "Hurry up; it take too long," became a signal that someone was about to die. Carrillo graduated to the lead for 1950's *Pancho Villa Returns*.

Five years before David O. Selznick produced *Gone With the Wind*, he learned some hard lessons with *Viva Villa!* To shoot in Mexico, MGM agreed to give script approval to a Mexican government full of Villa's enemies and final cut approval to Villa's widow. Accommodations were so primitive that cast and crew were living aboard a train—except sometimes star Beery, who often flew himself to El Paso, Texas, to sleep.

After two months of shooting, director Howard Hawks felt the film was in the can. Then a plane carrying three weeks of his footage crashed and burned.

As if that was not bad enough, second male lead Lee Tracy, playing a cynical journalist who befriends Villa, woke up hungover and, annoyed by noise outside his hotel, staggered, naked, out on the balcony, and urinated into the street, onto a military parade, dousing the cadets of Mexico's equivalent of West Point. MGM had to rush Tracy out of Mexico. To make amends, the studio not only apologized to the government but also fired Tracy, canceling his long-term contract, and cut every frame of him from the movie.

Back in Hollywood, California—between redoing all of Tracy's scenes with Erwin and the lost footage—two thirds of the movie had to be reshot. Not by Hawks—Selznick claimed he fired him, and Hawks claimed he quit—but by Jack Conway. Regardless of all the fiascoes, the movie turned out wonderfully.

Hecht's effort was followed up by Peckinpah and Towne's. In 1968's *Villa Rides*, the sophisticated Yul Brynner couldn't be any more unlike Beery's lovable bandit slob, and that was the problem: he wasn't willing to play Villa as a thug touched with greatness. Brynner complained Peckinpah had created a villain, not a hero. Paramount fired Peckinpah and brought in Towne to fix the mess. But all the action couldn't hide the half-hearted telling.

Mitchum, as a gunrunning pilot, is more fun than Brynner, and he gets more screen time. The film's greatest strength is its humor: Charles Bronson played Maj. Gen. Rodolfo Fierro, Carrillo's character from *Viva Villa!* The Brynner and Bronson teaming compares well with Beery and Carrillo. The biggest single mistake was casting Herbert Lom as Villa's nemesis, Gen. Victoriano Huerta. While Beery and his Teutonic-seeming enemy contrasted hugely, Brynner and Lom were so jarringly alike in looks, manner, and voice, that only Lom's hair would let you tell them apart—and bald-headed Brynner wore a wig!

With Savalas playing Villa and a supporting cast that included Clint Walker, Anne Francis, and Chuck Connors, the 1972 Euro-Western *Pancho Villa* should have been a winner. But director and story writer Eugenio Martín never decided whether to make an action picture or a farce, and he ended up with both. Savalas's performance is more than unsympathetic; it's clownish. In one scene, Villa thinks he's dying before he realizes that his clothes are actually full of lizards, because he doesn't change his underwear often enough.

The most recent of the Villa feature films is HBO's delightful 2003 movie *And Starring Pancho Villa as Himself*. Antonio Banderas stars as the savvy bandit using the American film industry to promote and finance his revolution. This is the first film on Villa since 1934 that's worth watching twice.

THE NATION'S WORST SINGLE LYNCHING

You might guess that the worst single lynching in US history took place in the Deep South and that the victims were black. But the remarkable truth is that it took place in the burgeoning California metropolis of Los Angeles in 1871, and its victims were eighteen Chinese men and boys. That crime is the culmination of the story of *The Jade Pendant*, the Western film based on the novel by Hong Kong immigrant L. P. Leung. It's a story he'd been wanting to tell for more than fifty of his eighty-plus years.

The Chinatown Massacre, wherein a gun battle between rival Tongs, over ownership of a girl, triggered the slaughter, is the film's climax. But the plot is about the girl, Peony (played by Clara Lee), who flees China to escape a disastrous arranged marriage. Educated by her father in English and martial arts, she believes she's sailing to *Jin Shan*—Chinese for "Gold Mountain," their name for San Francisco—to work as a florist. She doesn't realize she's been sold to a Tong.

Leung explains that although men came from China to work in the goldfields or on the Transcontinental Railroad during the 1800s, "[Chinese] women only came to America if they were forced to, sold to satisfy their father's gambling debts. Those girls were shipped to America as prostitutes."

Peony impresses the Tong brothel's Madam Pong (Tsai Chin) with her literacy and intelligence, and becomes her pet. Peony meets Tom (Godfrey Gao), who has left the violent goldfields to open a restaurant and sell his invention, *chop suey* (Chinese for "leftovers"). They fall in love.

But when Madam Pong considers letting them marry, the couple learns that merciless Tong boss Yu Hing (Tzi Ma) wants Peony for himself, and all Hell breaks loose.

Leung well understands the plight of Chinese immigrants of the era. Although the Chinese Exclusion Act of 1882, the only federal law ever to single out a race or nationality, was repealed during WWII, a quota remained until 1965.

"Only 108 Chinese were allowed to come to the United States a year," he says. "In 1958, a missionary arranged a work study program so that I could come."

The son of a poor minister, Leung left Hong Kong for California with $35 in his pocket. He studied accounting and was hired by Paramount Pictures to track spending on various productions, including *The Rifleman* and *Bonanza*.

"Many scenes were shot on the Western Street backlot," he says. "I always enjoyed going over there to watch during lunch hours."

He also tracked expenses and became friends with legendary producer A. C. Lyles. "Do you know he used to be a mailroom boy at Paramount? From there, he got to know the stars. When he finally got a chance to make his own movies, he was able to call in his markers for some of those older movie stars. The main studios would not hire them anymore. A. C. could get them a week's work for $10,000, making movies for less than $200,000 each," he says.

The primary market wasn't Americans. "Japanese viewers loved cowboy movies with famous stars, even in their fading years," he says. Lyles would produce more than a dozen such Westerns in the mid-1960s.

The years at Paramount planted the idea of the movie that would become *The Jade Pendant*. "But A. C. kind of told me that America was not ready for what I wanted to tell," he says.

In time, Leung wrote the novel and shopped it without success, until he was introduced to producer Thomas Leong. "I gave him the screenplay, and I said, 'If you're interested, I want the movie finished in one year, because I'm not young anymore. I can't wait.' I met him in February. By June, we were looking for a director. We started shooting in September and finished in November, so it was all done within one year," he says.

Despite his name, director Po-Chi Leong is English, Leung says, adding, "And he did most of his work in Hong Kong. Even though he can speak Chinese, he cannot read Chinese. So, he was really at home with *The Jade Pendant*, because it was in English, with the Western and Eastern thing combined; he was kind of perfect."

Of course, the modern-day cities of San Francisco and Los Angeles wouldn't do for a period film. "We built a whole Chinatown near Salt Lake City, Utah," he says.

Much has been written, some factual, some fanciful, about the mob that perpetrated the massacre and about the legal results: fifteen were indicted, seven were convicted of manslaughter and sentenced to a range of two to six years, and none of them served a day, due to an atrocious technicality: that Dr. Gene Tong's murder was never entered into evidence. The convictions were overturned; the charges were never refiled.

Before *The Jade Pendant*, little had been written about events from the Chinese point of view. The people of Chinatown didn't write it, Leung says, "and [the press] did not have access into a Chinese community because they don't speak Chinese, and the Chinese did not associate with journalists."

Though a fictional version based on history, the story has now been told in this romantic, tragic, and enlightening Western.

WESTERNS DOWN UNDER

In 1906, just three years after the twelve-minute *The Great Train Robbery*, the first ever hour-long film, *The Story of the Kelly Gang*, another Western, was made not in the United States, but in Australia. And before you say, "That doesn't count as a Western," consider this: it's set in the 1870s, in a pioneering region usurped by white settlers from indigenous people, during a gold rush, and it's about a gang of stagecoach robbers, although there, they're called bushrangers. If that's not a Western, then neither is *Stagecoach*.

Both Australia and America have a fondness for tales of pioneering, individualism, and daring. We see in Paul Hogan as Crocodile Dundee a shared exuberance and confidence. And that personality extends to the filmmakers as well as the films. Actress Laura San Giacomo fondly recalls going to Australia to star in *Quigley Down Under* and meeting the crew. "There was a very gung-ho, cavalier spirit of filmmaking, [as if] it was going to be very easy to do this Western, to do a *really difficult* shoot."

Ned Kelly and the Bushrangers

Australians also share our fondness for legendary "bad boys." We have our Jesse James and Billy the Kid; they have their bushrangers: Ben Hall, "Mad Dog" Morgan, and Ned Kelly. For good guys, we've got Wyatt Earp and Bat Masterson. And the Australians? "We don't have anyone like that," explains Simon Wincer, the Australian director of *Lonesome Dove* and *Quigley Down Under*. "The police were nearly all Irish, often pursuing their own, as in the case of Ned Kelly, who was Irish heritage. So the 'traps,' as they were known, were not liked."

And with good reason: while the settlers of the American West were there by choice, Great Britain expelled 164,000 English and Irish criminals and rebels to Australia. The bushrangers, particularly Ned Kelly, who famously beat plow shears into armor, are admired not for their robberies but for their opposition to the government. *Legend of Ben Hall* director Matthew Holmes explains, "The public cared for [them] because they knew what it was like to be oppressed by the British police. They also cared because the gang would pay them to provide shelter and information."

There are probably more biographical films about Ned Kelly than any other Australian.

The best of them, Tony Richardson's *Ned Kelly* (1970), features an unexpectedly strong and moving performance in the title role by Mick Jagger, who also sings the Irish/Australian rebel ballad, "There Was a Wild Colonial Boy." Notes Wincer, "[Its screenwriter] Ian Jones was the foremost authority on Ned Kelly. Ian created a television series called *The Last Outlaw*, that's probably the closest to being accurate."

Australian Heath Ledger played Kelly to great acclaim in 2003's *Ned Kelly*, with fellow Australians Gregor Jordan directing and Geoffrey Rush co-starring. Most recently, 2019's *True History of the Kelly Gang* is at its most interesting in Ned's early years, when bushranger Harry Power (New Zealander Russell Crowe) shows him the ropes of criminality. Wincer says, "I hated [it]. It was a whole revisionist look at Ned, and I didn't like it at all. It's just what I call a wank."

Dan Morgan's behavior marked him as psychotic even among bushrangers, so writer/director Philippe Mora was indeed fortunate to hire *Easy Rider*'s Dennis Hopper to play him, with Aboriginal star David Gumpilil (*Walkabout*) as his sidekick. *Mad Dog Morgan* is surprisingly watchable. It's even more surprising that it was completed. Hopper recalled that fueled by cocaine and rum, he crashed a truck through a cemetery, and the Victoria police, rather than jailing him, drove him directly to the airport and put him on a plane for the United States, with the shooting unfinished.

"Ben Hall was a successful landowner and cattleman," notes Holmes. "He had no criminal record until his life fell apart—his wife ran away with his friend and took their young son." *The Legend of Ben Hall* (2017) is a remarkably well-told story of Hall's attempts to do right by his son and to steal enough to finance a move to the States. Star Jack Martin is the spitting image of Hall, and a fine actor. "*Ben Hall* was made by a couple of young guys, literally on the smell of an oily rag," says Wincer. "They did a great job with the money they had.

"*The Proposition*, with Guy Pearce and Ray Winstone, was a very good movie. Gosh, it was bleak." Bleak indeed, the 2005 film is a Western *noir*. Outlaws Pearce and his kid brother are arrested by Police Captain Winstone, who makes a proposition: he will hang the kid brother on Christmas unless Pearce kills their much more dangerous older brother, played by Danny Huston.

Banjo Paterson and *Snowy River*

Beloved for writing the song "Waltzing Matilda," Banjo Paterson is also famous for his poem, "The Man from Snowy River." Written 130 years ago, it's about the chase to recapture an escaped horse, and just as much about social class and prejudice. The 1982 film was directed by George Miller. Its executive producer Simon Wincer recalls, "We had the poem, which is a great finale for a movie. But we had to invent the first ninety minutes before we got to what we call 'the ride.'" They wisely interwove a romance, involving the poor but honest protagonist and the headstrong, beautiful daughter of Harrison, the wealthy landowner. Miller cast the stunning Sigrid Thornton, whom he'd directed as Ned Kelly's sister in *The Last Outlaw*. The "man" was young Tom Burlinson, and when Kirk Douglas was offered the role of Harrison, he agreed, provided he could also play Harrison's brother, Spur. The classic adventure spawned a sequel and a series.

Family Fare

In 1947's wonderful *A Bush Christmas*, five children befriend a trio of campers, led by Chips Rafferty, not realizing that they are rustlers, until Dad's valuable horse disappears. The five friends strike out to recover the horse, with unexpected results. Reflecting attitudes similar to America's *Our Gang* comedies, the film features one Aboriginal boy, but race never enters into anyone's thinking. In 1958, twenty-five years before *A Christmas Story*, the Australian film *Smiley Gets a Gun* tells the story of a ten-year-old who wants the .22 rifle of policeman Chips Rafferty as much as Ralphie wants the Red Ryder BB-gun, and tries everything to earn it.

Quigley Down Under

Before *Quigley*, Wincer directed films about horse racing like *Phar Lap* and cavalry pictures like *The Lighthorsemen*. "I learned to ride when I was about four years of age and that was a passion that has never left me. I'm in my seventies now and still riding. Because of my interest in horses, and knowing what you can and can't do with them, people kept coming back to me to make more Westerns."

Quigley Down Under, the finest Australian Western, is the story of an American who answers an ad looking for the world's best long-distance marksman and finds himself in Australia, employed by wealthy rancher Marsten (Alan Rickman). Then Quigley realizes, to his fury, that Marsten hired him to slaughter Aboriginals. Star Tom Selleck remembers, "He became the avenging angel for the Aboriginal people. It was really a terrific script. I worked hard in preparation. I'm very, very proud of *Quigley*."

By the late 1960s, American Westerns were looking at the problems of Indians' assimilation, whether for or against their will, and Australian films were examining their parallel issues. With many echoes of *Tell Them Willie Boy Is Here* (1969), in the true turn-of-the-century *The Chant of Jimmie Blacksmith* (1978), Tommy Lewis is a half "Abo" young man raised by a well-meaning but clueless minister (Jack Thompson), leaving him unfit for either culture. Despite his incredible forbearance, the abuse he receives after marrying a white girl drives him to a homicidal spree. Lewis later played the terrifying escaped killer in *Red Hill* (2010), whose story is much akin to *Bad Day at Black Rock* (1955), with a small-town policeman uncovering a racism-based miscarriage of justice. In 2017's *Sweet Country*, set in 1920s Northern Frontier, and far away from law, an Aboriginal man (Hamilton Morris) shoots a white in self-defense but goes on the run, knowing he won't be treated justly.

Since filmmaking began, Australian's love of tales of pioneering and adventure has produced a steady stream of fine Westerns that stand up to the best of American work and are as enjoyable for their differences as for their similarities. One need look no further than Simon Wincer, who not only directed the finest of all Australian Westerns, *Quigley Down Under*, but first came to our shores and directed the best TV Western of all time, *Lonesome Dove*.

Boney and *Mystery Road—Longmire*'s Aussie Cousins

In 1971, a year after Tony Hillerman's *The Blessing Way* created the Rez mystery genre, Australian television filmed the first of Arthur Upfield's Inspector Napoleon Bonaparte mysteries, first published in 1929. The series *Boney* concerns a mixed-race police detective who moves seamlessly between the white and Aboriginal worlds to solve crimes. Caucasian New Zealander James Laurenson played the groundbreaking role. Forty-two years later, Aaron

Pedersen, an actor of Aboriginal descent, starred as indigenous Detective Jay Swan, investigating the deaths of young mixed-race girls in *Mystery Road*, a wise and tough drama that led to a sequel, *Goldstone*, and then a *Mystery Road* series.

CHAPTER 13

THE WIDE WORLD OF WESTERNS

THE BEST MOUNTAIN MEN FILMS

Unexpectedly, 2015 was a great year for mountain men. *The Revenant*, inspired by the true story of Hugh Glass's fight for life, earned more than $530 million internationally, the film rights to the character of Grizzly Adams were offered for sale and, across the country, hipsters dubbed "lumbersexuals" were sprouting facial hair and sporting flannel and buckskin.

Why the sudden appeal of the mountain man? Maybe because neither Grizzly Adams nor Hugh Glass ever said, "It takes a village."

As Charlton Heston's character says in 1980's *The Mountain Men*, "I can still walk for a year in any direction with just my rifle and a handful of salt and never have to say 'sir' to nobody. I reckon that's free."

Charlton's son, Fraser, who wrote that film, understands the appeal of the self-confident, independent man: "It's an archetypical Western; prototypical, really. It's an early version of America's drive West, before the country was settled, before there were gunslingers and ranchers and farmers and towns with sidewalks."

The men who cut the paths that became wagon routes for the pioneers have long fascinated filmgoers and filmmakers.

Here are ten mountain man movies worth seeking out.

#1: The 1971 Western, *Man in the Wilderness*, the first cinematic telling of the ordeal of Hugh Glass, stars Richard Harris as part of a grand trapper expedition. Horribly mauled by a grizzly, sure to die, the expedition's captain (John Huston) leaves two men behind to bury him, but fearing that Indians are coming, they abandon him. Yet he survives, driven by memories of his family, to try to catch up. It's directed by Richard C. Sarafian.

#2: *Jeremiah Johnson* features Robert Redford as a Mexican-American War veteran determined to make a life in the Rocky Mountains. Sydney Pollack's direction and John Milius and Edward Anhalt's script for the 1972 film create a man who, while speaking rarely, is accessible, romantic, and terrifying in his wrath, although the film tactfully skirts why he was known as "Liver-Eating Johnson."

#3: Clint Walker, on hiatus from *Cheyenne*, gave the screen its most clean-shaven mountain man in 1959's *Yellowstone Kelly*, directed by Gordon Douglas, from a script by Burt Kennedy and Heck Allen. Supported by fellow Warner Bros. TV stars Edd Byrnes's and John Russell's characters, Kelly must protect the Sioux, and his own traplines, from dangerously ambitious soldiers. He must also safeguard a beautiful Arapaho captive desired by both the Sioux chief and his ambitious nephew.

#4: *The Life and Times of Grizzly Adams*, a tiny-budget, sound-dubbed-in 1974 film, was such a success that it begat a slew of wilderness family films as well as a TV series for its star, Dan Haggerty. Falsely accused of murder, Adams disappears into the mountains, lives off the land, and raises a grizzly. Sometimes dismissed as *Jeremiah Johnson* Lite, the film has great beauty and charm. Haggerty, in his final interview, remembered fondly, "A lot of people don't know that the California State Flag is a representation of his bear. We did kind of a softened version [of his life]; couldn't do it hard and heavy in those days, the way James Capen Adams [lived], but that's how it was." The film was directed by Richard Friedenberg.

#5: The most filmed mountain man portrayal is of Albert Johnson, the "Mad Trapper of Rat River," filmed four times in nine years! (The 1978 comedy went unfinished.) In 1931, Inuits complained that Johnson was meddling with their traps. Mountie confrontations with Johnson led to them leveling his cabin with dynamite. When the smoke cleared, Johnson ran out, guns blazing, and the legendary Yukon manhunt began. Directed by Peter Hunt, the engrossing 1981 actioner *Death Hunt*, starring Charles Bronson as Johnson and Lee Marvin as the Mountie determined to catch him, is by far the best. Shot six years earlier, *Challenge to Be Free* is the kiddie version of the same story, starring legendary gangster-heavy Mike Mazurki, who plays Johnson like Grizzly Adams with a lobotomy.

#6: Charlton Heston and Brian Keith star in the salty and savage 1980 film *The Mountain Men*, directed by Richard Lang, an adventure story with plenty of humor and heart. Screenwriter Fraser Heston recalls, "Our story takes place in the 1830s, at the end of the fur trade era. The heyday was passed, so there's a feeling already of nostalgia for something that is lost." Victoria Racimo plays the Indian woman Heston's trapper character does not want but grows to love. Stephen Macht is Heavy Eagle, who will not give her up. Among the high points is the trappers' rendezvous sequence, an event Fraser describes as "part trade show and part rave, in buckskins."

#7: In "Wild Bill" Wellman's 1951 flick *Across the Wide Missouri,* Flint Mitchell (Clark Gable) bargains for a Blackfoot bride (María Elena Marqués) for trade reasons, assembles a battalion of fellow trappers, and leads them into rich beaver grounds. Mitchell finds himself loving his wife and her people, and he becomes drawn into a power struggle between her grandfather Bear Ghost (Jack Holt) and Ironshirt (Ricardo Montalban).

#8: Anthony Mann's 1955 Western *The Last Frontier* is a fascinating story of three cultures clashing: military, Lakota, and mountain man. When Red Cloud forces three trappers out, they scout for the nearby fort. As arrogant Colonel Marston (Robert Preston) drives the two sides inevitably to war, Victor Mature is the savage innocent of the trappers, who naively makes a play for Anne Bancroft's character, not caring that she's the colonel's wife.

#9: In 1969's *My Side of the Mountain,* directed by James B. Clark, Ted Eccles plays a twelve-year-old boy obsessed with Henry David Thoreau and science, who runs away to live in the mountains of Canada and tries to create a new food source—from algae! He also catches and trains a Peregrine falcon, skins deer to make his clothes, and befriends an itinerant folksinger played by Theodore Bikel.

#10: It's easy to dismiss *The Revenant* as superfluous, considering how well *A Man Alone* told the story of Hugh Glass. But if we said, "We don't need another Hamlet: we have Barrymore," we would not have Laurence Olivier. And *The Revenant,* a triple Oscar winner for director Alejandro González Iñárritu, cinematographer Emmanuel Lubezki, and star Leonardo DiCaprio is an excellent, enthralling, exhausting, and inspirational film.

Aside from their own work, according to some of the people who made the movies, which is the best mountain man movie? "I would guess *Jeremiah Johnson,*" says Heston. Haggerty concurred. "Robert Redford did such a great job on it; no one could have done it better."

THE BEST WEIRD WESTERNS

When Stephen King's *The Dark Tower,* an endlessly-in-the-works film finally premiered in August 2017, it disappointed fans because, unlike the novels, it's not a Western.

Readers found a lot of Spaghetti Western in the seven Dark Tower novels. As King says, "I saw . . . *The Good, the Bad and the Ugly* and before the film was even half over, I realized that what I wanted to write was a novel that contained [J.R.R.] Tolkien's sense of quest and magic but set against [Sergio] Leone's almost absurdly majestic Western backdrop."

But don't despair. There are some particularly fine Weird Westerns, a blend of Western with sci-fi and horror, from the mid-1930s to the more recent HBO's *Westworld* miniseries and the independent feature *Bone Tomahawk*. Here are some of the most entertaining selections.

The Phantom Empire

Mascot's delightfully nutty 1935 serial made a star of Gene Autry. His singing cowboy had to battle the advanced underground Muranian civilization in time for him to return to his ranch for his nightly radio show.

Riders of the Whistling Skull

Among the best of the B-Westerns, this 1937 film from Republic's "Three Mesquiteers" series features Ray "Crash" Corrigan, Robert Livingston, and Max Terhune as three buddies who find a man delirious in the desert. When the men learn he's a missing archaeologist on the hunt for the lost Indian city of Lukachukai, they join the expedition, led by an untrustworthy Indian (played by Yakima Canutt). Full of action and atmospherically photographed, the movie echoes *Gunga Din*, yet was made two years earlier.

Riders in the Sky

Inspired by a song penned by Death Valley Forest Ranger Stan Jones, this 1949 Gene Autry film features Rock McCleary (Robert Livingston), who sends his henchmen to arrange a fatal runaway wagon "accident" for Old Man Roberts (Tom London) after he witnesses a killing. Roberts sees the legendary ghost riders coming for him. Autry singing "Ghost Riders in the Sky" against a haunting and poetic montage is the film's highlight.

The Return of Dracula

A Weird Western made while the producers, director, and head writer were on hiatus for ABC's *The Rifleman*, 1958's *The Return of Dracula* is a sophisticated reworking of Alfred Hitchcock's *Shadow of a Doubt*. Instead of a serial lady-killer hiding out with his unsuspecting family, Francis Lederer's runaway Count Dracula blends in with an American household.

Curse of the Undead

A rogue's gallery of Western TV faces starred in this 1959 Gothic feature. *Rawhide* star Eric Fleming plays a rural minister in a romantic triangle with a lady rancher (Kathleen Crowley) and her suave hired gun (Michael Pate), who is torn between his love for the lady and the want of her blood. Watch for *The High Chaparral*'s future Manolito, Henry Darrow, in his first role.

Billy the Kid vs. Dracula

I once commented to Harry Carey Jr. that no matter how small his role, I always knew his movies were worth watching. He replied, "Then you haven't seen *Billy the Kid vs. Dracula*." John Carradine starred in that hammy reworking of 1958's *The Return of Dracula*.

This is no classic, but the 1966 flick is watchable hokum from Hollywood's most prolific director, William Beaudine. In her final role, Carey's mother, silent screen star Olive Carey, plays the doctor. It was released in a double bill with *Jesse James Meets Frankenstein's Daughter*, which isn't as good.

The Valley of Gwangi

A story by *King Kong* animator Willis H. O'Brien, concerning the search for a hidden dinosaur valley in Mexico, inspired two dinosaur Westerns. Talented actors Guy Madison and Patricia Medina struggle valiantly in 1956's *The Beast of Hollow Mountain*, but the film is utterly ruined by horrendous animation that makes them look like they are battling a Mattel tyrannosaurus in a Play-Doh jungle.

You'll want to see 1969's *The Valley of Gwangi*, which showcases thrilling and convincing dinosaur animation by Oscar-winner Ray Harryhausen, acknowledged as the finest stop-motion animator in the history of the art.

The Wild Wild West—the series

The popularity of James Bond films led in 1965 to the first sci-fi, spy Western series on television, *The Wild Wild West*. James West (Robert Conrad) and Artemus Gordon (Ross Martin) played President U. S. Grant's agents, using futuristic weapons to fight off villains bent on world domination. The CBS series is generally acknowledged as the birth of Steampunk.

The Hanged Man

One of the creepiest movies on the list is a cult classic by writer-producer Andrew Fenady, 1974's *The Hanged Man*. It takes the premise of 1968's *Hang 'em High*—a man who lives through his hanging extracts revenge—one step further. Steve Forrest's character dies on the gallows, then comes inexplicably back to life!

Westworld

Writer-director Michael Crichton's work was truly original, never more so than with 1973's *Westworld*. Set in a then fabulously expensive—$1,000 a day—Western-themed amusement park, the feature film was more light-hearted than the HBO miniseries but raised the same questions: How would we behave without consequences? And what would happen if the robots got sick of playing along?

High Plains Drifter

Clint Eastwood's first Western as a director, 1973's *High Plains Drifter* takes his Man with No Name character for a supernatural ride. He kills three thugs, only to learn a town hired them to shield it from a larger and more dangerous force. He becomes the town's protector, yet a series of nightmares suggest he may have been there before—and in a bad way.

Sundown

David Carradine, Morgan Brittany, and their band of vampires learn the value of sunblock in 1989's *Sundown*, a contemporary Western comedy set in a desert retirement community for bloodsuckers. It's full of great Western faces like John Ireland, M. Emmet Walsh, and Dabs Greer.

Grim Prairie Tales

In this eerie 1990 anthology, a bounty hunter (James Earl Jones) and city slicker (Brad Dourif) pass the night telling scary stories over a campfire.

Back to the Future III

From 1990, Marty McFly (Michael J. Fox) is stuck in the 1950s when he gets word that Doc Brown (Christopher Lloyd) has died in 1885, which will mess up everything that's happened since, and goes back in time to save him. Directed by Richard Zemeckis, produced by Steven Spielberg, this money-is-no-object production is a nutty delight.

Cowboys & Aliens

Weird Western stories have long thrived in comic books, but of the three adaptations in the 2010s—2010's *Jonah Hex*, 2011's *Cowboys & Aliens*, and 2013's *R.I.P.D.*—only one is enjoyable. The title tells you the plot. Starring Daniel Craig and Harrison Ford, *Cowboys & Aliens* grossed a whopping $100 million but is considered a flop because Universal spent $163 million to make it.

FEMALE-DOMINATED WESTERNS

Ever since *The Virginian*, Owen Wister's genre-defining Western novel, female characters have traditionally been portrayed as the civilizers. Even though in 1939's *Stagecoach*, we preferred the "bad" woman, Claire Trevor's Dallas, the respectable townswomen were hard at work civilizing their town by running Dallas out of it. But 1952's *High Noon*, richly borrowed (some might say plagiarized) from *The Virginian*'s final chapters, started changing the rules: the Mexican widow, played by Katie Jurado, was secretly the power of the town; and unlike *The Virginian*'s cowering schoolmarm, Marshal Will Kane's Quaker wife turned out to be the only sideman he needed in a shoot-out.

As exemplified in the recent crop of Westerns, the female characters have come so far to the fore that males are now weak, evil, or subservient to women. As the man who's built the largest private ranch in America, *Yellowstone*'s Kevin Costner is at the story's core. But while he and his estranged son, played by Luke Grimes, are the nurturers, it's his lawyer daughter, played by Kelly Reilly, who's the real family soldier. In the substantially true story of *Woman Walks Ahead*, Jessica Chastain's Barbara Weldon is for a time all that stands between Sitting Bull (Michael Greyeyes) and destruction (Sam Rockwell). *Westworld*'s season two is a battle of wits between several female characters, real and robot, played by Evan Rachel Wood, Charlotte Hale, and Thandie

Newton, who won an Emmy for her performance. The males by and large are reduced to henchmen and villains.

Perhaps the most striking example is *Godless*. Here a town has lost nearly all of its men in a gold mine collapse, and the town's women must hold things together and battle with crazy-evil characters like Frank Griffin (Jeff Daniels, who won an Emmy for the part). The "law" is represented by a wimp sheriff who's going blind (and his young, likable goofy deputy), and the sheriff is soon replaced by his sister, played by Merritt Wever in an Emmy-winning performance. The lead rancher who brings everyone together is a widow played by *Downton Abbey*'s Michele Dockery. As if Jeff Daniels needed villainy backup, Kim Coates is the hissable rep for the mining company. An exceptionally fine Western, written and directed by Scott Frank, *Godless*'s success with audiences might be a matter of the third time being the charm. A disaster leading to a Western town populated almost entirely by women was the premise of the sinister 2014 Lifetime series *Strange Empire*, as well as that of *When Calls the Heart* (yet another mine collapse), a romantic Western series, based on the novel by Janette Oke, which has been laboring with little fanfare on the Hallmark Channel since 2014 and began its tenth season in 2023.

Probably the most extreme of these role-switching Westerns was 1954's campy *Johnny Guitar*, in which a mannish saloon-operator (Joan Crawford) and a rancher (Mercedes McCambridge) battle over the romantic attentions of Scott Brady as the Dancin' Kid! There's also practically any Barbara Stanwyck Western—her ability to dominate all the men around her, yet remain feminine, was unique. More recently, we've had 2013's *Sweetwater*, when the husband of January Jones is murdered and the law won't help, she must go after the culprit. Then there are the girl outlaw gang films like 1994's *Bad Girls* with Madeline Stowe and Mary Stewart Masterson; 2003's *Gang of Roses*, the African American version with Stacy Dash and Lil' Kim; and 2006's *Bandidas*, the Hispanic version with Salma Hayek and Penelope Cruz.

It's easy to say that the current crop of woman-dominated Westerns is partly a response to the "me, too" movement. That might help a project get green-lit, but doesn't take into account how long development takes. One of the best such films of recent years, 2015's *Jane Got a Gun*, was a passion project of its producer-star, Natalie Portman. A director quit, cast members quit, and when the original distributor went bankrupt, who rescued and released the movie? The Weinstein Company.

WESTWORLD REBORN

When, in 1973, MGM, once the titan of Hollywood studios, found itself on the ropes after a string of flops, a tiny film saved the studio from oblivion.

With $1.25 million to work with, novelist-turned first-time screenwriter and director Michael Crichton created a darkly humorous contemporary sci-fi Western, about a high-priced ($1,000 a day!) resort where wannabe cowboys could live out their fantasies—be heroes or villains, guns blazing! Best of all, because realistic but remotely controlled robots populated the place, nobody could get hurt. That is, until one robot, played by Yul Brynner, in his *The Magnificent Seven* garb, got fed up with letting the tourists outdraw him. Other robots soon began malfunctioning in a deadly way.

Westworld, starring James Brolin and Dick Benjamin as businessmen who might have to die for their fantasies, was a smash with filmgoers but especially with fans of Westerns, because the 1973 film created a completely plausible world that they were desperate to enter. The movie spawned a sequel, a short-lived CBS series, and passionate fans.

But Jonathan Nolan, writer-director of the HBO series *Westworld*, notes that the movie spawned much more: "The original film anticipates *Terminator* and video games and artificial intelligence—so many ideas packed into that film. I probably shouldn't have watched when I was eight: Yul Brynner haunted my dreams for years to come. I loved it."

While updated technologically, the new *Westworld* is a thrilling, often heartbreakingly beautiful continuation of the predecessor's themes with, Jonathan explains, "An original set of stories within that world."

You'll be hooked from the moment the first group of "newcomers" (the paying visitors) is on the train, headed for Sweetwater, Wyoming, for their introductory meeting with their robot "hosts."

Jonathan wrote the series with his wife, Lisa Joy. Both writers are in their element with the premise. He wrote the original story for the brilliant 2000 amnesia film *Memento*; she contributed scripts to 2007–2009's *Pushing Daisies*, about a man who can bring the dead to life for a single minute.

"It's a synthetic Western," Jonathan says. "What Lisa and I were drawn to was the juxtaposition between Science Fiction and the Western, and the values they have in common."

"They're both basically frontier stories," Lisa elaborates. "The Westerns are classic frontier stories, and [Sci-Fi] is about the new frontier of space, the new frontier of technology. They're linked by this common theme—the individual versus the unknown."

Writing a successful adaptation is complex. "You need to understand and appreciate what was essential to the original property, but you have to be willing to be a bit of a heretic, and start anew," Jonathan says. "There were two things that we were very excited about from the original film; one, the idea of the emerging artificial intelligence robots, there to service our id, who eventually bridle at that job. And two, the environment where you're told that no one is keeping score, and you can behave as you want with no consequences."

While all of the characters in the HBO series are new, one bears a striking familiarity—Ed Harris's "Man in Black" in the remake has more than a passing resemblance to Brynner's gunslinger character in the original.

"We wanted to turn the narrative inside out and look at this world from the perspective of the robots. So, if the original film is about hapless humans in a park where the robots have gone crazy, our series is about the hapless robot inhabitants of a world in which the guests have gone crazy. And Ed sort of symbolically takes on that role of the villain that Yul played in the film, but in this case it's the guests who are the most villainous," Jonathan says.

Along with the villainy, the remake offers one trope not found in the original film: romance. Evan Rachel Wood plays host Dolores Abernathy to James Marsden's newcomer Teddy Flood. "The elusive love story; it's a timeless tale that has always appealed to me," Lisa says. "So much of a love story working [entails] first finding yourself. And that links deeply into Jonathan's theme, the problem with memory, because the hosts' memories are constantly being erased. So to pursue their dreams, they must first figure out which are *their* dreams and which are the dreams they've been programmed to have."

One of the great additions to the longform story not found in the 1973 film is the character of the visionary behind the Westworld resort, Dr. Robert Ford, a name inspired by Jesse James's killer, the Nolans admit. For that role, HBO cast a brilliant actor not primarily known for television—Oscar-winner Anthony Hopkins.

"I think Tony, or Sir Anthony, like a lot of us, has been watching TV," Jonathan says. "And I love the movies, but the work that's being done in TV right now is a little more sophisticated, a little more cerebral and a little more gripping."

By the second season's end, *Westworld* had virtually nothing to do with Westerns, and it was officially cancelled after four seasons in 2023. But when I spoke to the show's creators, not one episode had yet aired. When I asked how long they thought *Westworld* would run, Jonathan says, "Lisa and I came with a game plan for where the seasons would go and how the story would end. But the beauty of television is the journey is as long as the audience wants it to be. The goal will be to keep telling the story as long as it's vital and compelling."

YAKIMA CANUTT—THE SCREEN'S GREATEST HORSE STUNTMAN

The most memorable action sequence in *Stagecoach* comes near the end of the 1939 film. Shortly after the river crossing, the passengers expect a smooth ride into Lordsburg, New Mexico Territory, but Apache leader Geronimo and his men have other ideas. They swoop down from a hill to attack, and the stagecoach races for the Mojave Desert's Lucerne Dry Lake Bed, commencing a moving battle scene that runs relentlessly for an astonishing six minutes, from the moment the unsuspecting Samuel Peacock (played by Donald Meek) catches an arrow in the chest to the first sight of the cavalry led by Lieutenant Blanchard (Tim Holt).

Shot for three days on location, the Apache chase seamlessly intercuts with studio shots of the actors against rear projections. While doubles portray the other actors in this scene, John Wayne performs his role. With the chase moving at about forty-five miles per hour, the stage door swings open and Wayne is seen hanging on it. He scrambles up onto the roof of the coach, lies on his belly, and starts firing back at the Apaches.

In a truly death-defying sequence of stunts, Yakima Canutt, doubling for John Wayne, leaps from the top of the stagecoach to the first team of horses. *Courtesy United Artists*

Next comes the sequence that would make a legend. Yakima Canutt first performed this in 1937's Monogram release, *Riders of the Dawn*, doubling for Jack Randall, and he would do variations on it for the rest of his career. The stunt is frequently imitated, most notably in 1981's *Raiders of the Lost Ark*. Canutt, dressed as an Apache, rides up on the left of the stage's lead team, jumps from his pony over the near horse to the wagon tongue and begins to stop the lead team.

What comes next made this gag merely extremely dangerous, rather than suicidal. Not visible to the camera were metal bars Canutt had attached between the harness hames on each of the three teams, which kept the distance between the horses at three feet. When Wayne's Ringo Kid shoots him, Canutt drops between the horses, catching himself on the tongue and letting his back drag. Ringo Kid shoots him again, and Canutt drops all the way to the ground, between the horses.

Canutt crosses his arms across his chest as he falls, which may look odd, but he had good reason to do so. "The clearance under the coach is critical," Canutt recalled. "If you were to double your arms with your elbows up, the front axle would strike them. All in all, it is a gag that you could easily rub yourself out with if you make the wrong move."

When the stage passes over Canutt, he collapses and then rises to his knees—to prove that a person, not a dummy, was in the scene. That last move momentarily scared the hell out of director John Ford, a former stuntman himself, who'd expected Canutt to fall off the side of a horse, not between the teams. He thought the collapse was real, and that Canutt had been injured.

When the scene was finished, Ford's three cameramen were not sure they'd caught it. When Canutt told the director, "I'll be happy to do it again, Mr. Ford. You know I love to make money," Ford replied, "I'll never shoot that again. They better have it."

Of course, they did.

Next in the sequence, the stagecoach driver (played by Andy Devine) is shot in his right shoulder, nearly falls from the wagon, and loses the reins for the horses on the right side. He calls to Wayne's character, and Canutt, now doubling Wayne, leaps from the top of the coach to the first team, supporting himself on their backs (and those hidden bars), leaps to the second team, then the third, straddles the lead right horse and gains control. Although Wayne didn't perform this stunt, Wayne did act out the last shot of the sequence, in which he rides the horse, sans saddle, at breakneck speed.

Among the other stunts in the chase are numerous dramatic Apache horse falls, some done by Canutt, some by Iron Eyes Cody, and a horse drag, in which an Apache is shot out of his saddle, but his foot gets caught in the stirrup—he's dragged for several seconds. These actions were shot from a camera car with three cameras rolling, to provide three choices for each shot, so dangerous stunts did not need to be repeated. That these falls and drags were more impressive than in most Westerns was due largely to Canutt's skill in staging, along with Bert Glennon's brilliant cinematography; rather than the usual camera paralleling the action, the falls often come right at the camera. From *Ramona* in 1916 through the *Cheyenne* series in the 1960s, Glennon's artistry, particularly in black-and-white movies, would grace films in all genres, including eight of Ford's finest.

Dudley Nichols based his screenplay for *Stagecoach* on the Ernest Haycox story *Stage to Lordsburg*, which John Ford's son, Patrick, had read in *Collier's* magazine and brought to his father's attention.

When MGM made 1942's *Apache Trail*, based on yet another Haycox tale about folks on a stage trying to reach Lordsburg, New Mexico Territory, Lloyd Nolan got to play the outlaw-turned-hero. Interestingly, John Wayne had initially suggested Nolan play the Ringo Kid role in *Stagecoach*, before he took on the part himself. *Apache Trail*'s big Indian chase uses the alternative angles of horse falls and the horse drag from *Stagecoach*. When *Apache Trail* was remade as *Apache War Smoke* in 1952, with Gilbert Roland in the lead, the same horse falls and horse drag shots were featured in the movie.

Upon completion of *Stagecoach*, Ford told Canutt, "Any time I'm making an action picture and you're not working, you are with me."

Regrettably, at a studio party that night, the film's editor, Otho Lovering, was telling Ford, "I really think you're going to have one of the best Western action pictures ever made," when a tipsy Glennon interjected, "Yes, thanks to Yakima Canutt."

Glennon's comment was too much for the prickly Ford. Except for a single horse fall by Canutt in 1939's *Young Mr. Lincoln*—booked without Ford's knowledge—the screen's greatest Westerns director and the screen's greatest horse stuntman would never work together again.

JOAQUIN JACKSON—HOLLYWOOD'S TEXAS RANGER

Hell or High Water was the sleeper movie hit of the summer of 2016, nabbing four Oscar nominations. Tellingly, Jeff Bridges' performance is a matured echo of Nick Nolte's acting, nearly thirty years earlier, as Ranger Jack Benteen in 1987's *Extreme Prejudice*. Both characters share the same steely gaze, the white Resistol hats and dark Western shirts buttoned to the top, the stiff-shouldered amble, the raspy back-of-the-throat speech. Not surprising, since both men were coached by legendary Texas Ranger Joaquin Jackson, though decades apart.

Nolte shadowed Jackson on the job for weeks, absorbing his mannerisms and methods. Bridges, who describes Jackson as "My friend and technical advisor" and has called him "One of the greatest Texas Rangers of all time," says Jackson not only taught him how to think like a Ranger but also how to properly place his star and gather and tuck his uniform shirt.

Between Nolte's young lawman with a rage to stop wrongs and Bridges' soon-to-retire widower needing one last triumph before he fades, the two complementary parts bookend Jackson's screen career—but they do not entirely encompass it.

Retiring from the Texas Rangers in 1993, Jackson began coordinating security on Western film sets that included *The Good Old Boys*. Tommy Lee Jones, writer, director, and star—and *Lonesome Dove's* retired Texas Ranger Woodrow Call—asked Jackson to play the sheriff in the 1995 film. Jackson followed with roles in 1997's *Rough Riders*, 1999's *Streets of Laredo*, and 2009's *Palo Pinto Gold*.

Jackson's best and final performance was for *Lonesome Dove's* other retired Ranger, Gus McCrae, played by Robert Duvall. In 2015's *Wild Horses*, written, directed, and starring Duvall, Jackson plays, of all things, a retired Texas Ranger named Jackson, one who reluctantly gives advice on an investigation.

Duvall remembers him fondly. "Great guy, Joaquin Jackson."

THE "BEST" REEL TEXAS RANGER?

With more than two hundred feature films and TV shows to choose from, picking a favorite portrayal of a Texas Ranger is easier than selecting the best. For instance, many have played Ranger John Reid since the first screen appearance of *The Lone Ranger* in 1948, but Clayton Moore is the one who sticks.

When considering the more serious Texas Ranger films, Denver Pyle is memorable, but he dramatically misrepresents real-life Ranger Frank Hamer in 1967's *Bonnie and Clyde*, while Glen Campbell and Matt Damon are effective Rangers in their respective versions of *True Grit*, even though they are not the stars.

By far, the best portrayal of Texas Rangers was not on the big screen or small but on the radio. Starting in 1950, Joel McCrea starred as Texas Ranger

Jayce Pearson in ninety-three episodes of *Tales of the Texas Rangers*, a blend of radio's *Dragnet* and *Gunsmoke*; now in the public domain, the series is available on the Internet.

Most other shows that purported to show the Rangers in action were uninformed escapist fantasies, but every episode of *Tales of the Texas Rangers* was based on real case files, with consultant and legendary Texas Ranger Manuel Trazazas "Lone Wolf" Gonzaullas keeping the show accurate.

RUSTLED FOR HOLLYWOOD—FRANCIS, THE TALKING MULE

In the 1950s, Universal Pictures hit on an absurd premise that would delight millions and make millions: the Francis the Talking Mule military comedies. Audiences never guessed that Francis's true identity was a more guarded secret than the technique that made him appear to talk.

The inspiration for Francis came during WWII, in 1943, when David Stern III was stationed in Hawaii, co-editing a US Army paper, *Midpacifican*. "To pass the time, I wrote four pages of dialogue between a second lieutenant and an Army mule," he says. "I had no intention of writing more. But that little runt of a mule kept bothering me."

Those pages became a short story, then a string of them for *Esquire* magazine. The basic premise was that, while at war, an inexperienced soldier is aided by an experienced Army mule.

After Stern combined three of the stories into the book *Francis* in 1946, Universal snapped up the film rights. Director Arthur Lubin, whose Abbott and Costello comedies had made Universal a fortune, was an ideal talent to direct the series. The studio chose acrobatic star comedian Donald O'Connor to play the soldier. As the gruff, but lovable voice of Francis, former Minsky's Burlesque comic and George O'Brien sidekick Chill Wills perfectly filled the bill, although without billing, to maintain the illusion.

The most crucial casting was the role of Francis. Universal claimed Francis was played by a female mule, Molly, purchased from Jake and Jenny Frazier of Drexel, Missouri, for $350. The truth, published here for the first time, is that the mule who played Francis was, well, rustled.

As then ninety-three-year-old Tansy Smith told me in 2017, Francis, actually Judy, was the pet mule of her stepfather Archie Dean, who ran a mule pack train for tourists in Independence, California. "It was quite a popular place because Archie, as a young man, had worked for the studios," she says.

Dean regularly supplied horses and mules to the studios. Initially, Universal had bought a mule named Billy for $100 but returned him as unsuitable.

Universal wanted Judy. Dean was reluctant. "Archie'd raised her, and she was a favorite," Smith says. "Judy was a very pretty color, a bay mule with black points. She was very calm, affectionate. She roamed free around the pack station."

But the studio wore Dean down. While he would not sell her, "for love or money at any price," he agreed to loan her out, as long as she was returned for pack season in May. "But," Smith says, "that didn't happen."

After repeated requests for Judy's return, Dean was told by a studio representative, "Oh, you don't want her back: we have taught her to kick." He replied, "Yes I do. I've taught her practically everything she knows, and I can unteach her how to kick."

Archie hired an attorney to get Judy returned. "Universal just dug in their heels," says Petrine Day Mitchum, author of *Hollywood Hoofbeats* and daughter of actor Robert Mitchum. "Judy had become very famous and was worth a lot of money, and they just weren't going to let her go. He didn't want to sell her: he had made that very clear. Universal's ultimate position was they had bought Billy, he was unsuitable, and they exchanged him for Judy."

Archie never got Judy back. The statute of limitations for the theft had already passed.

So how did Hollywood get its rustled mule to talk? That job fell to Lester Hilton. "Les was a protégé of Jack 'Swede' Lindell, who was very well known for training Rex, King of the Wild Horses," the biggest equine movie star of the silents, Mitchum says. "He taught Judy to climb stairs, untie a rope, and wink. She flatly refused to sit, so another mule was brought in for those scenes. Les tried different ways to make her talk—chewing tobacco, gum— but nothing worked. So he devised a bridle or halter with a heavy filament thread running under her top lip, so that when the thread was pulled, she'd wiggle her lips."

When Francis made a rare live TV appearance on *What's My Line*, Hilton stood beside Francis, tugging the cord from the bridle. Theories abounded about how the mule talked, from the plausible—peanut butter under the lip— to the upsetting—electric shocks—but the trick was in the thread.

While the *Francis* films were a favorite with audiences, they weren't with Universal contract players; they certainly added no prestige to the résumés of Tony Curtis, Piper Laurie, and David Janssen.

Blonde bombshell Mamie Van Doren, who co-starred in 1954's *Francis Joins the WACs*, remembers, "I adored Francis more than any other actor on the set—believe me! But I really didn't want to play opposite a mule. The

Francis movies and the *Ma and Pa Kettle* movies were the ones you tried to escape. But when you're under contract, you have to do what you're told. Clint Eastwood was under contract, but I was further up the ladder. Clint asked me if I could get him into the movie. I said no, I was trying to get out of the movie. When they did the next one, *Francis in the Navy*, he was in it."

After six *Francis* films, the team disbanded. One more film was made, in 1956, *Francis in the Haunted House*. The original cast was replaced with top talent: Charles Lamont directed, Mickey Rooney starred, and Paul Frees voiced the mule. But even with Judy still in her role, the movie didn't have the magic, marking the end of *Francis* films.

Yet talking equestrian comedy was not finished. Lubin developed *Mister Ed* for television, with Hilton using his same technique to make the horse speak. Alan Young starred as Ed's befuddled owner, while Allan "Rocky" Lane, the former Red Ryder star for Republic Pictures, provided the horse's voice, like Wills, in secret.

Eastwood turned up in an episode of *Mister Ed* too.

THE GEEZER REDEMPTION STORY

One of the Western themes to recently find favor is the tale of the aging tough guy or, less sentimentally, the "Geezer Redemption Story."

The aging screen cowboy is not a new phenomenon. Yet for years, he was treated with far too little dignity. Many of the bit players in the 1930s and 1940s B-Westerns had been stars during the silent days. This dishearteningly common trend continued during the 1950s, when fans saw childhood heroes, including Bob Steele and Tom Tyler, play uncredited henchmen and stagecoach drivers on TV episodes. Of course, these roles allowed sentimental filmmakers to throw a little money their way; but when recognized in the bit part, the faded star felt humiliated in front of his fans.

Then came Sam Peckinpah's *Ride the High Country*, in 1962, where sixtyish stars Joel McCrea and Randolph Scott, at the end of their careers, not only carried the picture handsomely but also established the underlying theme of all such movies: a character sets out to make things right before he dies, often with a willingness to die to accomplish this feat. The appeal to an older actor is irresistible, offering a chance to play a part that values age and experience, instead of a throwaway role. For mature movie audiences, these films offered a cast with familiarity and shared—if imagined—experience, and the vicarious thrill of not feeling marginalized themselves.

Though an acknowledged classic today, critics overlooked *Ride the High Country* in its own time, and the theme lay dormant, except when played for laughs as in 1969's *The Over-the-Hill Gang*, until it was revived magnificently in 1976, in Don Siegel's *The Shootist* (Paramount), in which John Wayne, then age sixty-nine, closed his career playing a dying lawman.

In 2012, Ernest Borgnine, then making what would be his final film, *The Man Who Shook the Hand of Vicente Fernandez*, told me, "It's a Western, but it takes place in a nursing home."

Borgnine played a man recovering from a stroke and having to stare down a gang of assisted-living scooter-riding thugs, the lead villain played by Western stalwart Barry Corbin. Remarkably, the story shaved years off Borgnine's age, putting him in his eighties, instead of his true age of ninety-five!

In 2017, the Western genre featured a bumper crop of these films. In *The Hero*, the in-demand seventy-three-year-old movie icon Sam Elliott plays fictional Western movie icon Lee Hayden. He's been reduced to narrating barbecue sauce ads when he receives two pieces of life-changing news: he has cancer, and he's getting a lifetime achievement award from a fan organization. His stoned acceptance speech goes viral, creating a chance for a comeback, a romance, and a possible reconciliation with his neglected daughter (Krysten Ritter). Elliott's restrained but raw performance is a career highlight.

"Realism is a thing," insisted ninety-one-year-old Harry Dean Stanton, as the title character in the modern-day cowboy Western *Lucky*. The ancient realist lives in a small desert town, surrounded by numerous casual friends, but no close ones or family, and he's growing to fear his slow-coming demise.

Much of the story and character comes from Stanton's life, even the fact that he was a Navy cook in the Pacific during WWII. Although the setting looks like Arizona, only two days were shot there; the rest was in Los Angeles, California, to avoid making Stanton travel.

With a strong supporting cast, including James Darren, Ed Begley Jr., and Tom Skerritt, the movie is an amusing and moving character study by Stanton, who died shortly before the film's release.

In the only period film of the group, and a more direct descendant of *Ride the High Country* and *The Shootist*, Lance Henriksen stars in *Gone Are the Days* as Taylon, a one-time bank robber who hopes one more score will allow him to make things right for a young woman who doesn't know she's his daughter.

"Taylon is dying, but he's not giving up," Henriksen explained. "He'd done it all, and he regretted every minute of it, on the one hand. And on the other hand, he prided himself that he was still around. When I read the script, I said, 'Oh my God, this has an element of Buster Keaton in it—it's so physical.' Because of the long passages where I'm all alone. There's that feeling of being trapped in a great silence."

A star for decades, Henriksen also feels, as Taylon did, the sting of age. "I'm seventy-seven, and I don't feel no seventy-seven. The only thing that's changed is my hair got gray. And suddenly, people dismiss you. They're not interested; there's nothing to gain from talking to you."

In 2018, the then eighty-one-year-old Oscar-winner Robert Redford, now retired from acting, played his final lead in *The Old Man & the Gun*, as a real-life outlaw who busted out of San Quentin and, at age seventy-nine, robbed banks near his retirement community.

Impossible to see since its aborted release in 1975, *Mackintosh and T.J.* starred Roy Rogers in his last movie, nearly a quarter century after his final Republic feature, and it has just been released in a stunning 4K restoration. It was the best performance of his career. If he were younger, it could have been his *Stagecoach*. Directed by Emmy-winner Marvin Chomsky, *Mackintosh* was the passion project of Tim Penland, a stunning film that belies its $800,000 budget.

Roy, then age sixty-four, plays Mackintosh, a one-time top hand, now surviving on day-to-day ranch work wherever his disintegrating pickup takes him. He rescues teen T. J. (Clay O'Brien) from a shoplifting rap, and they throw in together. Working at the legendary Four 6s Ranch (recently bought by Taylor Sheridan), Mackintosh shows T. J. how to be a man, a lesson O'Brien first learned from John Wayne in *The Cowboys*, and could now teach anyone: he's in the ProRodeo Hall of Fame. It's a naturalistic, unsentimental story about the men who tend cattle and horses.

Roy's daughter Cheryl Rogers Barnett recalls, "He'd gotten so disenchanted with Hollywood that he told (manager) Art Rush not to bring him anything. But that script came, and he just fell in love with it."

"I'd never really considered Dad an actor," confides Cheryl. "He played himself. He was always saying, 'Old Roy wouldn't say it this way.' In *Mackintosh* he's not playing Roy Rogers; he's playing that wonderful character Paul Savage wrote." A contemporary tale, ethical Mackintosh must contend not only with broncs but with wifebeaters and Peeping Toms.

Sadly, the film was barely seen: Penland turned down $2,000,000 from Columbia and couldn't raise the money to distribute it outside of Texas. Since 2003, when he picked up a poor dub during the final week of Roy's Apple Valley Museum, Rogers aficionado Steve Latshaw has wanted to share

Mackintosh, and now he's done so, tracking the original negative to Technicolor labs.

The film industry's change of heart about its aging actors is heartening for fans and critics to see. Rather than just charitably throw old hands a bone, filmmakers throw them roles that, as with *Ride the High Country*, provide elegant cappers to fine careers.

THE BEST PATHFINDER FILMS

For all of the pathfinders' importance in the settling of the West, the films about those great pioneers comprise a short list indeed. The best treatment of John C. "Pathfinder" Frémont is Richard Chamberlain's star portrayal in the 1986 miniseries *Dream West*, which also featured Rip Torn as Frémont's frequent collaborator, Kit Carson.

Dana Andrews played Frémont as a supporting character in 1940's *Kit Carson* (United Artists), with Jon Hall in the lead. *Brady Bunch* dad Robert Reed played Frémont in Disney's 1977 *Kit Carson and the Mountain Men*, and Frémont turned up as a character once more in a 1966 episode of *Death Valley Days*, played by *Sergeant Preston of the Yukon* star Dick Simmons.

Not all of the films hit their mark. For instance, the title for *The Adventures of Frontier Fremont*, starring Dan Haggerty, suggested the 1976 movie would focus on the pathfinder, but it played more like *Grizzly Adams 2*.

One worthy entry in the Lewis and Clark filmography is 1955's *The Far Horizons* starring Fred MacMurray as Meriwether Lewis, Charlton Heston as William Clark, and Oscar-winner Donna Reed as Sacagawea. The history is iffy, but the production is grand.

Otherwise, aside from a 1967 episode of *Death Valley Days*, in which Dick Simmons played Lewis to Don Matheson's Clark and Victoria Vetri's Sacagawea, Thomas Jefferson's explorers have had little screen time. In 2005, HBO and National Geographic announced a miniseries based on Stephen Ambrose's enthralling history of the expedition, *Undaunted Courage*, starring Edward Norton and Brad Pitt, but never made it. Eleven years later, a version set for a 2018 release to star Casey Affleck and Matthias Schoenaerts never materialized. The slowpoke filmmakers were beaten to the punch in 2016, with the release of *Manifest Destiny: The Lewis & Clark Musical Adventure*, a musical featuring Muppet-ish hand puppets as well as human performers.

Probably the best film about pathfinders is 1960's *Ten Who Dared* (Disney). James Drury, who played Walter Powell, told me, "It was the story of the first party of white men who went down through the Colorado River rapids after the Civil War. It was led by Captain [John Wesley] Powell, a surveyor and explorer who had been a major in the Union Army and had lost an arm. They named Lake Powell after [him]. I don't think the picture made 10¢ for Disney, but it was just such a delightful show to be a part of."

THE BEST COWBOY FILMS

While cowboy characters proliferate in the vast majority of Westerns, not so many films deal with cowboying as a job, and yet the cowboy's labor was much of the backbone of Western life. With the work of a cowboy being so difficult, and so poorly paid, especially compared with acting, it seems perfectly sensible that many a real top hand made the transition from the range to the screen. Among the movies' genuine just-off-the-trail cowpokes were Hoot Gibson, Ben Johnson. and rodeo clown Slim Pickens.

Of course, the most densely populated arena for movies about cowboys was the B-Western. From the silent days through the 1950s, studios from Republic to Monogram produced hundreds of them. But whether these silver screen cowboys were Tom Mix, Johnny Mack Brown, or the Three Mesquiteers, cowboy life was usually not the focus but rather a springboard to stories about land grabs, murder, and the occasional Nazi saboteur. The most convincing portrayals of cowboy life in the B-Westerns were in the post-war films, principally Gene Autry's self-produced titles for Columbia Pictures and Tim Holt's remarkable RKO films.

The best overall cowboy picture, hands down? Howard Hawk's 1948 masterpiece, *Red River*, featuring John Wayne, Montgomery Clift, Walter Brennan, and every manly guy in Hollywood or environs. Delmer Daves' fact-based 1958 film *Cowboy* is another great cowboy flick, starring Jack Lemmon as a hotel clerk who quits to sign on with an outfit led by Glenn Ford's character and learns the unglamorous truth about cowboy life. Another classic is 1972's *The Cowboys*. Who among us wouldn't give his eyeteeth to be one of the adolescent boys who John Wayne hired for his character's cattle drive, deadly though the assignment may be?

Best rodeo cowboy movies? Sam Peckinpah's 1972 classic *Junior Bonner*, starring Steve McQueen, and 1994's *8 Seconds*, starring Luke Perry as rodeo legend Lane Frost.

The field is crowded when one considers the aging cowboy story. Exceptional films include 1970's *Monte Walsh* starring Lee Marvin and Jack Palance, remade for TV in 2003 with Tom Selleck and Keith Carradine. John Huston and Arthur Miller collaborated on 1961's *The Misfits*, showcasing soon-to-be

Western icon Eli Wallach and featuring nearly the last performances of Clark Gable, Montgomery Clift, and Marilyn Monroe. A tiny but exceptional film is 1975's *Macintosh and T.J.*, featuring the final, and maybe finest, performance by the King of the Cowboys, Roy Rogers.

For stories where a lone cowboy must make a stand, usually to protect the woman he loves, check out 1968's *Will Penny*, starring Charlton Heston, and 1971's *The Hired Hand*, directed by and starring Peter Fonda. Peter's father, Henry, played a humorous aging cowboy better than anyone, from 1965's *The Rounders*, teamed with Glenn Ford, to 1970's *The Cheyenne Social Club*, opposite James Stewart.

On television, the 1959–1965 series *Rawhide* showed a convincing view of life on an endless cattle drive and, most important, gave us Clint Eastwood. The 1962–1971 series *The Virginian* focused on Judge Garth and his family, but James Drury as the title character, and a bunkhouse full of drovers, were an important part of the tale, as were *The High Chaparral*'s bunkhouse boys, led by foreman Don Collier.

The best modern-day cowboy story, oddly enough, is a comedy, 1991's *City Slickers*, a loving tribute to the cowboy life. I must admit that, between the laughs, it has made me cry for my misspent adulthood as much as 1972's *The Cowboys* made me cry for my misspent youth.

INDEX

Note: Films, TV movies, and miniseries are followed by year. TV and radio series are followed by "TV" or "Radio." Page numbers in *italics* indicate photographs.

ABOUT THE AUTHOR

HENRY C. PARKE IS A BROOKLYN-BORN, L.A.-BASED WRITER AND GRADUATE of New York University's film and television program. He has been Film & TV Editor for *True West* since 2015; has written *Henry's Western Round-up*, an online report on Western film production, since 2010; and writes twice-monthly articles for the INSP Channel's blog. His screenwriting credits include *Speedtrap* (1977) and *Double Cross* (1994). He's the first writer welcomed into the Western Writers of America for his work in electronic media. Henry has recorded audio commentary for nearly thirty Western Blu-rays and is featured in the Turner Classic Movies documentary short *TCM Movie Fanatics: Westerns*. Henry has been married to his wife, Stephanie, for more than thirty years, and their daughter, Sabrina, is a documentary producer.